DELHI BET[W
TWO EMPI
1803-1931

DELHI BETWEEN TWO EMPIRES

1803–1931

*Society, Government and
Urban Growth*

NARAYANI GUPTA

OXFORD
UNIVERSITY PRESS

OXFORD
UNIVERSITY PRESS

YMCA Library Building, Jai Singh Road, New Delhi 110 001

Oxford University Press is a department of the University of Oxford.
It furthers the University's objective of excellence in research, scholarship,
and education by publishing worldwide in

Oxford   New York

Auckland   Cape Town   Dar es Salaam   Hong Kong   Karachi
Kuala Lumpur   Madrid   Melbourne   Mexico City   Nairobi
New Delhi   Shanghai   Taipei   Toronto

With offices in

Argentina Austria Brazil Chile Czech Republic France Greece Guatemala
Hungary Italy Japan Poland Portugal Singapore South Korea Switzerland
Thailand Turkey Ukraine Vietnam

Oxford is a registered trademark of Oxford University Press
in the UK and in certain other countries

Published in India
by Oxford University Press, New Delhi

First published 1981
Oxford India Paperbacks 1998
Third impression 2011

ISBN-13: 978-0-19-564102-8
ISBN-10: 0-19-564102-7

Printed in India at Anvi Composers, New Delhi 110 063
Published by Oxford University Press
YMCA Library Building, Jai Singh Road, New Delhi 110 001

To my mother
and
to the memory of
my father

CONTENTS

PLATES

(*between pages 96 and 97*)

The traveller's first view of Delhi

The Bridge of Boats

Contenders for Empire

The Delhi Bank in Chandni Chowk

St James's Church near Kashmeri Gate

The poet laureate of the city—Ghalib

Delhi Club before 1857

Delhi Club after 1898

Facade of a house on Chandni Chowk

The inner courtyard

MAPS

PREFACE

In the years that I have been burrowing in the Delhi Archives, the beautiful road on which it is located officially ceased to be called Alipur Road and was renamed Shamnath Marg; Pambari Road became Bhama Shah Marg; Phatak Habash Khan was renamed after Tilak, Delhi College after Dr Zakir Husain . . . The telephone directory rose to the challenge and had a two-column page of 'old names' and 'present names'. If someone were at pains to show that Indians lack a sense of history, that someone would be succeeding admirably. By the time my children grow up, many more landmarks and evocative names may disappear. Even now, most children in Delhi have their eyes blinkered against the incredibly rich historical past of their city, with their knowledge of localities chiefly in terms of cinema houses, and their awareness of Urdu unwittingly acquired through 'Hindi' films. Partly because Delhi has the misfortune to be the national capital, the national is crushing the city; Tilak Nagars and Nehru Roads proliferate, and hardly anyone knows of the poetry of Mir and Zauq, the humour of Ghalib, the quality of life that Chandni Chowk once symbolized.

The books written on the history of London could fill the best part of a small library. Delhi has a very long way to go in this respect. I hope that my attempt to recapture some aspects of life in Delhi in the last century will induce others to carry the story further back. I have opted to highlight issues and developments which appeared to have been significant at different points of time, because I lack the inclination or the resources for 'tunnel history'. This has necessitated some degree of selectivity, in an attempt to convey immediacy as well as perspective. In this attempt, in the words of Tocqueville, 'j'espère avoir écrit ce livre sans préjugé mais je ne prétends pas l'avoir écrit sans passion' (I hope to have written this book without prejudice but I do not claim to have written without feeling).

In the course of my research many people have helped me to gain insights and information. The least I can do is to acknowledge their help here and hope that any inadvertent omission may be forgiven. I would like to record my great debt to two remarkable individuals who are no more—Professor H. J. Dyos, who awakened my interest in the study of towns, and Principal Mirza Mohammed Begg, who introduced me to the *galis* and *kuchas* of Shahjahanabad. For being generous with their time I would like to thank Mr S. Ali, Professor Ashish Bose, Mr Maheshwar Dayal, Professor K. A. Faruqi, Professor Mohammad Hasan, Dr Abdul Haq, Dr V. C. Joshi, Professor Asok Mitra, Mr Durga Prasad, Professor Ralph Russell, Dr Percival Spear and Mr J. A. Wajid. I am grateful to Dr B. B. Misra, under whose supervision I began my research, and to Professor R. L. Shukla, who took over the task after Dr Misra's retirement. The Principal of Indraprastha College was kind enough to grant me leave for part of the period when I was doing my research.

I would like to thank the custodians of the archives and libraries where I worked; in India, the Delhi Archives, where helpfulness is combined with knowledgeability, the record room of the Delhi Municipal Corporation, the National Archives of India, the National Library, the Nehru Memorial Library, the Punjab State Archives, Rabindra-Bhavan in Visva-Bharati, and the West Bengal Secretariat library; in Britain, the British Library, the India Office Records and Library, and the library and archives of the Union Society for the Propagation of the Gospel. Mr Naresh Dayal lent me the manuscript memoirs of Sri Ram Mathur, and Mr A. P. Saigal gave me a copy of his father's *History of Delhi Municipality*—to them many thanks.

For tea and sympathy I would particularly like to mention the names of Mrs Pridmore and Miss Holland at the Archives of the U.S.P.G., Mr V. C. Suri at the Punjab State Archives, Mr Kaushik and Mr Shiv Charan of the Delhi Municipal Corporation, Mr M. L. Kachroo and the late Mr Wasson at the Delhi Archives. Mr L. D. Ajmani and Mr K. R. Perwahna did a splendid job of typing a largely illegible manuscript. The editorial and production departments of the O.U.P. and Mr P. K. Ghosh of Eastend Printers taught me a great deal, and with cheerful forbearance.

I owe a deep debt of gratitude to my mother, my parents-in-law, and Cherri. For helping, and even more for distracting, my very inadequate thanks to Niharika, Himadri, and Partha.

Indraprastha College, Delhi   Narayani Gupta

TWENTY YEARS AFTER

One afternoon in 1976, I walked into the comfortably shabby office of the Oxford University Press in Daryaganj, with my doctoral thesis in a shoulder bag. In the next three years, with the generous cooperation of the OUP staff, the thesis became a book, pictures, maps and all. At that time I hoped that in the next decade or two, my limited study would be supplemented by many others. What follows is a survey of what has been written on Delhi since then.

Towns are like people. They inspire pleasure, hostility, nostalgia, as well as scholarship, Attitudes to towns change, go through sudden swings. Take the examples of Calcutta and Bombay. For decades they were dismissed as 'colonial towns'. But the repeated reminders that they were going to be 300 years old by the end of this century inspired a great volume of literature and picture-books, a defiant pride in their history. Delhi has not done as well. At once older and younger than them, perhaps Delhi has lost out because it lacks a homogeneous past, because its various inhabitants relate to different parts of its history and its geography. While there is most definitely a growing popular interest in its history and a concern for its future, this has been manifested more in a dissemination and rehashing of available information, than in scholarly investigation.

Percival Spear, remembered as a teacher at St. Stephens College, was THE historian of Delhi, who lightened the dark years of World War II by writing one of the most charming books on Delhi.[1] It is fitting that a book of essays which surveyed Delhi's history from early historic times to the present should be in the form of a *festschrift* to Spear—Robert Frykenberg's edited volume gives an *aperçu* of the many faces of Delhi—shrine, capital, sanctuary, a changing landscape.[2] Dr. and Mrs. Spear's own lovingly written memoirs should be read along with these essays.[3]

Scholars in India find it difficult to locate many books published in the nineteenth century. This lack is being made up by collections of extracts and by reprints. A wonderfully 'dippableinto' book is that edited by Kaul.[4] We see Delhi through the eyes and with the pens of travellers over the centuries—Turkish, Arabic, Persian and French in translation, and numerous ones from British tourists writing in that golden age when the pen had to convey form, colour and dimensions, without the aid of photographs. The 1882 *Gazetteer* of Delhi, and the guidebooks by Fanshawe and Hearn have been reprinted. The trial of Bahadur Shah in 1857 has been printed as a book.[5] One of the best things to be printed has been Thomas Metcalfe's 'Delhie Book' (which I had read in microfilm at the India Office Library) in a handsome edition, interspersed with the lively letters of Metcalfe's daughter Emily, and—sometimes rather confusingly—the editor M.M. Kaye's own sprightly notes.[6] Her own expansive autobiography is also pervaded with golden sunlight, and has many evocative descriptions of Delhi.[7]

In the matter of reprints, the Urdu Akademi at Delhi is doing commendable work—Syed Ahmad Khan's book and that of Bashiruddin Ahmad, hard to come by in the 1970s, have been reprinted.[8] Sangin Beg's 'Sair-e-Dehli', a Persian manuscript of the early nineteenth century, has been translated into Urdu and published by the editor of *Shair-Ashoob*.[9] *Muraqqa-e-Delhi* (in Persian) has been translated into Urdu and, less satisfactorily, into English. Syed Ahmad Khan has also been partially and arbitrarily rendered into English.[10] Ahmed Ali's novel, written in English, has been translated into Urdu.[11]

Shahjahanabad as a Mughal city in the seventeenth century had not been studied till Stephen Blake arrived on the scene. His thesis, earlier familiar through articles, was published as a book in 1991—an important account of the city's morphology, where the homes of the rulers and of the aristocrats—*havelis* great and small—are seen in terms of ordered spaces and passages.[12] A vague nostalgia about these *havelis* is fed by a perfunctory picture-book[13] while the more serious explorer is led gently and competently through the *galis* of Shahjanabad and parts of the Civil Lines, with the help of an engaging little book by Barton and Malone.[14] The cartologist who is unlikely to gain access to the splendid but fragile 1842 water colour map of the city in the India Office Library which I used for my work can now rejoice in an exquisite copy, the work of the Geography

Department at the University of Bonn, published with a set of essays on Indian cartography, the city's history, it *mohallas* and shrines—an essential base-map for architects and planners as well as historians.[15]

Syed Ahmad Khan in his pioneering book on Delhi described not only its monuments but also its people. Biographies supplement town histories. Pavan Varma's excellent book on Ghalib[16] and Mushirul Hasan's on M.A. Ansari[17] (both in English) and Intezar Husain's on Hakim Ajmal Khan[18] are recent ones. Not central to Delhi's history but of tangential interest is the extraordinarily powerful Begum Samru, on whom Shreeve[19] and John Lal[20] have written recently. Dalrymple's[21] book is cleverly constructed as a diary which unfolds Delhi's history leaf by leaf, through conversations with imaginary and real people, including Dr. Yunus Jaffrey, who helped me translate the poem by Hali which appears in my book.

The year my book was published, Lutyens' New Delhi acquired a new visibility—again a case of celebrations helping to generate interest. The 50th anniversary of the founding of New Delhi was celebrated with discussions and an exhibition.[22] Robert Irving's book on the making of the capital was well timed.[23] His thorough study of the work of Lutyens and Baker can be supplemented by Sten Nilsson's lighter but perceptive analysis of New Delhi in the context of capital-building in South Asia.[24] For glimpses of what the new capital meant to the people of Delhi one can read Nirad Chaudhuri[25] and Patwant Singh.[26] The nostalgia of those who remember more tranquil times is part of Delhi, an index to its changing form—Ghalib, Ahmad Ali, Maheshwar Dayal, Khushwant Singh, Asok Mitra... The *Shair Ashoob* tradition in Urdu poetry is now expressed chiefly in English prose, recalling the animation of a car-free Chandni Chowk and the serenity of Lutyens' tree-lined avenues. But Delhi is not perceived simply in terms of the 'twin-cities' of the Mughal and British capitals, because beyond them are the older Delhis, where monuments became cowsheds and arches opened up vistas not of processions but of fields, which same fields became converted to housing estates after 1947. These transformations have been implicit in the nature of the city—commercial entrepôt and administrative capital are very demanding roles, and if they are both to work well, compromises have often to be made with history and morphology—sometimes somewhat mindless and unpleasing compromises.

The obverse of nostalgia is alienation, the perception of the city as an ensemble of 'problems', as heading towards 'crisis' and 'decay'. The debate in the 1930s about the need to 'decongest' the southern part of Shahjahanabad was resumed in 1975 when an official wrote a book proposing to 'rebuild' Shahjahanabad.[27] He suggested that the nomansland between Lutyens' New Delhi and Shahjahan's Delhi be developed as an 'extension' into which the inhabitants of Shahjahanabad could spill over, and that the 'walled city', now less congested, be developed like the Marais in Paris into a picturesque network of shops, coffee-houses and *havelis.* A little book on Shahjahanabad published by the Max Mueller Bhawan in Delhi[28] indicated a new respect on the part of architects and townplanners for a medieval city they had hitherto dismissed as chaotic and ill planned. The hierarchy of roads and *galis,* the importance of water channels, the sensible quality of the architecture, were noted.

The crisis of Partition strained the holding capacity of the city. The problem of rent control (which led to the deterioration of buildings) and of the large number of houses that had belonged to families who had migrated to Pakistan, and which now belong to the Delhi government, is addressed by Ajay Mehra.[29] 'Urban renewal' (a less ambitious task than 'rebuilding') has to be discussed always bearing in mind that Shahjahanabad (like Lahore, its mirror image) is not Warsaw or Dresden; 'renewal' here is to generate a better quality of life, not simply restore architectural facades.

A mix of nostalgia and anger at mindless 'development' comes across in a collection of articles edited by Patwant Singh and Ram Dhamija, selected from *Design* over the past years.[30] The title speaks of 'the deepening crisis', which reflects the deepening pessimism of the editors who hoped much from sensitive prime ministers and from the setting up of the Urban Art Commission in 1974. The crisis is that of Greater Delhi, where political parties, pressure groups and overlapping jurisdictions play havoc. Above all, the commercialisation of urban space has mired Shahajahanabad in squalor and pollution.

Linked to the 'problems' of urban governance is that of 'conservation', a term associated with the Archaeological Survey which, in the 1920s, was listing, documenting and mapping the 'monuments' of Delhi, of which only a few were in Shahjahan's city. For the ASI, Delhi was more a 'Pathan' city, with its vast expanse of Ilbari, Khilji, Tughlak, Lodi and Sayyid buildings. The 4 volumes of Zafar Hasan and Page's list of Delhi monuments (recently reprinted with a different and misleading title)[31] is an indispensable starting-point for any work of conservation.

The tragedy of the Lal Qila after 1857 has been described in my book. In 1981 the army agreed to vacate the Qila. It is however still in occupation of the fort, though it has transferred part of Salimgarh to the Survey. The thousands of visitors who stream through the areas open to the public get only a truncated view of the Mughal palace. The Jama Masjid has been enclaved by shops and the glory of its eastern entrance is obscured. The magic mix of colours, sounds, ceremonies, movement and mood that Delhi was in the nineteenth and early twentieth century can never be recaptured. All this is obscured by hoardings, loudspeakers, heavy buses and trucks and the irritations engendered by smoke and crowds. *But...* all these are reversible ..and there is increasing evidence that there are people who wish to help do this. The Conservation Society of Delhi conducts walks in different areas of Delhi, and acts as a watchdog to anticipate demolitions and encroachments.[32] A Court Order in 1996 has decreed that the house of Ghalib and the grave of Zauq be treated with the honour due to these two great poets (and rivals!). The major *havelis* and public buildings are being listed, to supplement and update Zafar Hasan's volumes.[33] Hopefully, in a few years, major steps will be taken to further the measures of conservation begun in Delhi in the 1930s. Too often the passion and eloquence heard at seminars evaporates beyond the airconditioned hall, but there is hope, given that the younger generation is now sufficiently distanced from the past to be concerned to retain, not demolish parts of the city. A section of the city *as* museum, as well as a city museum should not be an impossible dream.

Every book has to end somewhere. And so I had stopped short of the work of the Delhi Improvement Trust, since then so ably discussed by Douglas Goodfriend.[34] Patwant Singh's[35] and Sheila Dhar's[36] books convey the sense of the 1940s and 1950s, Usha Biswas' paintings the 1950s landscapes.[37] Anita Desai paints the portrait of a dreamy Urdu poet[38], Mukul Kesavan's novel takes us to Kashmiri Gate and Ludlow Castle and to Pandara Road in the 1940s.[39] All these reinforce the sense of a a major lacuna. The history of Delhi from the 1930s to the 1980s cries out to be written—from the time when the twin cities began to function in tandem, through the years of Partition and its aftermath, the growth of the planned and non-planned Delhis, through the silent days of the Emergency to the horrors of the 1984 riots, so meticulously documented by Uma Chakravarty and Nandita Haksar.[40] Since the years when I read documents in a cramped room in the Chief Commissioner's Office in Alipur Road, the Delhi Archives has moved to a spacious 6-storeyed building in South Delhi.[41] The revenue records at Tis Hazari are an untapped goldmine. Newspaper archives, and planning office record rooms are full of material which can be used. Any takers ?

Narayani Gupta

NOTES

1. T.G.P. Spear *Delhi: Its Monuments and History,* updated and annotated by Narayani Gupta and Laura Sykes, Delhi 1994.
2. R.E. Frykenberg (ed.) *Delhi Through the Ages,* Delhi 1986.
3. Percival Spear and Margaret Spear, *India Remembered,* Delhi 1981.
4. H.K. Kaul (ed.) *Historic Delhi,* Delhi 1985.
5. K.C. Yadav (ed.) *Delhi in 1857, Vol. 1, The Trial of Bahadur Shah,* Gurgaon 1980.
6. M.M. Kaye (ed.) *The Golden Calm: An English Lady's Life in Moghul Delhi,* Exeter 1980.
7. M.M. Kaye *Sun in The Morning: My Early years in India and England,* London 1990.

8. Sayyid Ahmad Khan, *Asaar us Sanadid,* reprint, 3 vols, edited by K. Anjum, Delhi 1991; Bashiruddin Ahmad, *Waqayat-ul-Dar-ul-Hukumat-e-Dehli,* reprint, edited by K. Anjum, Delhi 1996.
9. Sangin Beg, *Sair-e-Dehli,* Urdu translation, Delhi 1981.
10. R. Nath, *Monuments of Delhi: Historic Study,* Delhi 1979.
11. Ahmed Ali, *Twilight in Delhi,* reprint, Delhi 1991. Translated into Urdu as *Dilli ki Sham.*
12. S.P. Blake, *Shahjahanabad: The Sovereign City in Mughal India 1639–1739.* Cambridge 1991.
13. P.K. Varma and S. Shonkar, *Mansions at Dusk: The Havelis of Old Delhi,* Delhi 1992.
14. G. Barton and L. Malone, *Old Delhi: Ten Easy Walks,* Delhi 1988.
15. E. Ehlers and T. Krafft (eds) *Shahjahanabad/Old Delhi,* Stuttgart 1992.
16. P.K. Varma, *Ghalib, the Man, the Times,* Delhi 1989.
17. M. Hasan *M.A. Ansari, the Congress and the Raj,* Delhi 1987.
18. Intezar Husain's biography of Hakim Ajmal Khan was published (in Urdu) in Pakistan in 1996.
19. N.G. Shreeve, *Begam Samru,* West Sussex, 1995.
20. John Lall, *Begum Samru,* Delhi, 1997.
21. W. Dalrymple, *City of Djinns—A Year in Delhi,* London 1993.
22. An exhibition 'The Making of New Delhi' was organised jointly by the School of Planning and Architecture at Delhi and the British Council in 1980.
23. R.G. Irving, *Indian Summer: Lutyens, Baker and the Making of Imperial Delhi,* Yale 1981.
24. S. Nilsson, *The New Capitals of India, Pakistan and Bangladesh,* Lund 1975.
25. N.C. Chaudhuri, *Thy Hand, Great Anarch! India 1921–1952,* London 1987.
26. P. Singh, *Of Dreams and Demons,* Delhi 1994.
27. Jagmohan, *Rebuilding Shahjahanabad,* Delhi 1975.
28. B. Ghosh (ed.) *Shahjahanabad,* Delhi 1981.
29. Ajay K. Mehra, *The Politics of Urban Redevelopment,* Delhi 1991.
30. P. Singh and R. Dhamija, *Delhi, the Deepening Urban Crisis,* Delhi 1989.
31. *Monuments of Delhi: Lasting Splendour of the Great Mughals and Others,* Delhi 1997.
32. The Conservation Society of Delhi grew out of a more informal group set up in 1982; it aims to create public awareness about Delhi's historic past through conducted walks, slide-shows and workshops.
33. The Indian National Trust for Art and Cultural Heritage has a programme for listing heritage buildings all over India. The listing of Delhi's 'monuments' and other buildings of architectural and historic value was begun in 1985 and is being finalised in 1997.
34. D.E. Goodfriend, 'The Tyranny of the Right Angle: Colonial and Post-Colonial Urban Development in Delhi 1857–1957' *Design,* 26(2) 1982, and 'Shahjahanabad: Old Delhi; Tradition and Planned Change' *Ekistics* 49, 1982. It is a great pity that Douglas Goodfriend has not completed his thesis; in the course of doing research he published many excellent articles.
35. P. Singh, *op. cit.,* note 26.

36. Sheila Dhar, *Here's Someone I'd Like You to Meet: Tales of Innocents, Musicians and Bureaucrats*, Delhi 1995.
37. Usha Biswas, who generously contributed one of her paintings for the cover of this edition, has lived many decades in Delhi, and most of her paintings are of its monuments and streets.
38. Anita Desai, *In Custody*, Delhi 1985.
39. Mukul Kesavan, *Looking Through Glass*, Delhi 1995.
40. Uma Chakravarty and Nandita Haksar, *Delhi Riots: Three Days in the Life of a Nation*, Delhi 1987.
41. The Delhi Archives is now housed in the Qutb Institutional Area, and welcomes researchers. C.B. Patil and Purnima Ray of the Archaeological Survey of India have just published *Delhi: A Bibliography*, Delhi 1997. This is in two volumes, I History, Art and Culture, and II Urban Studies.

ACKNOWLEDGEMENTS

The publishers and the author wish to thank the following for their co-operation in making available, and for giving permission to reproduce, photographs in their possession:

The Archaeological Survey of India (photographs of the Palace from the river, the Bridge of Boats, the Palace, the Delhi Bank, Ghalib, the Delhi Club, Ludlow Castle, a house in Chandi Chowk, Jama Masjid, Delhi College, the Durbar of 1877)

The Delhi Archives (photographs of the Town Hall, Chandni Chowk and Fatehpuri Masjid)

The Cambridge Brotherhood (photographs of St James's Church, the Ram Lila, St Stephen's Hospital, Jama Masjid, the Durbars of 1903 and 1911)

The Librarian, Railway Board (photographs of a courtyard, Kashmeri Gate and the Pageant of 1931, all of which appeared in the *Indian State Railways Magazine*)

Mr Masrur Ahmad Khan (photographs of Hakim Mahmud Khan and his two sons, in his possession)

The Librarian, India International Centre (photographs of the *Lytton Gazette* and the *Curzon Gazette*)

ABBREVIATIONS

A.M.R.	Annual Reports, Delhi Municipality
B.M.S.A.	Baptist Missionary Society Archives, London
C.C.O.	Chief Commissioner's Office, Delhi (now called the Delhi Archives)
Cmd.	Command papers
C.M.D.	Cambridge Mission to Delhi
C.M.G.	*Civil and Military Gazette*
D.A.R.	*Delhi Administration Reports*
D.C.O.	Deputy Commissioner's Office Records (now housed in the Delhi Archives)
D.D.R.	Delhi Division Records (old records, consulted when at Punjab Record Office, Patiala; now housed in Financial Commissioner's office, Chandigarh)
D.G.	*Delhi Gazette*
D.M.C. Progs.	Delhi Municipal Committee Proceedings
D.P.I.	Director of Public Instruction
D.R.A.R.	*Delhi Residency and Agency Records, 1807–57* (Lahore, 1915)
Educ. Progs.	Educational Proceedings
Home (Ests.)	Home (Establishments)
Home (Mil.)	Home (Military)
Home (Munys.)	Home (Municipalities)
Home (Poll.)	Home (Political)
I.O.L.	India Office Library
I.O.R.	India Office Records
Int. Trade	Internal Trade
J.A.S.	*Journal of Asian Studies*
K.W.	Keep withs
Khutoot	*Khutoot-e-Ghalib*
L.S.G.	Local Self-Government
Mof.	*Mofussilite*
N.A.I.	National Archives of India

N.M.L.	Nehru Memorial Library
N.W.P.	North-Western Provinces
P.A.R.	*Punjab Administration Reports*
P.H.P.	Punjab Home Proceedings
P. Med. and San. Progs.	Punjab Medical and Sanitary Proceedings
P. Mun. P.	Punjab Municipal Proceedings
P.P.	Parliamentary Papers
P.W.D.	Public Works Department
R. and A.	Revenue and Agriculture
R.N.P.	*Reports on Native Newspapers published in the Punjab*
Rlys.	Railways
S.P.G.	Society for the Propagation of the Gospel
U.S.P.G.A.	Union Society for the Propagation of the Gospel, Archives

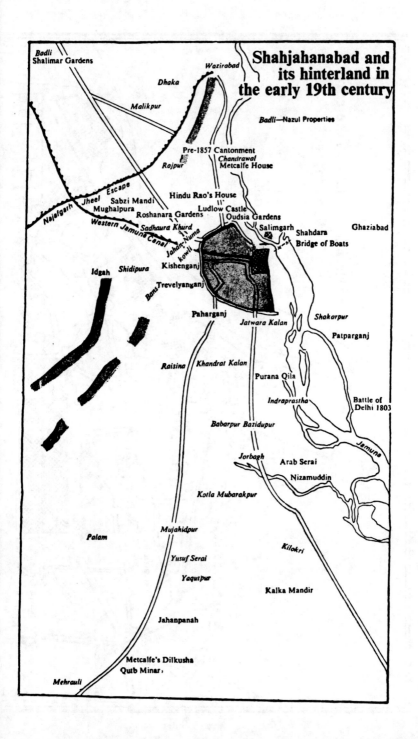

Shahjahanabad and its hinterland in the early 19th century

Badli—Nazul Properties

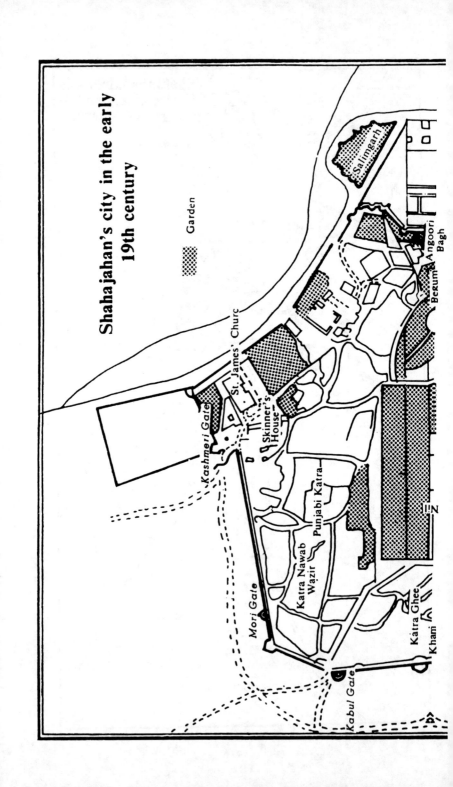

Shahajahan's city in the early 19th century

Garden

Salimgarh

St. James' Churc

Skinner's House

Kashmeri Gate

Katra Nawab Wazir

Punjabi Katra

Mori Gate

Katra Ghee

Khami

Kabul Gate

Begum

Angoori Bagh

N

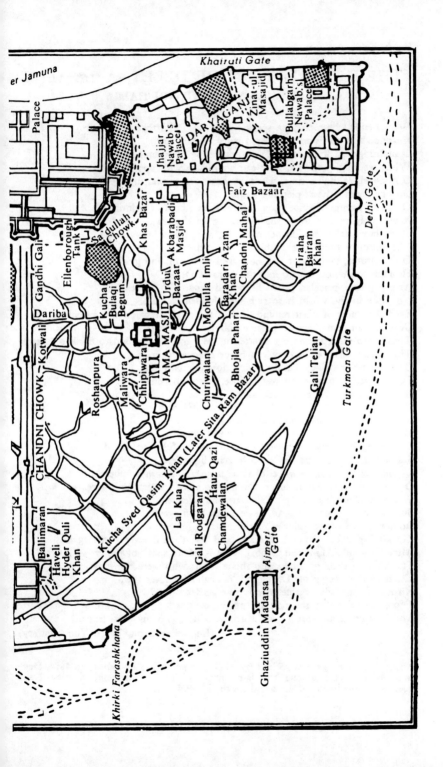

THE DEVASTATION OF DELHI—A LAMENT
KHWAJA ALTAF HUSAIN 'HALI'

Dear friend, I beseech you, speak not of the Delhi that is no more,
I cannot bear to listen to the sad story of this city.
O nightingale, I implore you, sing not a song of autumn,
While we laugh and talk, how can we mourn with you?
O minstrel, at such a time, when my heart craves pleasure,
Do not begin a heart-piercing *ghazal*.
O master-painter, do not open before us an album of paintings,
It will only remind us of the *musha'aras* of the past.
O my heart, take care, do not make me weep like a heavy cloud,
The ocean of blood is throbbing in my veins.
O adventurer, your heart will be seared with pain and grief.
Hearken to me, do not go into the ruins of Delhi.
At every step, priceless pearls lie buried beneath the dust,
No place in the world is so rich with hidden treasure.
Even the traces of what reminded us of the city's destruction are gone,
Dear heaven, can there be greater oblivion than that?
Those who are gone have forgotten us. We too have ceased to think of them.
Times have changed as they can never change again.
Can you point to any family which does not bear scars?
Dear heaven, that made us weep, cease, I beseech you,
But do not let strangers mock us.
If they were to know our plight, not only friends
But the whole world would pity us.
O cup-bearer, who passes the last round of wine.
Do not fill it to the brim, and let no thirst be fully quenched.
For now their long spell of good fortune lies asleep.
Do not awake them, O wheel of time, they are deep in slumber.
O mirth and joy, hasten hence, Delhi is no place for you any more,
Yes, once Delhi was the centre of art and science.
But the art of poetry is dead, never to be born again.
Do not grieve for the glories of the past.
'Ghalib', 'Shefta', 'Nayyar', 'Azurda' and 'Zauq' will never come again.
After 'Momin', 'Alavi' and 'Sehbai', who is left to speak of the art of poetry?
The light of their greatness also shone on us who were not great.
Listen to the poetry of 'Dagh' and 'Majruh', for after them
No nightingale will warble in this rose-garden.
Those *musha'aras* of the past are no more.
And it is unseemly that I should grieve others with my own lament.

(English rendering by Dr Yunus Jaffery)

NOTE: This *marsiya* was recited by Hali at a *musha'ara* in Lahore in 1874. Dagh
and Majruh were among the last survivors of the nineteenth-century Delhi
poets—Majruh lived till 1902 and Dagh till 1905.

نوحۂ دہلی

خواجہ الطاف حسین حالی

تذکرہ دہلیِ مرحوم کا، اے دوست نہ چھیڑ
داستاں گل کی خدا کی خداراہیں، نہ سنا اے بلبل
ڈھونڈتا ہے دلِ شوریدہ، بہانے مطرب
صحبتیں اگلی مصوّر، ہیں یاد آئیں گی
موج زن دل میں ہیں یاں خونی دریا اے چشم
لے کے داغ آئے گا سینے پہ بہت اے سیّاح
پتے پتے پہ ہیں یاں، گوہرِ یکتا تہ خاک
مٹ گئے تیرے مٹانے کے نشاں بھی، اب تو
وہ تو بھولے تھے ہمیں، ہم بھی انھیں بھول گئے
جس کو زخموں سے حوادث کے اچھوتا سمجھیں
ہم کو گر تو نے رلایا، تو رُلایا اے چرخ
یا رخود رویئں گے، کیا ان پہ جہاں روتا ہے
آخری دُور میں بھی، تجھ کو قسم ہے ساتی
بخت سوئے ہیں بہت جاگ چکے، اے دورِ زماں
یاں سے رخصت ہو سویرے کہیں، اے عیش و نشاط
کبھی اے علم و ہنر، گھر تھا تمھارا وہ ہی
شاعری مچلی، اب زندہ نہ ہوگی ہرگز
غالب و شیفتہ و نیّر و آزردہ و ذوق
مومن و علوی و صہبائی و ممنون کے بعد
کر دیا مر کے یگانوں نے، یگانہ ہم کو
داغ و مجروح کی کوشش لو، کہ پھر اس گلشن میں
رات آخر ہوئی اور بزم ہوئی، زیر و زبر
بزمِ ماتم تو نہیں، بزمِ سخن ہے حالی
یاں مناسب نہیں رو رو کے، رُلانا ہرگز

نہ سنا جائے گا ہم سے، یہ فسانہ ہرگز
ہنستے ہنستے ہیں ظالم، نہ رُلانا ہرگز
درد انگیز غزل نہ کوئی، نہ گانا ہرگز
کوئی دلچسپ مرقّع، نہ دکھانا ہرگز
دیکھنا ابرسے آنکھیں، نہ چُرانا ہرگز
دیکھ اس شہر کے کھنڈروں میں نہ جانا ہرگز
دفن ہو گا کہیں اتنا، نہ خدانا ہرگز
اے فلک اس سے زیادہ، نہ مٹانا ہرگز
ایسا بدلا ہے، نہ بدلے گا زمانہ ہرگز
نظر آتا نہیں، ایک ایسا گھرانا ہرگز
ہم پہ غیروں کو تو ظالم، نہ ہنسانا ہرگز
ان کی ہنستی ہوئی شکلوں پہ، نہ جانا ہرگز
بھرے اک جام نہ پیاسوں کو، پلانا ہرگز
نہ ابھی نیند کے ماتوں کو، جگانا ہرگز
نہیں اس دور میں یاں، تیرا ٹھکانا ہرگز
ہم کو بھولے ہو تو گھر، بھول نہ جانا ہرگز
یاد کر کر کے اسے، جی نہ کڑھانا ہرگز
اب دکھائے گا یہ شکلیں، نہ زمانہ ہرگز
شعرا کا نام نہ لے گا، کوئی دانا ہرگز
ورنہ یاں کوئی نہ تھا ہم میں، یگانہ ہرگز
نہ سنے گا کوئی بلبل کا، ترانہ ہرگز
اب نہ دیکھو گے کبھی، لطفِ شبانہ ہرگز

I

THE BRITISH PEACE AND
THE BRITISH TERROR
(1803–58)

'Shah-Jehan conceived the design of immortalizing his name by the erection of a city near the site of the ancient Delhi. This new capital he called after his own name, Shah-Jehan-Abad; that is to say, the colony of Shah-Jehan. Here he resolved to fix his court, alleging as the reason for its removal from Agra, that the excessive heat to which that city is exposed during summer rendered it unfit for the residence of a monarch.'[1]

Thus Shahjahanabad came to be built. This incarnation of Delhi survives today in a splendid fort, the Jama Masjid and many other mosques and temples, some broken walls and in the names of some *kuchas* and *mohullas*. It also survives as a culture and a way of life. Its ethos has been dimmed since the 1930s by the urban sprawl of New Delhi, and it will become increasingly difficult to recapture it. Three political episodes—in 1857–8, 1911–12 and 1947—affected Shahjahanabad as seriously as, and in many ways far more deeply than, earlier Afghan and Maratha invasions. This work is an attempt to illuminate some aspects of the town's history in the nineteenth and early twentieth centuries.

The site chosen was protected from the north-west by the Ridge, and was linked to the east by a bridge across the Jamuna, a glorified moat at the back of the Palace. The city was doubly fortified by the Palace and the city wall. Architectural and engineering skills designed the town with an eye to aesthetic appeal as well as to provide, for a limited population, military security, efficient tax-collection, an adequate supply of water and a functional drainage-system. Plots of land were allotted to noblemen, merchants and people of other professions. Bernier, who lived in the city soon after it had been built in 1638, was struck by the extent to which the economic and social as well as the

political life hinged on the monarch, the court and the *umara*.[2]
There were numerous *karkhanas* for craftsmen under the patron-
age of the aristocracy, but Bernier commented on the absence of
men of 'the middle state'. He saw great opulence and an abundance of provisions, but also great squalor. The city had some stone
and some brick palaces, ringed by mud-and-thatch houses. The
merchants worked in and often lived in second storeys of the
buildings and arcades along the two boulevards radiating from the
palace—Faiz Bazaar and Chandni Chowk. The other roads were
asymmetrical. Bernier explained this by their probably having been
built at different times by different individuals, but the more likely
reason was that this had been done deliberately to make ingress
more difficult for invading troops. *Katras* developed around
nuclei deriving their names from provincial groups or commodities (Kashmeri Katra, Katra Nil), and *mohullas* and *kuchas* were
named after commodities sold there or prominent men who lived
there (Mohulla Imli, Kucha Nawab Wazir). 'The city was aesthetically pleasing. The streets of Delhi are not mere streets. They
are like the album of a painter,' Mir, one of Delhi's great poets,
said affectionately.[3]

Some *umara* built houses outside the city wall, on estates gifted
or sold to them by the king, but there were no suburbs in the
sense of people moving out of a crowded city to more open spaces
beyond. This was to hold true till the nineteenth century. Bernier
used the word 'suburbs' not in the modern sense but to describe
the ruins of old cities near Shahjahanabad, and the pockets of
habitation around wholesale markets. These were akin to the
faubourgs of Paris and were separated by large royal or aristocratic preserves, gardens or hunting lodges, particularly Jahan-
numa in the north-west and Shalimar in the north. There were
palaces and hunting grounds also on the left of the river, which
were reached by crossing the river on elephants,[4] until they came
to be linked to the city by the bridge of boats beside the Fort
and Salimgarh. Delhi was fed from the Doab and from the grain
emporia east of the river in Shahdara, Ghaziabad and Patparganj.
These were linked to the intramural market near the Fatehpuri
mosque; vegetables and fruit came from the north-west and were
sold in the wholesale market of Sabzi Mandi in Mughalpura, outside the city wall, on the Grand Trunk road to Lahore.[5]

In the decades between Bernier's visit and the British conquest in 1803, Shahjahanabad withstood the ravages of civil war and invasion. The basic map of the city remained unchanged, though there was some building activity as well as cases of some areas becoming gradually or suddenly deserted. Masjids, temples, houses, markets, streets and gardens were laid out by individuals at different times. Maliwara and Chhipiwara, and suburban Teliwara originated in the period of Maratha control, as indicated by the Marathi suffix 'wara'. During the vicissitudes of struggle for power at the imperial level, troops, merchants, artisans and intellectuals often withdrew to the provinces. Even as late as the 1780s, however, there were sixty bazaars in the city and abundant supplies of food. The wall of the city, which was not proof against Nadir Shah or the Marathas, did protect the inhabitants to a considerable degree from the Mewatis and Gujars of the hinterland. When imperial authority declined, that of the *Kotwal* increased proportionately. From his office in Chandni Chowk, he and his twelve *thanadars* policed the town, collected duties, regulated trade and industries, and kept a count of the population and of immigrants, through the agency of the *mohulla* news-sheets. The extent and incidence of tax-collection appears to have varied depending on whether Mughal or Maratha was in power, as well as on the efficiency of individuals.[6]

This city, battered but not ruined, uncertain of its fate but with enough sense of kinship and a cultural and social tradition to check its morale from flagging, was taken over from the Marathas by the British in 1803. It was a city that Bernier would have recognized, and in the following half-century it changed only to a limited extent. Bernier had carried away an impression of a city consisting largely of 'wretched mud-and-thatch houses' which appeared less a town than 'a collection of many villages'. A century and a half later, Forbes was disparaging about one of the boulevards, Faiz Bazaar, which he saw as 'a long street of very miserable appearance', of a piece with many houses which were 'low and mean'.[7] The disparity of status noticed by Bernier was also apparent to Forbes, who said that the houses of the *umara* and the rajas were on a larger scale than those of nobles in Europe, 'on account of their immense establishments'. This was also the impression of Heber in the 1840s, who said the houses at Delhi 'far exceed in grandeur anything seen in Moscow'.[8] Bernier's disappointment at the absence of window-display (indicating lack of familiarity with Indian styles of salesmanship) is echoed by the Englishman of 1815 who commented that the bazaars were poorly furnished.[9]

The *Gazetteer* of 1815 claimed that the value of land in the city had doubled in the first ten years of the 'British Peace'. There was building activity in these years, one of the most spectacular constructions being the *haveli* built by Bhawani Shankar, a shrewd Indian who had backed the Marathas and later the British, and was locally nick-named *Namak-Haraam*.[10] In a census of houses in 1843, over 23,000 were counted, of which over 17,000 were listed as being made of brick and stone.[11] 'The largest city in India' was the phrase of a European soldier who saw Delhi in 1844, after travelling up-country from Calcutta[12]—a far cry from Bernier's 'collection of many villages'. The Palace buildings and the houses of the rajas in Daryaganj did not acquire additional storeys, for the traveller approaching by river or across the bridge of boats saw the domes and minarets as a distinctive skyline, with date-palms and acacias showing over the wall.

After the British conquest, there was an impression that the population of the city was increasing. Available estimates for the size of the population in the previous centuries are unreliable, and specific enumerations are available only from 1843. Lord Lake in 1806, and other officials in 1808, were convinced that there was an increase, which they attributed with complacency to the novelty of a regime of 'security, comfort and impartial justice'.[13] In 1833, a detailed census indicated that there were 119,860 people in the city, excluding the Palace.[14] The censuses of 1843, 1845 and 1853 show the population rising from 131,000 to 137,000 and then to 151,000; in 1854, half the population of Delhi District (306,550) was said to be concentrated in the city.[15] By 1850, the pressure of population led to a row of houses being built down the length of the two main streets of Chandni Chowk and Faiz Bazaar[16] along the centre of which flowed the two major canals of the city.[17] Pockets of settlements developed outside the wall. Many extramural markets had been closed or shifted into the walled city in the course of the previous century. Some of these appear to have shifted out again in the early nineteenth century. The settlements west of the city wall, described inaccurately as thirteen villages, had a largely non-agricultural population. Sabzi Mandi, 'consisting of houses ... high walls, gardens etc.',[18] was located in Mughalpura, the property of a Mughal *maafidar*. South of this were Dargah Nabi Karim (around the shrine of Qadam Sharif), Teliwara and Shidipura (granted to Meher Ali Shidi. in 1773). These were all in the revenue estate of Jahan-numa village.[19] But these settlements were not formalized by being made into extra-mural wards, as in nineteenth-century Pune, where the increasing population was settled in new wards adjacent to the city.[20]

The increasing population of these settlements was explained as being caused by 'the annual increase ... by births, the influx of strangers and travellers and other causes incidental to large and thriving suburbs'.[21] The 'strangers' were chiefly from the Punjab, whence a dispersal of *khatris* occurred early in the nineteenth century. In the north, Rajpura Cantonment was separated from the city by large royal gardens rich with fruit trees.[22] The army's bazaar was located at 'Khyber Pass' on the Alipur Road. Though Mughal power declined, this did not lead to any exodus of Muslim families from Delhi, for the numbers of Muslims and Hindus remain fairly consistently equal in these years; the immigration rate of both communities was fairly equal.[23]

An Indian chronicler, writing in the early nineteenth century, who remarked on the extent of Calcutta, the buildings of Jaipur, the abundance of goods in Lucknow, thought that Delhi was chiefly remarkable for its *aadmiyat*, its polished urbanity.[24] And the culture of Delhi was contained within its walls. 'The culture of the time was obstinately, narrow-mindedly urban, seeking protection within the city walls against a surrounding barbarism. The desire to be closer to nature would not take a man outside the city, because it was believed that nature fulfilled itself in the gardens ... and the breezes of the city.'[25]

There was in those years a camaraderie between Hindus and Muslims, at the Court and at Delhi College, at the gatherings in Chandni Chowk and Sa'dullah Chowk, around the *dastan-gos*, at festivals, especially *Basant* (when the whole city was 'dressed like a bride') and the *Phulwalon Ki Sair*, during weddings and *musha'aras*.[26] Weekly *musha'aras* were held at Ghaziuddin Madarsa (where Delhi College classes were held) and on those nights Ajmeri Gate was kept open late into the night. The spirit of the age has been described as having been characterized by three addictions—to mysticism in Islam, to a frenetic gaiety, and to the salons of the courtesans—all explained as being a form of escape from the political insecurity of the late eighteenth and early nineteenth century.[27]

In Delhi, this half-century saw the establishment of the first Indian press for Persian and Urdu lithography, and the publication of some of India's first newspapers.[28] By 1852 the mushrooming of private presses in Delhi led to a sharp fall in the price of books. The most exciting thing that happened was a literary and scientific efflorescence which C. F. Andrews called 'the Delhi Renaissance'. The focus of this was Delhi College.

Rs 7,000 out of the funds collected by a short-lived Town Duties Committee in 1824 were spent on repairing Ghaziuddin Madarsa.[29] This housed a school which had been set up in 1692, to which the newly-formed Committee of Public Instruction gave a grant in 1824 equivalent to that allocated from *waqf* funds.[30] Three years later, English classes were added to it under the encouragement of Charles Trevelyan. The local inhabitants were not too happy at this, suspecting it to be the thin end of the wedge of Christian proselytization.[31] In 1829 Nawab Itmad-ud-daula of Lucknow (a native of Delhi) gave a generous endowment for the College, to be managed by British officials. (This was variously described as the Itmaduddaula Fund and the Fazl Ali Bequest.) This helped the school to win back local allegiance. From that time on the English and 'Oriental' sections were separate. The school attracted boys from all over north India, and the Committee of Public Instruction gave many scholarships. The English courses were initially wider in scope than the 'Oriental', but by 1848 the two sections were on a par. This was because of the remarkable enthusiasm of both teachers and students, which made the College a dynamic instrument of change.

Delhi College (and later those in Agra and Benares) achieved something which was qualitatively very different from the contemporary Calcutta 'Renaissance'.[32] Delhi had a well-defined and broad-based school curriculum and a native language. On to this were grafted European philosophy and science. The students showed a decided predilection for a scientific rather than a literary education. It is remarkable that this should have been the preference of a people renowned for their love of literary Urdu. It was not a question of making a choice. The students and teachers found it possible to be enthusiastic about mathematics and astronomy and to compose Urdu verse at the same time. The joint efforts of Indians and Europeans led to Urdu transforming itself from a language of poetry to the transmitter of western knowledge. The college set up a Vernacular Society, which translated as many as a hundred and twenty-five books, chiefly Greek classics, Persian works and scientific treatises, into Urdu, all in the space of about twenty years.[33] There were inevitable, but not insurmountable, hurdles such as Syed Ahmad Khan's reluctance to give up his Ptolemaic vision of the world and accept the Copernican view. C. F. Andrews has given a vivid account of young Zakaullah running all the way home from College; a more sedate pace was impossible because of his sense of excitement at the wonders of mathematics he had just imbibed. The work of the Vernacular Society was supplemented by that of the Society for the Promotion of Knowledge in India through the vernacular, the executive committee of which consisted of Thomas Metcalfe of Delhi, Boutros, the Principal of Delhi College from 1840 to 1845, Charles Grant and Dwarkanath Tagore.

The European teachers who were remembered for their sense of involvement were Boutros, a Frenchman, and Sprenger, a German. This was perhaps the reason why learning English was not, as in Bengal, regarded as vitally important. 'We regarded the English section as a means of getting a job, not an education,' commented Altaf Husain Hali, one of the most renowned alumni of the College. Nazir Ahmad, who became a well-known novelist in Urdu, recounted how 'my father . . . told me . . . he would rather see me die than learn English.'[34] This would explain why visitors such as Bishop Heber, Jacquemment and Shah Abdul Aziz felt that the educated classes of Upper India had been touched very little in feeling and life-style by the British presence.[35]

The teachers at the College included Mamluk Ali and Mufti Sadruddin 'Azurda' of the Court. Among the students were 'Master' Ram Chandra, whose work on differential calculus was published and noticed in Europe, Dr Mukand Lal, one of the first allopathic practitioners in north India, Maulvi Ziauddin, an eminent scholar of Arabic, Mohammed Husain Azad, author of *Khumkhan-e-Javed*, a work of literary criticism, Maulvi Zakaullah, historian, Pyare Lal 'Ashoob', and Master Nand Kishore, well-known educationists, and Syed Ahmad Khan, a versatile person who moved from mathematics to theology to archaeology, and later was to found the Muslim Anglo-Oriental College at Aligarh in 1877, the year that Delhi College was forced to close down.[36] Even as late as the nineteen-thirties, the Delhi College ethos could be seen in the *kayasths* of Delhi who studied Persian not because it was useful but because of the family tradition.

In the years before 1857, in sharp contrast to the subsequent period, relations between the prominent Indians of the town and the British officials were characterized by an easy conviviality, because Englishmen as well as Muslim *umara* and Hindu *kayasths* and *khatris* all subscribed to the vibrant Urdu culture and etiquette. Apart from the literary and academic meeting-grounds, there were many other points of contact, formal and informal. Magistrate Gubbins' Relief Society had Indian and European members, and the amount of subscriptions from the Indians was soon larger than that from the Europeans.[37] The Delhi Bank, pioneered by Lala Chunna Mal, had Hindu, Muslim and European shareholders.[38] An Archaeological Society was formed to study the monuments and ruins near Delhi. Its members included British officials, and Master Ram Chandra, Syed Ahmad Khan, Maulvi Ziauddin, and other scholars of Delhi College. Syed Ahmad Khan was curious enough and agile enough to scale the sides of the Qutb in a basket manipulated from the top storey, in order to decipher the inscriptions at the higher levels. He presented a paper to the Society on his findings, and tried to make them accept his belief that part of the Qutb was built by a Hindu ruler.[39] From these discussions and papers resulted his massive book *Aasar-us-Sanaadid* (*The Ruins of the Cities of Delhi*), published in 1846, and considerably revised again in 1854. This was well before the Archaeological Department started focussing attention on these 'ruins'. On the strength of this book, he was made a Fellow of the Royal Asiatic Society, but there was no attempt to translate this remarkably comprehensive work into English.[40] It was, however, translated into French by Garcin de Tassy, a scholar of Urdu.

Religious zeal often bubbled to the surface, but did not destroy the harmony. Excited debates were held in the Jama Masjid in the 1850s between local *maulvis* and Dr Pfander of the Church Missionary Society (similar debates were held in Agra). These were not prohibited by the Resident, as were the lectures of the

Waha'bi leader Shah Mohammad Ismael.[41] The officials became
uneasy because Shah Abdul Aziz, the son of Wali'allah, declared
that 'in this city [sc. Delhi] the *Imam-al-Muslimin* wields no
authority, while the decrees of the Christian leaders are obeyed
without fear [sc. of consequences]'.[42] From the British side, the
Baptist Missionary Society (from 1818) and the Society for the
Propagation of the Gospel (from 1852) alienated conservative
sections of people in Delhi by their proselytizing activities. They
had their moment of triumph when they won two prestigious
converts—Master Ram Chandra and Doctor Chiman Lal. Their
baptism in 1852 generated a lot of interest, and the officials feared
that there might even be a riot. But though 'the whole Hindu
population turned out and surrounded and filled the Church', the
'greatest order and decency prevailed', commented the Reverend
Mr Jennings. 'We had near at hand, though not visible, a body
of Muslim *chokadars* and *chaprasses* whose services, however,
were not required.'[43] Adopting Christianity did not make Ram
Chandra break with Urdu and the cosmopolitan culture of Delhi.
He edited two of Delhi's earliest Urdu newspapers—the *Fawaid-
ul-Nazarin* (aimed at the general reader) and the *Qiran us Sa'adain*
(which published articles on scientific subjects). In July 1847, he
published a translation of Macaulay's Minute on Education, and
commented sadly '*Dekhiye Hindustan ke dinen kab phirenge?*'
('When will the great days of India return?').[44]

The British and Indians met over leisurely soirées at the houses
of Colonel Skinner (who was the son of an English father and an
Indian mother), Raja Hindu Rao, Lala Chunna Mal, the nawabs
of Jhajjar and Ballabgarh, or Court *umara*. Ghalib, like others,
realized that the British had come to stay, and shrewdly thought
that a *qasida* to the Queen would be a useful investment. But he
went that far and no further. When Thomson, the provincial
Secretary, treated him boorishly, Ghalib sacrificed the offer of an
appointment at Delhi College, though he desperately needed a
steady income to cushion him against his extravagances and his
gambling debts.[45]

The British administrators in Delhi often thought it their duty
to act so as to keep the balance between the communities. This
was to be done, depending on the occasion, by arbitration or by
the show of force. In 1807 there was tension in the city because

of demonstrations against a Jain banker who sponsored a *Rath-jatra* procession with great fanfare. Charles Metcalfe, on whom we are dependent for an account of the incident, claimed that a riot would have ensued had the civil authorities not acted in time and called out the army.[46] Tension between the Jains and Hindus occurred in 1816 and 1834, after which such processions were banned. In 1837, Magistrate Lindsay altered the traditional proclamation about *tazias* in favour of the Shias. The Sunnis, twice as numerous as the Shias, petitioned against this order to Thomas Metcalfe, who had it repealed.[47] In 1853 and 1855 the Resident called out troops to prevent possible clashes during the celebration of Id and Ram Lila.[48] The Mughals had a simple device for minimizing clashes. They reserved Chandni Chowk for their own cavalcades. The Ram Lila procession traditionally passed from Mori Gate to Nigambodh Ghat, skirting the Palace along its northern face. This was modified when Bahadur Shah ordered that it should pass in front of the Palace so that he could also have the pleasure of viewing it.[49]

By prohibiting cow-slaughter the Mughal rulers had scrupulously avoided offending the Hindus.[50] At the Id of 1852 Bahadur Shah sacrificed camels and his subjects goats. In 1853 Thomas Metcalfe issued a decree permitting cow-slaughter on festive occasions. Bahadur Shah as well as Hakim Ahsanullah Khan, the court physician, were unhappy at this decision. The Magistrate, who was a Hindu, ordered that meat should be screened before sale. The butchers went on strike, confident they would win. An abortive attempt was made to replace them with butchers imported from Meerut, but ultimately the officials had to yield to the butchers.[51] Shortly before the Revolt, Egerton permitted Muslim butchers to kill cows in a locality which was largely Hindu. The shops owned by Hindus observed a *hartal* for three days, till the decision was rescinded.[52] These acts of the rulers were not so much an attempt at creating tension as an extension to Indian towns of the practice of the slaughter of cows for consumption by British officials and soldiers.

When the British captured the city, they found that it had been divided into spheres of control by neighbouring Gujar tribes for purposes of plunder. Ochterlony (the Indianized Englishman, who had thirteen Indian wives and whom the local people called 'Loony Akhtar') organized a force of volunteers to check them.[53]

Later, the Assistant who had charge of the criminal court was made superintendent of the city police, which was directly under the *Kotwal* and his twelve *thanadars*, as in Mughal times. Under him were 148 infantry and 230 guards, all paid by the Government. They were supplemented by 400 *chowkidars* on night-duty, paid by the inhabitants.[54] In both cases there was one guard or *chowkidar* to every four hundred of the population. The judicial powers of the Resident, fortified by the contingents of the army in and near the city, gave security from external aggression and from raids by the Gujars and Mewatis.

By the Act of 1837, applied to Delhi in 1841, the charge of the *chowkidari* tax was given to the *Bakshi*, in place of the citizens' *panchayats*. This was so strongly resented by the inhabitants that the traditional system was restored.[55] The British image of themselves as the bulwark of impartiality led the editor of the *Delhi Gazette* to suggest that a European be appointed *Kotwal*, or at least that Hindus be appointed alternately with Muslims, and the local police force be recruited from Europeans and from Hindus of the North-Western Provinces rather than from local men.[56] This fetish of maintaining an artificial communal balance was endorsed by the officials, for Magistrate Lindsay in 1837 was said to have 'broken through the very unjust rule of giving preference in nomination to Muslims only'.[57] The last *Kotwal* before the Revolt was young Gangadhar Nehru, the father of Motilal Nehru.[58]

Whatever tension flared up occasionally seems to have been caused often by sections of the inhabitants playing off different authorities against each other—*Kotwal* against Magistrate, or Commissioner against Resident. Charles Metcalfe expressed this clearly in 1807: 'Two authorities exist in the town, which circumstance gives rise to much trouble and confusion.'[59] An episode of 1837 illustrates how the inhabitants sought to divide the civil authorities to their own advantage. A grain 'riot' occurred because some *banias* cornered the supplies. This was aggravated by the Commissioner fining those who asked that prices be fixed. The protesters asked Thomas Metcalfe to intervene.[60] Subsequently the export of grain from the city was regulated by the Magistrate and the police, to reduce the power of the *Kotwal*, who had been helpless in 1837.[61] We have no evidence as to how many people took part in these 'riots'.

There were problems for the administrators at Delhi, especially if a foreign power was sovereign, because Delhi was such a compact city, with a dense population, with well-defined religious, caste and *mohulla* affiliations and a strong historical tradition. At all times, the British were on the alert against a local rising, not against an invasion from outside. It became a standard practice for the Resident to call out the army when an Emperor was about to die—as Seton did in 1806, when Shah Alam II died. In 1852 Bahadur Shah was seriously ill, and the *Delhi Gazette* urged that 'it would be unsafe to diminish the number of troops in Delhi... The death of the king, which is likely to occur any day, is sure to unsettle people's minds in this populous city.' The fear of a Waha'bi outbreak might have contributed to this, and might have been why, the following year, the guards at the Palace gates were increased in anticipation of the Emperor's death. 'The Wahabee movement seems to have affected Delhi', reported the *Delhi Gazette* in September 1852. 'Last week several houses, including those of Husain Baksh, the Punjabi merchant, were searched.' The same issue quoted a local Muslim-owned newspaper, *Urdu Akhbar*, as expressing surprise at anyone 'opposing such wise and powerful rulers'. Syed Ahmad Khan, like many others in Delhi, went through a 'Waha'bi phase' in the early 1850s, but this was perfectly consistent with maintaining a rapport with the officials and with the Delhi College teachers. In 1850 the Waha'bi leader Wilayat Ali had given lectures at some mosques in Delhi. He had been received by the Emperor and by the Resident, but the attitude of the Resident made him deem it prudent to leave Delhi soon after.[62]

In 1828, to humour the Emperor, the European troops had been moved out from the city to the cantonment on the Ridge, and only Indian soldiers were left within the walls.[63] In the 1840s Napier and Ellenborough repeatedly pointed out how dangerous it was to continue to have the arsenal in the city, where an accidental explosion could occur any time.[64] Lord Wellington, making suggestions from London, thought that the Resident should barricade himself inside 'a citadel comprising the Residency and the Magazine'. He went on to add: 'There are in the town many houses pucka built... These, by degrees, must be bought and destroyed... It would be very desirable to endeavour to prevail upon the Mughal to construct no more buildings of this description within the precincts of the palace, at least not within the distance of cannonshot of the citadel.'[65] Fortunately for the inhabitants of Delhi, these remarkable instructions were not put into effect. The main arsenal was shifted from the city to the bank of the river in 1851, in response to a petition from the local inhabitants, who, like Napier, feared an accidental explosion.[66] Only a small magazine was retained between Kashmeri Gate and the Palace.

The Treaty of 1803* restricted the Mughal Emperor's domain and jurisdiction to his Palace, and his revenue to the income from territories north-west of the town of Kabulpur, which was farmed out and was under the management of the Resident. The Emperor and his family received regular but frugal pocket money, and *nazars* on the occasion of festivals.[67] The British succeeded in making the Emperor politically functionless, but the mystique of the court kept Delhi essentially a Mughal town. 'In heart we are united, though in appearance there is disunion. And this circumstance is perceptible to the whole world,' wrote the gentle Bahadur Shah to the Governor-General's Agent in 1843, with the fortunate ability to sublimate his discomfiture by verse.[68] His consolation lay in versification and flying kites. Debendranath Tagore, who visited Delhi shortly before the Revolt, wrote that the first thing he saw as he approached the city by boat was a large crowd gathered to watch the Emperor's prowess at flying kites.[69] The *musha'aras* held at the court were relayed to the people outside, and the rivalry of the poet laureate, Zauq, and Ghalib were discussed animatedly in the town.

The Emperors and Residents co-existed on fairly amicable terms. There were some stray incidents of cold war, when the Emperors complained about tributes or honours. Once the British magis-

---

* Shahjahanabad was the chief city of Delhi Territory, which was acquired by the East India Company from the Marathas by the Treaty of Surji Arjungaon in 1803. It comprised Delhi and Hissar Divisions, which were sub-divided in 1819 into the districts of Haryana, Rohtak, Panipat, Gurgaon and Delhi; in 1848 and 1853, 193 square miles from Meerut and Bulandshahar (the 'Eastern Parganah') was added to the Territory east of the river. Lying on the route from Calcutta to the yet unconquered Punjab, Shahjahanabad had, for the British, the strategic importance of a frontier town. It also linked the North-Western Provinces with the principalities of Rajasthan, and the British conducted their diplomatic relations with these from Delhi.

trate empowered the banker Lala Chunna Mal to seize the property of the heir-apparent, to which the latter retorted by moving his worldly goods to the immunity of the Palace precincts.[70] The empress Mumtaz Mahal offered to adopt Resident Seton as her son. If this had been accepted, it would have had bizarre consequences for the issue of sovereignty![71] When Simon Fraser accepted a title from the Emperor, Governor-General Bentinck was annoyed and made it clear that this should not be allowed to form a precedent.[72] The Resident was a powerful official, the representative of the sovereign power. But the British officials never ceased to covet the less tangible aura attached to the court of the powerless Mughals. The British officials repeatedly suggested that they should occupy the Palace. Thomas Metcalfe, in a detailed Minute in 1848, proposed to move the Emperor to the Qutb Charles Napier suggested Fatehpur Sikri.[73] Metcalfe was enthusiastically supported by Dalhousie. If the accident of the Revolt had not occurred, this plan would have been put into effect when the long-lived Bahadur Shah died.[74]

'The British Resident [sc. at Delhi] was very important in those days,' wrote a newspaper in 1868, referring to the years before the Revolt. It was 'the most coveted job in India'[75] because Residents elsewhere in India were only concerned with diplomatic relations. The Delhi Resident 'ostensibly [sc. represented] the British Government at Court but, in fact, . . . his business is rather to watch the straw sovereign, pay him his pension and regulate his intercourse with strangers'.[76] These powers were sometimes felt to be too much of a responsibility for one man. In 1816 Charles Metcalfe complained to the Court of Directors that the Resident's work was more that 'of a subordinate Government than of a political Resident'.[77] So, when Ochterlony replaced Metcalfe in 1819, the Resident was asked to share his responsibilities with a Civil Commissioner. But Metcalfe, who returned to Delhi in 1825, did not find his own earlier recommendation palatable, and the post of Civil Commissioner was scrapped. In 1830 he wrote a Minute to justify 'the completeness of control and unity of authority' of what came to be known as his Delhi System.[78] Bentinck, after his tour of the Territory in 1831, decided that the offices of Collector, Judge and Magistrate should not be vested in the same person. The Residency was abolished, and the Territory thereafter administered by a Commissioner, with increased power given to the Board of Revenue and the Agra High Court. The junior Officers were English, Bengali and Delhi men. One of the most promising of them was Syed Ahmad Khan.

'Delhi is a very suggestive and moralizing place,' wrote the inimitable Emily Eden in 1838. 'Such stupendous remains of power and wealth passed and passing away—and somehow I feel that we horrid English have just "gone and done it", merchandised it, revenued it and spoiled it all.'[79] 'Merchandising' and 'Revenuing' were the functions of any imperialist goverment. What appeared to be a new concept was one spelt out by Governor-General Amherst in 1823, that town duties be earmarked for local 'improvements', and that even direct taxes might be levied for this purpose. The follow-up action on this in Delhi was that a Committee was set up to administer town duties. Its work was made easy by the very comprehensive report prepared by Fortescue in 1820, cataloguing the customs and town duties prevalent in Delhi.[80] But before the experiment had got under way, the Committee was disbanded by the masterful Charles Metcalfe, and the nascent Municipality crushed under the weight of his centralizing policy. Charles Trevelyan, in his Report of 1833, criticized town duties, which, he held, had made Delhi decline as a trade-centre, just as their absence had helped Bhiwani, Rewari and Shahdara to flourish.[81] Town duties were, accordingly, abolished first in Bengal and then in the North-Western Provinces.

To people in Delhi the civil administration at this time connoted not a place or an office—as it did after the 1860s—but individual officials. This was because the British accepted the walled city, and did not segregate themselves in a 'Civil Lines'. Land beyond Kashmeri Gate was handed out by the Mughals very generously. Ochterlony laid out Mubarik Bagh, four miles north of the city.[82] In 1839, one of his begums, Mubarik-un-nissa, claimed 180 *bighas*, and was allowed 42 as her due.[83] A more complicated and bizarre issue of succession rights was about a Jorus (?) Bagh beyond Qudsia Gardens. This had been given to Begum Samru and then to her heir David Ochterlony Dyce Sombre. In 1883 compensation for this property (which was requisitioned by the Canal Department) was claimed by seven members of an Italian family called Solaroli—their claim being based on the marriage of Baron Solaroli to Georgiana, sister of

Dyce Sombre (another sister had married an Englishman). The original 25 *bighas* 'had increased' mysteriously to 40, for which 'full compensation' was given. The sum paid—Rs 5019—was converted into Italian currency and helped support the family of an indigent Italian nobleman![84] There were some Englishmen who had such an attachment to the city that they built private palaces and pleasure-domes near it. Ludlow built his 'Castle' (the area retains the name though there is no trace of Ludlow Castle).[85] This was on a site beyond the Qudsia, purchased in 1820. Thomas Metcalfe built his 'House' (it is still standing) on the river front in 1830. He and his brother Charles patronized the Mughal gardens at Shalimar and the Qutb, where Thomas built a country house in 1844.[86] William Fraser owned the large stone house spectacularly located on the Ridge and described by Jacquemment as 'an immense Gothic fortress'. This became popularly known as Bara Hindu Rao, after that nobleman bought it in 1835[87] (this, too, is perpetuated in the name of the hospital built on the site).

'The works of the Europeans at Delhi', commented a visitor in 1845, 'are confined to a magnificent canal, an arsenal . . . a church, a college and a printing press.'[88] Some of the palaces were requisitioned for offices. These were scattered south of Kashmeri Gate. The *Kotwali* continued to function from the traditional building in Chandni Chowk. In 1849 the Joint Magistrate's office and residence were moved from outside to inside the city, a move commended as evincing 'consideration for the people and for the safety of Delhi'.[89] Safdarjang's house was used as a guest-house for British travellers. The post-office and the arsenal were located south of St James' Church. The area thus acquired the appearance of a Christian enclave, adding another dimension to a cosmopolitan city. The Swedish author of a work on European architecture in India has described the church as 'a very unusual building in Indian territory'.[90] It was this fact— that the British lived and built in 'Indian territory'—that made Delhi before 1857 different from the Presidency towns, where there was racial segregation. British officials lived in rented houses in Daryaganj and inside Kashmeri Gate. When in 1847 Begum Samru's palace in Chandni Chowk fell vacant, it was suggested that the *kachahri* move there, so as to be near the *Kotwali*. The

Delhi Bank was, however, quicker in getting together the necessary funds to buy the house.[91]

In such a situation, where British officials and Indian citizens
lived and worked side by side in a confined area, the civilian
officials could not afford to be indifferent to questions concerning
the maintenance of the city, road repair and traffic regulations.
In the early years, before town duties came to be earmarked for
local improvement, Seton undertook to replant trees along the
Chandni Chowk at his own expense.[92] In 1830 Trevelyan spent
his own money to establish a small suburb outside Lahore Gate.
A classic Whig amalgam of altruism and financial hardheadedness,
he wrote enthusiastically about his experiment. 'The population
of Delhi is crowded within the walls, around which immense
fields of ruins extend ... A portion of them I have purchased off
the Government to lay out in streets and squares, giving to each
person as much as he will undertake to build good houses upon,
thereby raising up new towns and converting into valuable property what was before a mere sightless [sic] nuisance. Even now
the example has had great effect, and the people are applying ...
to buy up these rubbish lands, with a view to their improvement.
My new suburb will soon become a handsome city, without my
laying out a Rupee on it except the original purchase money of
the ground.'[93]

The city wall was kept in good repair and well fortified with
bastions and glacis. A contemporary noted that 'the shopkeepers
have encroached on to the roads in the bazaar', and their shops
were demolished by the British and returned to the state in which
they were under Shahjahan. His judicious comment was '*Durushti
aur narmi bahamdar bahast*' (a mixture of the firm and gentle is
good).[94] The shortlived town committee used the duties to repair
drains and bridges and the Canal which had been reopened two
years earlier. In 1822 the *taiul*, *waqf*, *zabt* and *nazul* properties
held in trust by the British Government for the Emperor were
removed from the control of the city *Kotwal* and put under a
special *daroga*.[95] Middleton reported with pride that the subsequent cleaning of mosques and their environs was appreciated by
the local Muslims.[96] Bishop Heber noticed in 1828 that the Jama
Masjid was repaired by a special grant from Government (he was

2

in error, for the grant was from *waqf* funds); it was 'a measure which was very popular in Delhi'.[97] It was decidedly not popular with the squatters who had long lived undisturbed in the smaller mosques and who were now unceremoniously ejected.[98]

The *Delhi Gazette* frequently complained that the city roads were neglected; this referred not only to cantonment roads but also to areas of the 'native city'. It was insinuated that only the 'exhibit' roads were kept in repair, and that 'the lanes and back slums [sc. were] worse than Edinburgh'.[99] The Local Road Committee (a Provincial Department) was advised to borrow money from the Delhi Bank to expedite road repair. The sharp tongue of the *Delhi Gazette* was equally unsparing on the local inhabitants. It criticized the Hindu residents of the road from Shahbula-ka-Bad to the Chidiyakhana, who would spend thousands on a wedding but would balk at giving forty rupees to repair their road. In 1837 the local authorities tried to induce prominent local men to subscribe towards improving roads. The response was poor, being limited to Raja Hindu Rao and Ahmad Ali Khan. The Rajas of Pataudi and Ballabgarh are known to have made generous grants.[100] Diwan Kishan Lal, who had been in the service of the Raja of Jhajjar and later was made Deputy Collector by Thomas Metcalfe, founded the *ganj* in the western suburbs which came to be named after him.[101] Near it were the eleven acres which were gifted to the grain merchants of the city in 1853 when trade with Punjab had started to pick up after its conquest by the British. This area was to serve as 'a grain ganj', so that the procession of carts carrying grain did not need to enter[102] the city. The local merchants and bankers agreed in 1856 to raise a loan for building a permanent bridge over the Jamuna which would enable the railway line from Calcutta to be extended to Delhi.[103] They were also enthusiastic about a project to introduce steam navigation between Delhi and Mathura at their own expense, provided the government met the initial cost of the steam engine.[104]

Questions of public health were discussed frequently because of Delhi's importance as a military encampment and because of the possibility that it might be made the capital of the North-Western Provinces. In the early nineteenth century the British only imperfectly understood Indian diseases and problems of public health, but attempts were made to pinpoint causes and find solutions. The diseases prevalent in Delhi—cholera, malaria, and the 'Delhi Sore', were thought to be caused entirely by waterborne contagion, transmitted through running water, brackish well water and water-logged pools. A proposal was made to drain the Najafgarh *Jheel* in 1817, but this was not done, probably because of the expense involved.[105]

The sanitary arrangements within the city had from its inception been linked to the water supply in the hinterland. The Ali Mardan Canal had dried up. Soon after the British conquest, Mr Mercer offered to reopen it at his own expense, if he were given the canal revenues for the next twenty years. Accordingly a survey was made in 1810, and work begun in 1817. Charles Metcalfe formally opened it four years later. It was to provide healthy drinking water for the city-dwellers, who greeted the flowing water with offerings of ghee and flowers. But the farmers in Delhi Territory used up so much of it that the quantity flowing into the city decreased and the Canal finally dried up again.[106] During the eighteen-twenties and eighteen-thirties, when the canal did provide potable water, the wells were neglected. This was possibly why in 1843 as many as 555 of the 607 wells in the city were pronounced to be brackish. In 1846 at the suggestion of Lord Ellenborough, the Provincial Ways and Means Committee constructed a large tank (popularly known as 'Lal Diggi') between the Palace and Khas Bazaar to be linked to the canal and to serve as a reservoir. The officials somewhat ineptly tinkered with the Shahjahani drains; this led to flooding in the city, with the drainwater flowing back. This, and the canal, rather than the Najafgarh *Jheel*, were now blamed for the city's ill-health.[107] In 1852 the question was thought sufficiently serious to merit a very comprehensive report on the city's drainage.[108]

The barren Ridge, with its extremes of temperature, was considered such a health hazard for the soldiers that regiments were stationed at Delhi only for two years at a time.[109] Napier was puzzled. 'If Delhi be unhealthy, what made it such a grand city?', he wanted to know. 'A rigid police to keep the town clean, sound sanitary rules about irrigation from the canal, which runs much too rapidly to produce malaria if the banks are kept clean, would perhaps make Delhi as healthy as any part of India,' he said.[110]

Generous contributions were made by men of the Court,

bankers and merchants towards a projected dispensary, to be built 'in a manner worthy of the Imperial City'. As against nearly Rs 10,000 from local subscriptions, the Government grant amounted to only Rs 2,500.[111] An Act of 1850 sanctioned for British India the establishment of Committees in towns to levy taxes for public health. Apart from the Presidency towns, this was followed up in Ahmedabad where a 'wall-tax' was levied for conservancy expenses.[112] There was nothing similar in Delhi but in 1849 an appeal in Urdu was circulated in the city, urging the inhabitants to accept taxation for the purpose of a conservancy scheme. The example of Ahmedabad was cited as worth following.[113] Thomas Metcalfe, Commissioner of Delhi, was sceptical as to 'whether among the most influential members of the native community there exists that degree of public spirit which would induce them to originate a system of conservancy which will not only entail upon them their personal exertion and responsibility but a taxation to which they are most sensitively opposed'.[114]

The exigencies of the Rising of 1857 jeopardized good relations, not as between Muslims and Hindus but as between those who supported the rebels, for reasons of conviction or of self-interest, and those who either sat on the fence or helped the British troops. Nawab Hamid Ali Khan supported the Mughal ruler, Nawab Amiruddin the British. Mufti Sadruddin 'Azurda' was opposed to the Rising, though he stood by the Emperor. Of the merchants and bankers, Ramji Das, Saligram, Qutbuddin and Husain Baksh helped Bahadur Shah, though many others stayed neutral or secretly aided the British. These names are examples to indicate that the cleavage cannot be simplistically stated as being between a declining Muslim aristocracy and a nascent Hindu bourgeoisie, but between those who sided with the Emperor and those who were far-sighted enough to back the British and thus set up a store of security and rewards for the future.

During the siege the British on the Ridge waited anxiously for Id, on 3 August 1857, hoping that the Purbias and Muslims would clash, for then 'Delhi will fall to the British'. They misunderstood Bahadur Shah and said: 'It is a great satire on Muslims fighting for their faith that at Id no one was permitted to sacrifice a cow.'[115] Mughal Beg's last words on the gallows in Chandni Chowk were to be '*Hindu Musulman mere shurreek ho/meri yaad rahen*[116] (Hindus and Muslims be my witnesses/May I never be forgotten). The British then and later were to persist in holding to the stereotypes of their own creation—the treacherous Muslim and the loyal Hindu.

The immediate sequel to the fall of Delhi was that a vast quantity of wealth was seized by the British forces, thousands were killed and the surviving inhabitants expelled. The British soldiers encamped on the Ridge had kept their spirits up through the long hot summer by dreaming of the riches in Delhi—'a nice little diamond or two' from the 'rich old niggers'.[117] After the city was stormed, their pent-up tension was released in an orgy of violence. 'For several days after the assault every native was . . . killed; the women and children were spared,' wrote the wife of C. B. Saunders, the Commissioner of Delhi.[118] The officers themselves frankly admitted that often there was no discrimination between the guilty and the innocent. 'It was a war of extermination—in short, one of the most cruel and vindictive wars the world has seen,' admitted a participant.[119] Theophilus Metcalfe's sense of shock at the ravaging of his father's house was transformed into the anger of a maddened bull. He plunged into a welter of killing Indians.[120] Mrs Saunders put this in her own way when she wrote home that Metcalfe was a 'great help' to her husband, 'from his local knowledge and great activity'.[121] Saunders himself sympathized with Metcalfe and wanted the Supreme Government to give him compensation. When news of the activities at Delhi began to trickle through, many senior officials, particularly John Lawrence, repeatedly urged restraint and some action against Metcalfe for taking the law into his own hands.[122] All along, most of the people concerned described what was happening in curiously impersonal, third-person terms. Later they were affected by a kind of amnesia. 'The days following the assault . . . were ones of great excitement and he [i.e. Gen. Wilson] may not have been able to recall what exactly took place at that eventful juncture,' wrote Saunders to the Secretary of the Government of India. His words were to be repeated as late as 1884 in the official *Gazetteer*.[123]

The 'Delhi Prize' was a temptation to all officers, civilian or military. Their anxieties were not about the rights and wrongs of private aggrandizement but about the quantity it was possible to collect. 'The troops have amassed enormous plunder, though

contrary to orders,' said an official helplessly in November 1857.[124]
A latter-day Clive said, unconsciously using the words of the
first marauder of them all, 'I showed great moderation in possess-
ing myself of only a small portion of the plunder.'[125] Even Mrs
Saunders, who immediately after the siege patriotically professed
to 'loathe' anything Indian 'unless it is of Punjab manufacture',
was soon after happily sending home silver vases and gold-
embroidered shawls 'given to us by the Prize Agents'.[126] William
Muir heard with anguish that 'a great number of valuable Persian
and Arabic books were wantonly destroyed by our troops'.
Lawrence wrote to Calcutta to make a clarification. 'Prize does
not include the property of merchants, *sahukars* and artisans. If
it did so, Delhi would be reduced to pauperism and the trade of
the country will be paralysed.'[127] Sacred reasons of trade thus
provided stronger arguments than humanitarian considerations.
Eventually, the officially-collected loot figured in a major legal
case, the Delhi Prize Case, between the Indian Government and
the conquerors of Delhi.[128]

'When the angry lions entered the town, they killed the helpless ... and burned houses ... Hordes of men and women, com-
moners and noblemen, poured out of Delhi from the three
gates and took shelter in small communities and tombs outside
the city,' wrote one of those who was lucky enough to be able
to stay on in the deserted city—Ghalib.[129] The exodus was
partly the impulsive reaction of the terror-stricken inhabitants,
partly the result of government decree. When the soldiers entered
Delhi they found 'the *taikhanas* filled with the old and infirm
who could not join the general exodus. There was no means of
feeding them in the city, where their presence would have raised
a plague. So, by the orders of the General, they were turned out
of the gates ... Hundreds passed through the gates every week.
We were told that provisions had been collected for them at
some place—but ... we had our doubts. I fear many of them
must have perished.' The same writer said that when the population of the town was turned out it drew forth 'exclamations of
sympathy even from the rough soldiers on guard'.[130] 'Numbers
of people are daily dying of starvation and want of shelter,'
wrote Mrs Saunders. Ghalib's language was more poignant—'Had
you been here you would have seen the Begums of the Qala
walking about, their faces like the full moon, clothes dirty,

trouser-legs torn and shoes worn out.'[131] Devoid of emotion and concerned only with what he thought was efficiency, General Burn informed Lawrence that 'Delhi is nearly cleared of its inhabitants...I shall let no one back without a *parwana* setting forth who he is...All men allowed to return I shall register in the *Kotwali*.' By December he was permitting some people to re-enter. 'Hindu artisans and also those Muslims whose services were required by...the Public Works Department have been admitted...I have also allowed some ten men, women, and children per street...I am now admitting more Hindus to the extent of one *bania*, one *punsaria* and one *halwai* per street... 50,000 are within the walls...The number of Muslims is... small. One month more of suffering may be endured by the people who are outside without any great evil...to secure us against sickness in the city from the accumulation of filth which we could not remove while so many of the gates are closed.'[132] Lawrence, again in December, heard from Muir that a visitor to Delhi had reported on the prevalence of 'wanton sickness among the lower orders, specially about the Qutb and Nizamuddin's Tomb'. Bholanath Chunder in 1869 quoted an eye-witness account of 1858 about miserable sheds along the roadside, inhabited by 'perhaps rich *banias*, merchants and shopkeepers'[133]—an erroneous impression, because in 1858 only the Muslims were still outside the wall, in Paharganj, at the Qutb, Nizamuddin and the Purana Qila. Bholanath Chunder himself was to be struck by 'the old withered *Musulmanis* and gipsy-like Mughals' at the Qutb.

Some individuals were lucky enough to secure immunity. 'The Prize Agents have on payment down of a certain sum by the inhabitants of a street, ransomed its wealth or rather guaranteed it from search,' wrote Saunders in November 1857. 'Nil ka Katra, the richest quarter of the town, has been ransomed and guards placed to protect the inhabitants from further molestation. The consequence has been that all the wealth of the city which escaped the plunderers was transferred by the owners at night-time to this quarter.'[134] Katra Nil was the *haveli* of Lala Chunna Mal, one of the richest bankers in Delhi and a supporter of the British. Similarly, the *Hakims* of Billimaran, Mahmud Khan, Murtaza Khan, Ghulam-ullah, whose 'double row of...extensive houses stretches some distance', were protected by the guards of their patron, the ruler of Patiala. This lane too therefore became a refuge of the Muslims and, learning this, 'the administrators entered . . . and took away sixty innocent refugees'. In December 1857 Ghalib wrote that he was apprehensive of describing the true condition of the city (*Mufassil halath likhne dartha hoon*).[135] Individuals who were *en rapport* with the British—Master Ram Chandra, his brother Ghanshyam Rai, Behari Lal, an assistant clerk, Girdhar Lal, a local banker—were among those who were given 'protection tickets' and allowed into the city when the rest of the population was still outside the wall.

In January 1858 the Hindus were allowed to return to the city, but 'the Muslims' houses remained so long empty . . . that the walls seemed to be made of grass' (Ghalib).[136] In February Lawrence took charge of the administration, and the campaign of retaliation assumed a more rational character. The debate was now whether the inhabitants had been punished enough or whether, as suggested by Saunders, the property of the guilty should be confiscated and the others made to pay a punitive tax. The Punjab government agreed that legally this was possible, but wondered whether the inhabitants had not suffered enough already. The final decision was to confiscate the property of the Muslims and any guilty Hindus, and allow the rest to reoccupy their houses on showing proof of their innocence.[137] A general pardon was issued in November 1858, but many prominent Muslims were kept under house arrest.[138] It was not till January 1859 that the Muslims were readmitted to the city (but the attachment on their houses was kept).[139] This was done by Canning in response to a petition from the Delhi Muslims. They had neither food nor shelter, they said. Another winter faced them, and if they were not readmitted, they had no option but beggary.[140] Ghalib wrote with his unshakeable optimism that he had heard that Muslims would be admitted in January 1859, and pensioners would be given bagfuls of money![141] Till August 1859 nobody was allowed in without a 'pass'[142] This was not as satisfactory a measure of security as intended because, Saunders complained, the Sikh guards were equally unable to read Urdu and English passes, and therefore, 'we cannot keep out the Muslim population'![143] When the 'pass' system was discontinued, it was noticed that many Muslims and some Hindus had left the city. The *Delhi Gazette* suspected that they had left 'far more wealthy than when they came'.[144] What actually happened was that many Muslims departed, with their meagre belongings, to seek a new life in the courts of Jaipur, Hyderabad, and elsewhere. Delhi was still a deserted city. 'All houses are lying vacant, if they have not already been demolished by the government or by the rains,' said Ghalib dismally in November 1859.[145]

'When will the agitation of European nerves subside?' demanded the *Mofussilite* angrily in June 1860. 'There is no reason for it ... The people are abject because they are starved out, banished and plundered. Thousands of Muslims are wandering houseless and homeless; the Hindus, pluming themselves on their assumed ... loyalty, strut about the streets giving themselves airs ... Let not the public think that Delhi has not been punished. Wend through the empty grass-grown streets, mark the uprooted houses, and shot-riddled decaying palaces. We must not overpunish ...' From the silence of the unfortunate Delhi rose the tragic dirge of its poets mourning this latest calamity to hit the city—the lament of Delhi, the *Fugan-e-Delhi*, the kind of poetry which only a dearly loved city and the elegant language which was part of the city's culture, could summon. These poems were part of the genre of Urdu verse known as Shair-Ashoob, the elegy on the death of the town, which had appeared on earlier occasions in Delhi, first in the 1740s. 'What can I write,' moaned Ghalib. 'The life of Delhi depends on the Fort, Chandni Chowk, the daily gatherings at the Jamuna Bridge and the annual *Gulfarosham*. When all these five things are no longer there, how can Delhi live? Yes, there was once a city of this name in the dominions of India.'[146] How little even a sympathetic man like John Lawrence understood these feelings is seen by his statement, 'But for those who are dead and gone, and a little loss of property, public and private, all would seem like a dream.'[147]

For an Imperial Government, the commercial and historic *raison d'être* of a town is often obscured by military considerations. For some months after the capture of Delhi there was a debate as to whether the city should be retained or destroyed. Charles Trevelyan wrote to John Lawrence pleading that the city be spared and be rebuilt into the metropolis of India.[148] But as late as April 1858 Lawrence was not sure whether the Government of India wished the city to be maintained.[149] Only in May that year did the Secretary of State decide to agree with Lawrence 'that the political objects to be gained by destroying the Palace will be gained by occupying it.'[150] The *Lahore Chronicle* that month said that the destruction of the city would be a wise measure, 'symbolic of the invincibility of British power'.[151] A year later, the same newspaper publicized Trevelyan's suggestion that the Palace be destroyed and a Fort Victoria built.[152] The *Friend of India* in March 1858 wanted the Delhi people to pay for a new capital city which would symbolize 'the living, active, Anglo-Saxon power.'[153] About the same time Lord Egerton had suggested that the Jama Masjid be demolished, and others wanted a Christian cathedral to be built in its place. None of these suggestions materialized. Delhi was neither destroyed nor made into the capital city. It was allowed to survive, and 'the political punishment pronounced of transfer to the Punjab', to use the curious phrase of the 1884 *Delhi Gazetteer*.[154] 'Don't imagine that Delhi is like the N.W.P. districts,' wrote Ghalib. 'It is now in the Punjab. There is neither law nor constitution. Whichever officer is in charge does what he likes.' Reports would go from Delhi to Lahore and thence to Calcutta—which, to Ghalib's mind, was a very roundabout method. For some time, the city remained in a state of paralysis.[155] In August 1859 the Lieutenant-Governor, Montgomery, expressed regret that Canning, in the course of his north India tour, would have to pass through Delhi—'a city on which there seems to be a curse'. He was emphatic that no Durbar could be held there, since there was no one of 'sufficient wealth and respectability' in the city.[156]

Once it had been decided to retain Delhi, accommodation had to be found for the large European and Indian army contingents that were to be posted there. Immediately following the capture of the city, the army had been quartered in many buildings in and outside the city—among others, in Colonel Skinner's house, the palace of Ahmad Ali Khan, Khan Mohammad's house, Bara Hindu Rao, the Jama Masjid, the Ghaziuddin Madrasa (the Delhi College premises), the Idgah and the Palace itself. All through 1858 and 1859 it was not certain whether the Delhi Muslims would ever be allowed to pray again in the Jama Masjid. Lawrence's line was consistent—Delhi was to be retained as a fortification, but the people of Delhi should not be punished any longer. He scotched the proposal to remove the tank of the Jama Masjid (for the convenience of the Punjab Infantry), and ordered that the Infantry be shifted from the Masjid to cattle-sheds in Daryaganj.[157] By contrast, A. A. Roberts, an official who had worked in Delhi in the 1840s, did not want the Masjid or the Idgah to be returned to the Muslims—'Let us keep them as tokens of our displeasure towards the blinded fanatics ... [158] As in the case of Metcalfe, it was those British officials who had worked in Delhi and been happy there who now were the most vindictive against the inhabitants for their real or supposed treachery. In January 1860, a year after the Muslims had been allowed to enter the city, the *ulema* were spurred on by a *fatwa* of Rahmatullah urging them to petition for the use of the Jama Masjid.[159] This was to be granted only two years later, when the Waha'bi and Hanafi factions were able to come to an agreement and nominate a committee, headed by Mirza Ilahi Bux, the Mughal Louis Philippe and a British puppet, to take charge of managing the mosque.[160] The Fatehpuri Masjid was sold to Lala Chunna Mal, a banker, and the Zinat-ul-Masajid was used as a bakery.

There was much discussion as to whether Delhi would be better defended from within or from without; this was tied up with the question of whether the danger to be feared was external or from within the city. It was decided to station the European troops within the walled city, in Daryaganj and the Palace (henceforward called the Fort) and some outside the wall, in Hindu Rao's house. Thus the pre-1857 civilian and military positions were reversed. Some thought that the ideal location for a cantonment was between the Fort and Kashmeri Gate; therefore this area was also requisitioned by the army, and remained with it till 1873. An ancillary requirement was that a clear space of about five hundred yards should be available as a shooting range around the Fort. Napier worked out a 'Memorandum on the Military Occupation of the City of Lucknow' in March 1858, and one for Kanpur as well.[161] Both suggest defence measures similar to those of Delhi.

At one sweep the face of the city, so lovingly built by Shahjahan, was transformed. What the Government decided was necessary for its security led to some of the loveliest buildings of the city being destroyed—Kucha Bulaqi Begum, the Haveli Nawab Wazir, the Akbarabadi Masjid, the palaces of the Nawabs of Jhajjar, Ballabgarh, Farrucknagar and Bahadurgarh. Ghalib stated that thirty lakhs' worth of property had been destroyed.[162]

Canning was prepared to make a concession to the Hindus, when he said that 'small temples', which were within the area to be cleared, be allowed to remain.[163]

When the five hundred yards' radius was found to include much of the Dariba, where the shops of many 'loyal' Hindu merchants were located, the matter was referred to Canning. He compromised on four hundred and fifty yards, which would include only part of the Dariba.[164]

Within the Palace, in March 1859 the *Delhi Gazette* noticed 'a good deal of blowing up' going on. It was not till a year later that Canning ordered that old buildings 'of architectural or historical interest' should be preserved;[165] by that time much damage had been done. Half a century later Curzon was to bemoan 'the horrors that have been perpetrated in the interests of regimental barracks and messes and canteens in the fairy-like pavilions and courts and gardens of Shahjahan.[166] In the excess of patriotic fervour that prevailed in the early 1860s, the Lahore and Delhi Gates of the Red Fort were renamed Victoria and Alexandra Gate. An eccentric thought of a moment and a sketchy knowledge of the French Revolution led to the cleared space in front of the Fort being christened Champs de Mars.[167]

In February 1858 the military authorities ordered that the city wall be demolished. Lawrence was strongly convinced that this was unwise. He pleaded that there was not sufficient gunpowder in Delhi to blow up seven miles of wall, but that, in obedience to the order, the stones of the wall were being manually removed one by one.[168] This might have been deliberate delaying tactics, for by the end of the year the Supreme Government had come to accept his arguments and decided to retain the wall. This in turn implied the need to retain the city 'ditch' and another 500 yards of cleared area around the wall. Ghalib wrote in February 1858, 'The British have said that people should not build houses outside the wall, and any which have been built should be demolished.'[169] There were to be many attempts by Delhi Municipality to make the government revise its policy, and permit the wall, or parts of it, to be demolished, to allow for ventilation. In any case, there were so many points of egress that it afforded little protection to the inhabitants.

Between 1858 and 1862, a land transaction of bewildering com-

plexity was carried through. The confiscation of the houses of
all Muslims who could not prove themselves innocent, the demolition of a large number of houses in order to build the Cantonment and the railway line, and the necessity to compensate the
owners of these houses, were all linked up into a single operation.
It led to one of the most remarkable revolutions in the owner-
ship of urban property. Broadly speaking, it gave much of the
property which had belonged to suspect Muslims into the hands
of comparatively few individuals who had liquid cash, and involved the government, because of its own amateurishness, in an
unnecessary loss. Canning proposed that confiscated houses be
given as compensation to the individuals whose houses were to
be demolished as part of the Fort and railway clearances.[170] To
enable them to choose freely, they were given 'tickets' stating the
value of the property to be demolished, which could be exchanged
for confiscated houses of equal value. In theory, the government
would, by this measure, have had to pay out very little in compensation, whereas, in normal times, they would have had to pay
some lakhs. What complicated the process was the 'introduction
of trafficking speculators'.[171] The rich bankers entered the fray
zestfully, and the 'tickets', like the *assignats* of the French Revolution, became negotiable currency which changed hands rapidly
and were chiefly concentrated in the hands of a few millionaires.
The total number of ticket-holders was fifteen. These included
Chunna Mal, Sahib Singh, Ramji Das, Narain Das, Mahesh Das,
Janki Das, Mohun Lal, Debi Sahai, Jwala Nath, Gouri Mal, Meher
Chand, and Mirza Ali (there were three others, whose names
cannot be deciphered).[172] The first six were to be actively associated with the officials when a Municipality was set up in 1863.

An account by one of those involved illustrates how the opera-
tion was carried out. The S.P.G. Mission wanted a house within
the city, and was allowed to occupy the residence of 'rebel'
Nawab Jang Bahadur. When the government decided to sell all
confiscated property, this house was offered to the Mission for
Rs 20,000. 'When we decided to buy the property already in our
possession, a Civil Official arranged for us with one of the rich
Delhi merchants for paying in tickets. The Rs 20,000 worth of
tickets was procured for Rs 13,000.'[173] The government then
decided it would be more profitable to dispose of the confiscated
property by auction, instead of by simple exhanges, as had been

originally intended. They planned to divide the profit from these
sales among all the householders; this was subsequently modified,
and limited to a few individuals. The fifteen ticket-holders protested at the manner and amount of the profit distributed, and
appointed as arbitrator De Kantzow, the local magistrate. The
Deputy Commissioner chose Master Ram Chandra, but he was
not acceptable to the ticket-holders. The bankers included *khatris*
and Jains, of whom three—Chunna Mal, Sahib Singh and Narain
Das—were among those who the next year were to petition to
have the railway routed through Delhi and the first two were to
be nominated members of the Municipality. The case, like many
which went up to the level of the Secretary of State, was incon-
clusive. The ticket-holders, however, had already become millionaires, by large-scale purchases at a time when the price of land
in Delhi had reached an all-time low, and some by securing for
themselves confiscated property which they claimed had been
mortgaged to them by the Muslim occupants,[174] and also by forming a closed shop to corner the royal jewels being auctioned.[175]
The chief purchasers of the land auctioned in June–July 1861
were Mahesh Das, Ajodhya Pershad, Ilahi Bux and Narain Das
(it is not clear if the last was Gurwala or Naharwala)—three
bankers and one Mughal who had made his peace with the British.
The 'Ticket Case' and individual cases of householders who
refused to surrender their property to bullying local officials at a
grossly unfair low price showed that at least some of the inhabitants of Delhi were far from craven and servile. Their 'loyalty'
to the British did not extend so far as to induce them to accept
things lying down. For their part, the local officials acquired 'an
abiding horror of professional lawyers'.[176] In the ultimate analysis,
therefore, in the counter-attack it was not the army or the civil
authorities who emerged really as the gainers, but the new 'Lala-
cracy'.

When the dust of the demolitions had settled down, the people
of Delhi rubbed their tired eyes and looked in vain for their
familiar landmarks, and did not find them. 'Where is Delhi?'
moaned Ghalib. 'By God, it is not a city now. It is a camp. It is a
cantonment...'[177] Delhi was a vast cantonment and an undeve-
loped civil lines, with the indigenous inhabitants huddled into
two-thirds of the walled city and into the ragged western suburbs.
A sentry guarded the Jama Masjid, and an entrance-fee was

charged at the gate of the Fort. The morale of the people was low, the city was battered, and politically it was a cipher. Ghalib symbolized the schizophrenia of many of the inhabitants of Delhi. In an introspective mood he wrote, 'We had only one thing left/ the wish to reconstruct the city/Everything else was plundered' (*Ghar men tha kya jo tera gam usay gaarat karte/Voh jo rakhte the ham ek hazrat-e-tameer so hi*).[178] But Ghalib the sycophant could gush that 'John Lawrence's *firman* [i.e. the Queen's Proclamation] has transformed the city into a festival of light' (*bahar-e-chiraghan*, an allusion to the illuminations on the day of the Proclamation).[179]

APPENDIX

Confiscations in Delhi City and District, 1858-59
(SOURCE: Compiled from two handwritten lists in Files nos. 4/1858 and 1/1868, of the Deputy Commissioner's Office, now housed in the Delhi Archives)

I. *Maafi* plots in Delhi District (100 above ten bighas+95 under ten bighas = 195 plots. The smaller plots are listed in detail, and of these 46 belonged to the family of Bahadur Shah.)

Location :

The plots were in Alipur, Aslampur, Badli, Babarpur-Wazidpur, Banskowli, Chandrawal, Dhaka, Ghiaspur, Indraprastha, Jahanuma, Jatwara Kalan, Jor Bagh, Khandrat Kalan, Kilokri, Kotla Mubarakpur, Malikpur, Mehrauli, Mubarikabad, Mujahidpur, Narhaula, Nizampur, Palam, Raisina, Rajpur, Sadhaura, Sadhaura Kalan, Salimpur, Shairpur, Shekharpur, Sikandarpur, Wazirabad, Yakutpur, Yusuf Sarai.

II. Plots within the walled city (86 plots occupied by houses and/or shops were sold as adjustment of the claims of those whose property was demolished for railway construction or military purposes. The former owners of these were Bahadur Shah, Zeenat Mahal, Azizabadi Begum, Kutbi Begum, Moti

Begum, Adina Begum, the Nawab Wazir, Nawab Ziauddin, the Rajah of Ballabgarh and the Nawab of Jhajjar.)

Location :

(a) Plots belonging to Bahadur Shah and his Begums were in Kashmeri Gate, Fatehpuri Bazaar, Bhojla Pahari, Ajmeri Bazaar, Faiz Bazaar, Dariba, Chandni Chowk. (37 plots in all)

(b) Plots belonging to the Nawab Wazir were in Lahori Gate, Turkman Gate, Hauz Qazi, Faiz Bazaar, Chandni Chowk, Bhojla Pahari. (35 plots in all)

(c) Plots belonging to the rulers of Ballabgarh and Jhajjar were in Daryaganj and Faiz Bazaar.

NOTES

1. F. Bernier, *Travels in the Mogul Empire 1656–68* (Paris, 1891) (S. Chand and Co., 1968), p. 241.
2. Ibid., p. 252.
3. Mir Taqi Mir, quoted in M. Sadique, *History of Urdu Literature* (Oxford, 1964), p. 100.
4. *Mofussilite*, 16 June 1868, p. 8.
5. H. K. Naqvi, *Urban Centres and Industries in Upper India* (Delhi, 1968), p. 87; *Gazetteer of the East India Company* (London, 1864), p. 112.
6. Revenue Report by Fortescue, in *Delhi Residency and Agency Records 1807–57*, Vol. I (Lahore, 1915).
7. J. Forbes, *Oriental Memoirs* (London, 1813), Vol. IV, p. 61.
8. R. R. Heber, *Narrative of a Journey through the Upper Provinces of India* (London, 1828), Vol. I, p. 563.
9. *East India Gazetteer* (London, 1815), p. 334.
10. Syed Moinul Haq (ed.), *Akbar-e-Rangeen* (Karachi, 1962), p. 207.
11. *Delhi Gazette 1843*, 24 May 1843, p. 326; A. A. Roberts, *Report on Selections*, NWP (1849), I, p. 13; *D.G. 1853*, 23 February 1853, p. 126.
12. G. Browne to Mawes, 12 April 1844 (Browne MSS, National Library of Scotland).
13. Quoted in J. Holmes, 'Administration of Delhi Territory, 1803–32' (Ph.D. thesis, London, 1955).
14. L. Visaria and P. Visaria, 'Population in the Indian Sub-Continent 1757–1947' (in D. Kumar (ed.), *Cambridge Economic History of India*, Vol. II, in press).

15. *Delhi Gazette 1843*, 24 May 1843, p. 326; A. A. Roberts, *Report on Selections*, NWP (1849), I, p. 13; *D.G. 1853*, 23 February 1853, p. 126.
16. F. Parks, *Diary of the Wanderings of a Pilgrim in Search of the Picturesque* (London, 1850), Vol. II, p. 219.
17. J. Forbes, op. cit., Vol. IV, p. 61.
18. F. Roberts, *Letters Written During the Indian Mutiny* (London, 1924).
19. D.C.O., MI(67)/46-General/1902. 'Memorial from the Muslims for the grant of the revenue of Jahanuma in favour of the Jama Masjid'.
20. V. D. Divekar, 'Political Factor in the Rise ·and Decline of Cities in Pre-British India with special reference to Pune' in J. S. Grewal and I. Banga (ed.), *Studies in Urban History* (Amritsar, 1981).
21. *Gazetteer of the East India Company*, p. 264.
22. H. H. Greathed, *Letters Written from Delhi During the Mutiny* (London, 1858), p. 260.
23. *D.G. 1843*, 24 May 1843, p. 326: 66,503 Hindus and 64,157 Muslims. Ibid., *1853*, 23 February 1853, p. 126: 71,530 Hindus and 66,120 Muslims.
24. Syed Moinul Haq (ed.), *Akbar-e-Rangeen*, p. 22.
25. M. Mujeeb, 'Ghalib—I', in *Islamic Influence on Indian Society* (Delhi, 1972).
26. Akhtar Qamber, *The Last Musha'irah of Delhi* (a translation of Farhatullah Baig's *Delhi Ki Akhri Shama*) (New Delhi, 1979).
27. Professor Mohammad Hasan, oral interview.
28. R. B. Saxena, *History of Urdu Literature* (Allahabad, 1927), p. 315; R. Zakaria, *Rise of Muslims in Indian Politics* (Bombay, 1970), p. 210.
29. *Delhi College Magazine*, 1953, Old Delhi College Number, p. 105.
30. Extract from *Bengal and Agra Gazette 1842*, Vol. I, p. 88, (C.C.O., Education, File 3A, August 1917).
31. A. Haq, *Marhum Delhi College* (Delhi, 1945), p. 6.
32. For the 'Bengal Renaissance', see S. Sarkar, 'Rammohan Roy and the Break with the Past', in V. C. Joshi (ed.), *Ram Mohun Roy* (Delhi, 1975); for a nostalgic vignette of the Delhi Renaissance, see C. F. Andrews, *Zakaullah of Delhi* (London, 1929). Also C. W. Troll, *Sayyid Ahmad Khan: A Reinterpretation of Muslim Theology* (New Delhi, 1978).
33. A. Haq, op. cit., pp. 6, 36; *Delhi College Magazine* (Delhi, 1953), p. 13.
34. M. Mujeeb, *Indian Muslims* (London, 1966), p. 531.
35. R. Russell, *Ghalib—The Poet and His Age* (London, 1972), p. 55.
36. A. Haq, op. cit., p. 8.
37. *D.G. 1847*, 4 August 1847, p. 501 and *1852, passim*.
38. C. N. Cooke, *Rise and Progress and Present Conditions of Banking in India* (London, 1863), p. 234. For lists of Indian shareholders, *D.G. 1845*, 23 July 1845, p. 495, and ibid., *1847*, 3 February 1847, p. 77.
39. *D.G. 1847*, 31 March 1847, pp. 209-10. On the strength of this book Syed Ahmad Khan was made a member of the Royal Asiatic Society.
40. An English edition which has appeared recently is R. Nath, *Monuments of Delhi* (New Delhi, 1979).
41. Rev. P. I. Jones, 'Coming of the King to Delhi', *Church Missionary*

Review, LXIII, 1912; Imdad Sabri, *Asar-ur-Rahmat* (Delhi, 1967), *passim*.
42. M. Mujeeb, op. cit., p. 390.
43. Memoir of Rev. M. J. Jennings (typescript, USPG Archives).
44. *Delhi College Magazine*, p. 50.
45. Altaf Husain Hali, *Yadgar-e-Ghalib*, p. 32. Peter Hardy in R. Russell (ed.), *Ghalib—The Poet and His Age*, p. 65.
46. J. Kaye, *Life of C. Metcalfe* (London, 1858), Vol. I, p. 155.
47. D.G. *1837*, 12 April 1837, not paginated.
48. D.G. *1853*, 15 October 1853, p. 674 and ibid., *1855*, 15 September 1855, p. 894.
49. Sri Ram Mathur, 'Waqa-e-Sri Ram', Vol. II, fol. 91.
50. P. Spear, *Twilight of the Mughals*, p. 197.
51. D.G. *1854*, 29 July 1854, p. 494 and 2 September 1854, p. 587.
52. *Mof.*, 28 May 1868.
53. J. Holmes, op. cit.
54. T. T. Metcalfe, 'Reminiscences of Imperial Delhi', Dehlee, 25 November 1844, 'Delhi Book' (Metcalfe Papers, I.O.R. MSS.), not paginated.
55. D.G. *1841*, 25 August 1841, p. 268.
56. D.G. *1837*, 5 July 1837, not paginated.
57. D.G. *1837*, 12 April 1837.
58. J. Nehru, *An Autobiography* (London, 1936), p. 2.
59. J. Kaye, op. cit., Vol. I, p. 155.
60. D.G. *1837*, 11 October 1837, not paginated.
61. Ibid., and *1853*, 5 October 1853, p. 650.
62. Q. Ahmed, *The Wahabi Movement in India* (Calcutta, 1966), p. 120.
63. *East India Company Gazetteer*, p. 113.
64. C. J. Napier, *Defects, Civil and Military, of Indian Government* (London, 1853), p. 270.
65. Lord Wellington to Lord Ellenborough, 27 September 1842, in Lord Colchester (ed.), *History of the Indian Administration of Lord Ellenborough in His Correspondence with the Duke of Wellington* (London, 1874), p. 306.
66. *East India Company Gazetteer*, p. 113 and F. Cooper, *Handbook for Delhi* (London, 1863), p. 35.
67. J. Kaye, op. cit., Vol. I, pp. 149–52.
68. T. T. Metcalfe, 'Delhi Book'.
69. Debendranath Tagore, *Atma Jeebani* (Calcutta, 4th Edn., 1962), pp. 180–1.
70. D.G. *1843*, 8 July 1843, p. 439.
71. K. N. Panikkar, *British Diplomacy in North India* (Delhi, 1868), p. 37.
72. *D.R.A.R.*, Ch. XII, No. 8.
73. C. J. Napier, op. cit., p. 270.
74. *D.R.A.R.*, Ch. XVI, No. 3 and Ch. XVII, *passim*.
75. J. Kaye, op. cit., Vol. I, p. 240.
76. J. H. Stocqueler, *A Handbook of India* (London, 1845), p. 444.
77. I.O.R., Bengal Political Consultations, No. 12 of 1 June 1816.

78. J. Kaye, op. cit., Vol. I, Appendix, p. 445.
79. Emily Eden, *Up the Country* (Oxford, 1937), p. 98.
80. Fortescue's Report, *D.R.A.R.*, Ch. VI.
81. Trevelyan's Report (1833), *P.A.R. 1866–67*, Appendix I.
82. Bashir-ud-din Ahmad, *Waqayat-e-dar-ul-Hukumat-e-Delhi*, Vol. II, (Delhi, 1919), p. 501; T. T. Metcalfe, 'Delhi Book', n.p.
83. D.C.O., F. 3/1867.
84. D.C.O., F. 4/1882.
85. 'Press List of Delhi Residency Records' (Punjab Archives, Patiala), No. 57, p. 17.
86. T. T. Metcalfe, 'Delhi Book'.
87. F. Parks, op. cit., p. 222; H. Trevelyan, *The India We Left* (London, 1974), p. 30.
88. J. H. Stocqueler, *A Handbook of India* (London, 1845), p. 444.
89. *D.G. 1849*, 27 October 1849, p. 693.
90. S. Nilsson, *European Architecture in India 1750–1850* (London, 1968), p. 130.
91. *D.G. 1847*, 10 March 1847, p. 157; *D.G. 1848*, 16 February 1848, p. 109.
92. J. Holmes, op. cit., For a similar picture in another British Indian town, see B. Cohn, 'The British in Benares', *Comparative Studies in Society and History*, Vol. IV, 1961–2.
93. Trevelyan Papers, information kindly supplied by Lord Trevelyan; 'Press List of Delhi Residency Records', p. 69 (No. 259) (Punjab Archives, Patiala); H. Trevelyan, op. cit., p. 42.
94. *Akbar-e-Rangeen*, No. 23, p. 17.
95. *D.R.A.R.*, Ch. VII, No. 1. *Nazul* was crown property, *waqf* the property of religious trusts, *zabt* was property which had been forfeited, *taiul* was personal royal property.
96. Ibid., No. 5.
97. R. R. Heber, op. cit., Vol. I, p. 556.
98. *D.R.A.R.*, Ch. VII.
99. *D.G. 1858*, 29 July 1858, p. 724.
100. *D.G. 1837, 1847, 1853, passim.*
101. Sri Ram Mathur, 'Waqa-e-Sri Ram', Vol. II (MS., 1903), fol. 236.
102. D.C.O., F. 1/1853.
103. *D.G. 1856*, 11 October 1856, p. 981.
104. I.O.R., India and Bengal Despatches, 6 October—25 November 1857, p. 1233, Public Works, No. 44 of 18 November 1857.
105. *D.G. 1837*, Vol. V, 9 August 1837, n.p.
106. L. M. Jacob to Dunlop Smith, 11 December 1905 (N.A.I. Microfilm, Minto Papers, Vol. I, No. 22); R. R. Heber, op. cit., Vol. I, p. 550.
107. *D.G. 1840, 1843, 1845, 1856, passim.*
108. W. H. Greathed, *Report on the Drainage of the City of Delhi and on the Means of Improving it* (Agra, 1852).
109. *D.G. 1854, 1855, passim.*
110. Napier, op. cit., p. 270.
111. *D.G. 1854, 1855, 1857, passim.*

112. K. L. Gillion, *Ahmedabad* (Berkeley, 1968), pp. 110 ff.

113. *D.G. 1849*, 30 May 1849, p. 341.

114. T. Metcalfe to Secretary, Industrial Department, NWP, I.O.R., Legislative Consultations, June 1850, No. 2694.

115. H. H. Greathed, *Letters written during the Siege of Delhi* (London, 1858), p. 166; *Illustrated London News 1857*, 10 October 1857, p. 354.

116. *Mof.*, 1862.

117. A. C. Warner to Dick, 31 May 1857 (I.O.R., MSS. Eur. C 190).

118. Mrs Saunders to Eliza, 26 October 1857 (I.O R., Saunders Papers, IV, i, 44A).

119. C. J. Griffiths, *Narrative of the Siege of Delhi* (London, 1910), p. 99.

120. W. Muir to J. Lawrence, 14 December 1857 (Saunders Papers, III, i, p. 25).

121. Mrs Saunders to parents, 22 November 1857 (Saunders Papers, IV, i, p. 46).

122. Mrs J. Lawrence to C. Trevelyan, 23 April 1858 (I.O.R., Lawrence Papers, p. 290).

123. C. B. Saunders to Secy., Govt. of India, 31 December 1857, I.O.R., NWP Progs (Pol.), 1 January to 4 February 1858, 736; *Gazetteer of Delhi*, 1884, p. 30.

124. Stewart to Eden, No. 332 of 27 November 1857 (I.O.R., India Cons. (Secret)).

125. Griffiths, op. cit., p. 253.

126. Mrs Saunders to Eliza, 29 November 1857 (Saunders Papers, IV, Pt. I, p. 47); and Mrs Saunders to Saunders, 6 October 1857 (Ibid., II, p. 342).

127. *Records of Intelligence Department, Govt., NWP, during Mutiny of 1857* (Edinburgh, 1902), Vol. 2, pp. 288 and 297.

128. *Index to Law Cases 1854–80*, p. 263 (No. 74).

129. Asadullah Khan Ghalib, *Dastanbuy* (trans. K. A. Faruqi, Delhi, 1970), pp. 40–1.

130. Griffiths, op. cit., pp. 199–200.

131. *Khutoot-e-Ghalib* (ed. Meher, Lahore, n.d.), Vol. I, p. 185.

132. Burn to Lawrence, 4 October 1857 (Lawrence Papers, 19A, No. 5); same to same, 19 December 1857 (Ibid., 19A, No. 62).

133. Bholanath Chunder, *Travels of a Hindoo* (London, 1869), p. 371.

134. Saunders to Muir, 16 November 1857, Records of Intelligence Department, Vol. 2, pp. 298–300.

135. Ghalib, *Dastanbuy*, p. 42; *Khutoot*, p. 145.

136. Ghalib, *Dastanbuy*, p. 58.

137. Secretary to the Chief Commissioner, Punjab, 21 April 1858 (N.A.I., Foreign Political Consultations, 30 December 1859, No. 88/8, K.W.).

138. *Khutoot*, pp. 169, 390.

139. R. H. Davies, Secretary, Government of Punjab to the Secretary, Government of India, Foreign Department, 11 August 1859 (N.A.I., Foreign Political Consultations, 30 December 1858, No. 86–7).

140. N.A.I., Foreign Political Consultations, 31 December 1858, No. 226B 'Abstract translation of a Petition from the Musulmans of Delhi'.

141. *Khutoot*, p. 280.
142. Secretary to Government of India, Foreign Department, to Secretary, Government of Punjab, 19 January 1859 (N.A.I., Foreign Political Consultations, 30 December 1859, No. 86–7, K.W.). The *Imperial Gazetteer*, Vol. XI, 1908, is incorrect in stating that the Muslims were readmitted in January 1858.
143. C. B. Saunders to Secretary, Punjab Government, No. 105, 18 April 1859 (N.A.I., Foreign Political Consultations, 30 December 1858, No. 83–5).
144. *Mof.*, 18 August 1859, p. 793.
145. *Khutoot*, p. 404.
146. Ghalib, *Dastanbuy*, Introduction (quoting *Khutoot-e-Ghalib*), p. 285.
147. J. Lawrence to Col. Fraser, 27 October 1857 (Lawrence Papers, D.O. No. 12, p. 62).
148. J. Lawrence to C. Trevelyan, 16 December 1857 (Lawrence Papers, F. 90, 12, 173–4).
149. N.A.I., Foreign Political Consultations, 30 December 1859, No. 88, K.W., pp. 11–12.
150. Enclosure to 9 in India: Secret Letter No. 68 of 1857 (I.O.R., India and Bengal Secret Despatches, India Public No. 63 of 1858, 5 May.)
151. *Lahore Chronicle 1858*, 15 May 1858, p. 309.
152. Ibid., *1859*, 26 March 1859, p. 199; H. Trevelyan, *The India We Left*, p. 66.
153. *Friend of India*, March 1858.
154. *Delhi Gazetteer*, 1884, p. 30.
155. *Khutoot*, pp. 468, 357.
156. Lt. Governor, Punjab to Viceroy, 27 September 1859 (I.O.R., Canning Papers, 23/6).
157. C.C.O., F. 238–Vol. II/1858, Military Secretary to Chief Commissioner, Punjab to Officiating Chief Engineer, Punjab, 14 December 1858; Engineer, Delhi Division, P.W.D. to C. B. Saunders, 18 December 1858.
158. Financial Commissioner to Secretary, Government of Punjab, No. 899, ibid.
159. Imdad Sabri, *Asar-ur-Rahmat*, p. 228.
160. C.C.O., F. 238–Vol. II/1858, Deputy Commissioner, Delhi to Commissioner, No. 203, 19 April 1862.
161. Veena Talwar Oldenburg, 'Peril, Pestilence and Perfidy: The Making of Colonial Lucknow 1856-1877', unpublished doctoral thesis, University of Urbana, Illinois, 1979, p. 27.
162. Delhi Division Records 11/a, 45, Punjab Record Office, Patiala.
162. Secretary, Government of India, to Secretary, Government of Punjab (Military), 13 January 1860, No. 82 (D.D.R., 11/a, 45).
164. *Khutoot*, p. 70.
165. Ibid.
166. Curzon, *Speeches* (Calcutta, 1900), Vol. I, p. 223.
167. *Mof.*, 30 January 1869, p. 6.

168. N.A.I., Foreign Secret, 25 January 1858, 11–15, p. 51, Chief of Staff, to Officer Commanding Meerut Division, 27 January 1858.
169. *Khutoot*, p. 283.
170. D.D.R., 11/a, 45.
171. Ibid.
172. Ibid.
173. Skelton, 'Revival of Delhi Mission After Mutiny', *Delhi Mission News*, January 1897, pp. 10–11.
174. *Mof.*, 9 January 1869, p. 7.
175. Campbell to Saunders, 12 June 1858 (Saunders Papers, III, ii, 299).
176. *Mof.*, 6 June 1868, p. 6.
177. *Khutoot*, p. 293.
178. Ibid., p. 228.
179. Ibid., p. 340.

2

PORTRAIT OF THE CITY
(1858–1931)

It took some time for the shadow of death to lift in Delhi. The court dependants were dead or in exile and many Muslim artisans had fled. Ghalib said as late as 1863 that, in contrast to Lucknow, which had also suffered in 1857–8, Delhi was still a deserted city. Neither he nor Shaikh Mohammad Riyazuddin Amjad, who saw Delhi in 1861, noticed any large-scale return of the inhabitants.[1] But after a sharp drop in population in 1857–8 there was a steady increase from the 1860s. The census officials did not count the exiles from the city who huddled round the Qutb, Nizamuddin and the Purana Qila, but in the 1860s there was a considerable increase in the population of the western suburbs, much greater than that within the walls. This was because many of the shopkeepers who had been displaced by the clearance around the Fort were given cheap plots of land in the new Sadar Bazaar outside Lahore Gate. This Bazaar was initially established for the needs of those soldiers who were quartered in the Idgah and on Pahari Dhiraj.[2] The labourers working on the new railway line also lived there. There was also some dispersal from the city, because the Muslim dwellers of Punjabi Katra, which was demolished for the railway station, migrated to Kishenganj.[3]

Poverty and demoralization were the legacies of 1858. Ghalib's anguish was that of all the inhabitants and of the stragglers who returned. As stunning as the desecration of the Jama Masjid was the military occupation of the Palace and Daryaganj, the demolition of houses, and the sudden construction of the railway embankment that arbitrarily divided the city into two vertical slices. But in spite of this, many of the people of Delhi opted to lose themselves in the familiar environment rather than seek a new life outside. And what was touching was that there was not so much bitterness and anger as determination to build up Delhi again, to revive some of the elegance and gaiety of the earlier way of life before it was lost totally. In the 1860s many of the *melas* were revived, and the town went gay for the *Pankhe Ki Mela* and the *Phulwalon Ki Sair*,[4] and the *Mofussilite* commented on the '*Kangal bankas*' (penurious dandies), who had 'passed into a proverb for ostentation abroad and abstinence at home',[5] those with '*moonh chikna aur pet khali*',[6] the aristocrats of former days whom the *bouleversement* of classes had impoverished. They preferred to live on in Delhi on charity or by manual work rather than migrate. Most of the people in Delhi in the 1860s chose to be there because its familiarity gave them security. It was only a few individuals who found Delhi a place of economic advantage—those men of property who had come unscathed through 1857, made fortunes in 1858, and now found tenants for their property and patrons for their goods in the European population.

By the mid-1860s there was a large European population at Delhi—both civilian and administrative and military personnel. Later, in the wake of the railway, came the tourists. In the 1860s most people, even the Europeans and the Indian clerks and officials, lived within the walls. The house-owners in the city, many of them richer after 1858, made huge profits—in the 1860s the rent of a small house was as much as Rs 30 per month, and a medium-sized city house was priced at Rs 20,000.[7] There was a mushrooming of hotels—Hamilton's, Courtenay's and the Western Indian Commercial Association Hotel, all inside Kashmeri Gate, and Mrs Benn's Hotel near the station[8]—all catering to a European clientele. The increase in *ticca* (*theka*) *gharries* and in palanquin carriages[9] testified to this rise in the tourist traffic.

Delhi's role as a centre of trade and handicrafts became important once again because of this increased population and because of the presence of the rich Hindu and Jain men of business. The increase in the number of shops and the rising trade figures[10] are direct pointers to this recovery. In 1858 Ghalib noticed that the Parsis' shops were full of champagne and French wine, and the *sahukars*' shops full of goods. Lord Roberts was surprised in 1859 to see that Chandni Chowk 'is as gay as formerly with draperies ... the jewel and shawl merchants [sc. carrying] on their trades as briskly as ever and ... just as eager in their endeavours to tempt the *sahiblog* to spend their money as if trade had never been interrupted. So quickly do Orientals recover from the effects of a devastating war.'[11] The 'Orientals' who had 'recovered' were a

few bankers and merchants, Hindu, Jain and Muslim. 'The capital
is in the hands of one or two men like.Chunna Mal and Mahesh
Das,' wrote Campbell in 1858. 'I fancy these men have obliged
the subordinate jewellers with loans to enable them to purchase
[the crown jewels] so that there will be no fair market price.'[12]

The recovery of Delhi was perceptible not only in the growth
of trade, which was to be expected, but in the revival of its handicrafts. In 1858 it had seemed as if this would not happen. 'There
is no bookseller or binder or artist in Delhi,' Ghalib had complained.[13] Mrs Saunders wrote that 'Artificers of all kinds are not
in the city of Delhi now. They are scattered to the four winds,
and many are believed to have died.'[14] 'Delhi's fallen back in the
manufacture of gold lace, shawls and gold and silver jewellery ...
she's been beaten by Cuttack and Madras.'[15] This could have been
because some of Delhi's craftsmen had fled to those cities. It was
Muslim craftsmen from Delhi who made Jaipur a centre for brass-
ware, bangles, dyeing and the shoe-making industry.[16] But even
Bholanath Chunder, whose loyalty to Calcutta was obvious,
admitted that the 'mosaics, enamelling of jewellery, carpets and
shawls, miniature portrait painting' of Delhi were of 'great excellence'.[17] A *Guide Book* in 1866 recommended to European tourists
some jewellers and a shawl merchant (all Hindu), three shops
owned respectively by a Parsi, a Hindu and a Muslim, and two
Muslim painters of miniatures (in Khari Baoli and Chandni
Chowk);[18] Ghalib had said in 1858 that the British had allowed
some artists to settle in Delhi, and were buying their pictures
cheaply. The craft which gave a livelihood to a much larger
number of people now than formerly was the manufacture of
gota, gold and silver thread, and of *kinari* and *salma sitara*. Small
entrepreneurs and big merchants made money from *tarkashi*
workshops, which became the mainstay of hundreds of destitutes
from the Court, particularly women.[19] The display of this ornate
and glittering ware, so characteristic of Delhi, was not appreciated
by the austere Glaswegian traveller Matheson who said that in
'Chandni Chowk, the Regent street of North West India [the]
array of tinsel and ornaments far outshone and outnumbered the
products of sober usefulness'.[20]

The recovery of trade was accelerated when the East India
Railway was built through Delhi. The rich *khatris, baniyas*, Jains
and Sheikhs of Delhi, who controlled the finances and the retail

trade of the city, and some of whom controlled its handicraft industries, were obviously interested in the prospect opened up by a Punjab–Calcutta railway. This had been first mooted in 1852. After the Revolt, the Indian Government suggested that the railway line should pass through Meerut and not Delhi. This was received with dismay in Britain and at Delhi. 'The original decision was made not only with regard to Delhi's military and political importance but also the trunk line to the Punjab,' the Directors of the East India Railway Company protested, but the Governor-General insisted that this railway line was 'more completely an Imperial and Political line as distinguished from a commercial line'.[21] In Delhi a meeting was called in 1863 to urge that the town should not be deprived of its railway line. This was attended by some officials and 'many hundred respectable Indians' —quite a large number to muster five years after the debacle. The vocal members of the audience included Hindu and Jain bankers, one Hindu, one Muslim and one Parsi merchant, and five Muslim aristocrats.[22] In a petition to the Secretary of State they said that diverting the railway line would affect the city's trade and be unfair to those who had bought shares in the railway. This was significant; generally very few Indians invested in British Indian Railway Companies' ventures but it was stated in 1863 that some of the Delhi plutocrats had bought shares. Pressure from them and the Punjab Railway Company (which wanted a junction with the East India Railway at Delhi and not at Meerut, which was more distant) led to Charles Wood reversing the Viceroy's decision.[23] At midnight on New Year's Eve 1867 the railway whistle sounded and the first train steamed into Delhi.[24] This 'road of iron', a curiosity to Ghalib, was to change the life of the city.[25]

The railway line was built partly as a famine-relief project. It reached Delhi at a time when trade had not yet picked up after the famine, and some merchants had left for other towns. Local merchants became pessimistic as to whether, after all, the railway would benefit them.[26] But the opportunities provided by it were soon evident. Delhi was already an established distributing centre for Punjab, Rajasthan and the North-Western Provinces, so that wholesale trade was bound to increase once the railway was built. There was a scheme to establish a big cotton-growing area in the neighbourhood of Delhi, to take advantage of the railway and of the challenge of the American Civil War, but this did not get off the ground because of the depression in the early 1860s.[27] But the benefit from the railway was seen in the low cost of food in Delhi in 1869, particularly of sweetmeats and fruit (in contrast to Calcutta, noted Bholanath Chunder). This came as a welcome relief after the years of distress, 1863–4, when the cost of living in Delhi had doubled.[28]

From 1872, Delhi had the largest share in the volume of Indian trade compared to other towns in Punjab. By 1877 Delhi was drawing away trade from Amritsar.[29] Half of Delhi's trade was with the North-Western Provinces, a quarter with Calcutta and the remaining quarter with the rest of the country. Of the five 'blocks' demarcated in Punjab in 1876 for registering inter-provincial trade, Delhi formed one in its own right, and accounted for the largest share when compared to the other four. She imported rice, refined sugar, iron, brass and copper (which was manufactured into finished products locally), and a vast quantity of European cotton piecegoods. Her exports were raw cotton from the hinterland, Indian piecegoods, wheat from Punjab, hides cured locally, and leather goods manufactured locally. The great money-maker was European piecegoods, and Delhi was the obvious entrepôt for this because her Municipality from the beginning exempted piecegoods (and grain) from octroi duties, the only town in Punjab or the North-Western Provinces to do so.

The only rich people in Delhi, according to Ghalib in 1869, were the *sahukars*. There were three Muslims among them, though the majority were Hindus. Bholanath Chunder was obviously generalizing when he said categorically that 'the little merchandise that there is in Delhi is in the hands of Hindus—merchants, shopkeepers, jewellers, upholsterers, coach-builders and stable keepers'.[30] Lala Chunna Mal's wealth, which Bholanath Chunder wrongly attributed entirely to his piecegoods trade, became legendary.[31] There were also, however, many Muslims in the cloth and oil trade and some Europeans engaged in whole-sale trade.[32] The highest amount of income-tax from any individual realized in Punjab in 1869 was from 'a person in Delhi District', and 'a Delhi banker' had the distinction of being one of the two individuals in the province with an income of over a lakh.[33] The person was not named, but was obviously either Mahesh Das or Chunna Mal. Between 1868 and 1869 the number of bankers, piecegoods merchants, grain merchants and traders in food in Delhi District doubled in number, and the total tax collected from them doubled in amount. Even allowing for part of this to be explained in terms of more careful tax-assessment, and with the qualification that the figures cover the entire District, it is not unreasonable to assume that the increase occurred chiefly in Delhi, the only big town in the District, and was due to increased trade and to some immigration of merchants as a sequel to the railway.

The Delhi Bank of 1850 was resuscitated in 1859, with a large number of Indian shareholders, indicating that there was much liquid capital available in the city.[34] The bulk of the financial transactions in Delhi were carried on in the traditional indigenous system. The bankers at Delhi repeatedly protested against the stamp law which operated to the disadvantage of native banking and discriminated in favour of government currency notes. The Khatri-Marwari monopoly of the banking business, well entrenched since before 1857, was still very strong.

From the 1870s there were twice as many people in Delhi engaged in 'manufacture and production' as in trade. The railway, which made possible the increase in the volume of trade, had been the first and indirect incentive. After a generation, local manufacture, both traditional and mechanized, became more direct boosters of trade. But though there was a steady increase in the number of people engaged in crafts and manufactures, it was sometimes felt that this increase was at the expense of quality. Lockwood Kipling in the early 1880s deplored the fact that 'the crafts of Delhi only precariously survive' and that 'the tendency of the leading castes... is more towards trade... than towards craftsmanship'.[35] The trade or the craft which made the fortunes of the merchant or the middleman often gave him his name—Chawalwala, Gurwala, Gotewala and Tarkashi, were some well-known surnames in Delhi (the first three can still be found in the telephone directory).

The population of Delhi—intramural and suburban—rose steadily. This occurred in most Indian towns; but because the volume of increase was very small when compared to the massive increase .after the 1940s, this has been termed 'erratic urbanization'.[36] One peculiarity of Delhi's demographic history was that the three occasions of marked change—the depopulation of 1858, the increase after 1911, and the sharp climb after 1947—were all caused by political decisions. The rate of natural increase in Delhi was negligible; it was kept down by a very high death-rate till the end of the nineteenth century. The famine years 1861, 1867, 1877 and 1898 led to much 'distress migration' to the city from places as distant as Rajasthan. In Delhi the rate of overall increase in the nineteenth century was greatest in the late 1860s and 1870s. There were frequent statements to the effect that in Delhi there was much immigration.[37] The causes and the consequences of this immigration were to give the lie to the statement of the *Friend of India* in 1858—'Delhi is not a mercantile but a dynastic capital',[38] and to lead to Delhi becoming 'the seventh largest town in British India' by 1891,[39] 'the richest town in the Punjab' by 1896,[40] and the largest railway junction in India by the beginning of the present century.

The number of men living in the suburbs in the 1870s was far higher than the number of women, in contrast to the city, where the proportion was more even; it was most marked in the age-group 15–45. This indicates that a large number of men living in the suburbs had come initially as labourers or petty shopkeepers. This is corroborated by the fact that only one in twenty of the adult males of the suburbs was literate, whereas the very high proportion of 1 in 4 obtained for the city. Half the number of males in the city and suburbs were engaged in 'manufacture or trade'; as many as half the men in the suburbs were manual labourers, whereas only 1 in 3 were of this category in the city. One in fourteen of the city-dwellers were professional workers and clerks, as against a sparse one in eighty in the suburbs.[41]

Not till the end of the century did the intramural population become as numerous as it had been before the Revolt. But the room available for it was cut by one-third because of the decision to locate the Cantonment within the city and to have a wide open space around the Fort. Therefore the density of the intramural city increased at a higher rate than did the number of the inhabitants. The census of 1846 had counted over 25,000 houses within the walls (of which 18,000 had been *pucca*) and in 1853 over 38,000 houses were listed.[42] Bholanath Chunder, coming from Calcutta in 1869, commented that 'not only have the people multiplied but ... they have built substantial houses'.[43] He chose to observe only the upper strata of Delhi's inhabitants. J. Wilson's

POPULATION IN THE DELHI
MUNICIPAL AREA

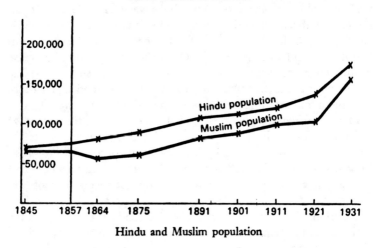

Hindu and Muslim population

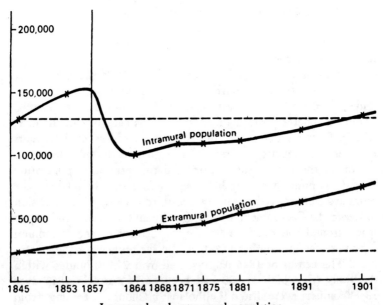

Intramural and extramural population

(Separate statistics for intramural and extramural population are not
available after 1901.)

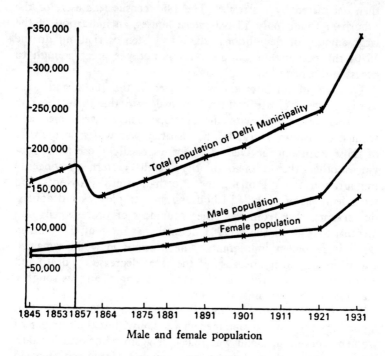

Male and female population

N.B. Sources of graphs:

Census of North-Western Province, 1853
Census of Punjab, 1864, 1881, 1891, 1901 and 1911
Census of Punjab and Delhi, 1921
Census of Delhi, 1931
Punjab Gazette, 1875

recollection of Delhi in 1875 was quite different—that it had consisted largely of 'mud buildings washed down by rains, thousands of people cooped up within the town walls, every now and then decimated by malaria'.[44] The 1881 census (inclusive of the suburbs?) found only 17,498 *pucca* houses, an indication of the large amount of demolitions which had been carried out. In the 1870s the pressure of population was not yet great enough to necessitate private building activity.

The rate of immigration was slower in the 1880s, and two-thirds of the increase consisted of males. In the 1890s the rate increased once again with the disproportion between men and women even more marked. The disparity was widest in the case of those born outside Delhi District, especially those from provinces other than Punjab or the North-Western Provinces.[45] Immigration from Punjab, the North-Western Provinces and Rajasthan was of unskilled labourers, shop employees and domestic servants, that from the other provinces of professionals and merchants. The census of 1901 noticed that most of the Jains in Delhi were recent immigrants. The Muslims in Delhi remained always in a minority because of the great decrease by death and exile in 1857–8, but the rate of increase among them was roughly the same as that amongst the Hindus.

The number of working men in Delhi was 75,000 in 1901. This figure was the same as obtained in Lucknow, but the number of women workers in Delhi was 16,000 as against Lucknow's 5,000. This is accounted for by the large number of women engaged in *kandlakashi* and *tarkashi*, and by the smaller, but increasing, number of women working in factories and workshops. Half the men workers were engaged in manufacture, only a quarter in commerce. The official comment in 1910 was that 'the city population is steadily expanding, as is to be expected from the growth in the area of the city, of factories and railways, and the increase in commercial business'.[46] In 1921, even after the transfer of the capital, the proportion of those engaged in professional occupations, to those engaged in commerce and industry was 1: 6: 8.

In contrast to the 1870s, there was much building activity in the 1880s and 1890s.[47] This was more often done to accommodate an increasing population than merely to have the luxury of more rooms per family. The wealth of the few was not translated into any significant constructions of aesthetic value;[48] but rather into buying adjacent plots or encroaching on public roads, and building extra storeys. Smaller merchants and professional men bought small houses in the more squalid parts of the city and added rooms to them, or bought small plots in the suburbs. The poorer families could get a foothold by 'squatting' on public property and making it tiresome for the administrative authorities to evict them. In these decades the number of houses within the walls did not increase much (only from 17,498 to 18,746) but there were a large number of rented flats.[49] A writer at the end of the century described graphically 'poor clerks, schoolmasters and lower middle class people [sc. living] in flats like rabbit-warrens in labyrinths of back streets'.[50] Many of the 'clerks', particularly from the early years of this century, were Bengalis. The characteristic feature of this increased congestion was that it was as obvious in the more well-to-do areas as in the poorer, and it was not till the twentieth century that the notion of living in more healthy and open suburban houses became popular.

The pressure of the increasing population was most evident in the walled city south of Chandni Chowk. Conservatism and poor transport facilities kept commerce as well as banking confined to Chandni Chowk; conservatism, poverty and fear made many thousands huddle into the region south of Jama Masjid. Only from the 1890s did traders and shopkeepers begin to move out to the western suburbs. Chandni Chowk, as far north as Queen's Road, and south to the Dariba, was flanked by the wards with the highest land values in the city (though in 1880 it was still possible for an adventurous young Bengali doctor, Hem Chandra Sen, to afford strategically-situated premises on Chandni Chowk for his clinic). In 1900 these wards paid the heaviest house-tax. Though the total number of people living there was proportionately higher than in other wards in ratio to the number of *houses*, the ratio of *flats* to *houses* was also highest there.[51] At the time of the transfer of the capital in 1912 land values in Chandni Chowk were very high in comparison to the outer circle of the intramural city and to the euburbs. Many plots around Chandni Chowk had been given to Hindu and Jain merchants and bankers as early as Shahjahan's days, but many houses and *havelis* which had belonged to Muslim nobles were bought by rich Hindus and Jains, and in the late nineteenth and early twentieth centuries the old families as well as the later Marwari immigrants clustered in this area and

4

in Katra Ashrafi. The *haveli* of the *khatri* Chunna Mal family in Katra Nil, with access to the railway station and to the retail business of Chandni Chowk and with its location adjacent to the Town Hall, the centre of local government, symbolized their enhanced status.

Ghalib had mourned the 'ending' of the life around the canal in the 1860s but, quite soon after, the canal and Chandni Chowk were again throbbing with life. Private trade, public business, public worship and politics were concentrated here. Its narrowing width (120 ft in 1890, 84 ft in 1919)[52] testified to pressure of trade and business. The canal causeway ran down the length of it, and one side was a broad drive for carriages, the other narrow, for carts and wagons. The causeway, shaded with trees, was the converging point where business, politics, social problems, were discussed. The spacious 'Company Bagh' around the Town Hall was another outdoor club where the *maulvis*, *hakims*, bankers and teachers met, while the Hall itself was used as the municipal office and, till the end of the century, also housed the public library and the European club. Religious as well as secular activity was concentrated in Chandni Chowk—the massive Jain temple, built in the 1870s, the Sisganj Gurdwara, the Baptist Chapel, St Stephen's School, the Fatehpuri Masjid. The Christian missionaries held lectures near Northbrook Fountain in the 1880s, the Hanafi and al-Hadis Muslims held disputations in the Fatehpuri Masjid, and argued with the missionaries near the Fountain in the 1890s, the Arya Samaj preachers joined in with their preaching in the early 1900s. As the currents of politicization grew stronger, the Company Bagh became an arena for preaching the new religion—nationalism. Other areas used for public meetings were the Pipal Park (sometimes called the People's Park and today covered with shops) and the King Edward Park (on the site of the former Akbarabadi Masjid).

Chandni Chowk symbolized solid prosperity but also the cosmopolitan spirit. It was much loved by the inhabitants, because it symbolized continuity. The essential point to understand when speaking of any Indian city is that a European and an Indian view of it are so totally different. If in London in the nineteenth and early twentieth centuries the slums of the East End had a greater sense of community than the hygienic well-planned areas that replaced them, how much more so was this true of Delhi.[53]

The depressing Dickensian picture painted by the outsider visiting Delhi cannot be reconciled with the nostalgia of the poet who said '*Kaun jaye Zauq par Dilli ki galian chhorkar*'. Privacy and the absence of congestion were not regarded as necessary for comfort and well-being. Unhappiness was exile from the city, even to its suburbs. Delhi was unique, wrote Sri Ram Mathur, with some degree of poetic exaggeration but a great deal of conviction. 'Its culture, its conversation, its dress-styles, its *galis* and *kuchas*, its canal, its bazaar more beautiful than heaven', made it different from all other towns.[54] This pride in the city was most marked on the part of the Delhiwala—that stereotype who has been attributed certain characteristics—his dislike of innovations, his lack of any sense of deferring to another, his lack of interest in issues outside his narrow ken. Changes came to Delhi despite these people, and because of the British presence and the immigrant traders and businessmen and, later, immigrant politicians.

Continuity could be seen in the fragrance of fresh flowers and of watered earth in the back lanes, in the five variations of Urdu spoken in the city[55] which made it a cultural oasis in a rural desert, in the story-spinning by the *dastan-go* on the steps of the Jama Masjid, in the wrestling-matches, *patangbazi*, *kabutarbazi* and *satta* gambling, in the gatherings during the evening in the Urdu Bazaar, with its culinary and bibliophile attractions, in the free ministering to the poor by the *hakims* every morning, in the bathing at the Jamuna in the course of the morning, the gathering in the evening by the canal. Change clashed sometimes and coexisted often with continuity. The most fundamental change was the *bouleversement* of classes. 'Now everyone from all classes wears beards,' Ghalib complained in 1859.[56] Another significant comment of his was 'where is the language of Delhi now? Is it camp language, Punjabi or what?' The old hierarchy was upset, it appeared to the Delhiwalas, by a new brash order where it was money and servility to the British that determined one's rank, rather than the degree of culture. But actually the two coexisted, and there was much in Delhi after 1858 which was still the same as it had been earlier. That cross-class and cross-communal camaraderie that had thrived on the implicit recognition of the separateness of each group remained. The events of 1858 made many of the former aristocrats paupers, *karkhandars* and schoolmasters, and led to many of them having to live in a few rooms in the *imambaras* that had formerly belonged to them.[57] Their distress evoked pity and philanthropy, not contempt. One of the features of the earlier part of the century—the extravagant style of living which was symbolic of the last days of the Mughals—continued to be seen in the behaviour of these *nouveaux pauvres*, symbolic now of the uncertainty of their own lives. In earlier days *karkhanas* had been attached to the *imambaras*—now the owners of those *imambaras* were themselves often forced to do manual work in the *karkhanas*. The dialect of the *karkhandar* proper was distinct and different from the *Urdu-e-moalla* of the aristocrat, but sartorial class distinctions were easier to obscure than the cultural distinctions. The *karkhandar* sported white clothes sprinkled with *itr*, and wore spangled caps.[58] Hindus often dressed like the Muslims. 'How did this matter?' Subuhi was to ask himself, and answer cynically, 'But only by these idle distinctions was Shahjahanabad different.'[59] Entertainment was cheap and democratic. The great *musha'aras* of former days were held no more; with the Palace and Delhi College gone, they were held in private houses only. As the character of the town changed at the end of the century, and it became more obviously a commercial metropolis rather than a cultural one (by contrast to Lucknow), the Delhi tradition and the Delhi language became more obscured, and later people were to ask 'Who is a Delhiwala?' and to argue that there had been no significant difference between Lucknow and Delhi even earlier.[60] In the early twentieth century, as the gentle rhythm of the *doli* and the *ekka* and the swagger of the tonga was jostled by the tram and later the motor car, as the attraction of the 'bioscope' edged out the *dastango*, the old culture became more musty, and had an appearance of genteel decay.[61]

The areas around the Jama Masjid were the quieter regions, where elegance and genteel poverty coexisted without either being regarded as an affront to the other. There are two Ghalibs, the poet had said half-humorously. 'One is the Seljuk Turk who mixes with *badshahs*, the other is poor, in debt and insulted.'[62] Ghalib longed to live in the comfort of Ilahi Bux's house when the roof of his own dwelling caved in after a heavy shower of rain (many houses had remained uninhabited for years, after 1857, and their bricks had been stolen, so that they caved in under pressure).[63] These *mohullas* too were prone to congestion, but had more stable land-values. Here there were none of those 'solid blocks of houses of semi-European style'[64] that lined Chandni Chowk, but there were the substantial and comfortable houses of families like those of the 'Orleanist' Ilahi Bux,[65] and of the propertied writer, Rashid-ul-Khairi, and of the *Hakims* of Ballimaran, best known of whom were Abdul Majid Khan and his brother Ajmal Khan. Many of these *baradaris* were large but no longer grand. 'But even a dead elephant weighs 100 maunds', as Bashir-ud-din Ahmad said of Ilahi Bux's Chandi Mahal.[66] Many more had been broken up and been bought by loyalist middle-class men after 1857—Baradari Nawab Azam Khan by the Jutewala family, Syed Ahmad Khan's houses in Tiraha Bairam Khan by Sheikh Nasir Ali, the house of Shah Alam II's son by Bishamber Nath, Haveli Nawab Muzaffar Khan by Pandit Jwalanath, Haveli Hamid Ali Khan by Hardhyan Singh; Gali Telian was the property of the family of Lala Sheo Pershad, and Kucha Mai Das near Sita Ram Bazaar was bought up in sections by Badri Das.[67] Roshanpura and Chhelpuri were inhabited by *kayasth* Mathurs, and Sita Ram Bazaar by *kayasth* Saxenas. Chhipiwara and north Ballimaran were owned and inhabited by Hindus, Gandhi Gali was inhabited by *khatris*, South Ballimaran, Lal Kua and Haveli Hyder Quli Khan owned partly and inhabited wholly by Muslims.[68] Many Muslims who had owned houses here before 1857 found these being auctioned in 1858, and had to seek more modest quarters elsewhere.[69]

Here one saw—till as late as the 1930s—the unmistakable faces of poverty-stricken Mughal children and women, in Motia Khan.[70] Here lived that bizarre category of erstwhile nobles designated as 'pensioners' by virtue of the conscience-money the government paid them, some of whom succumbed to temptation and 'sold' their pensions (i.e. commuted them) and frittered away the money on *kulfis*, and others lived in debt in order to live in style and be able to hand out munificent *bakshish!*[71] Some of the *mirzas* and *nawabs*, particularly from the end of the century, compromised by working as school teachers.[72] Others, more penurious, had to lower themselves to the status of craft apprentices, or *karkhandars*. Some set up small shops. A typical example of downward mobility followed by upward mobility was that of an aristocratic family which lost two of its members on the Chandni Chowk gallows in 1858; the survivors camouflaged themselves in Gali Rodgaran, hitherto considered a very low class locality (*rodgaran* means gut-workers). In the 1860s and 1870s, the older children became shoe-maker's assistant, *kandla* worker and *karkhandar*, in that order. The two youngest ones went to school and became, in the 1880s, a municipal clerk and, in the 1890s, an accountant, respectively. By the turn of the century the family was sufficiently well-off to build an additional storey to the little house which they had first occupied, and then bought. Mirza Mohammad Begg, the son of the municipal clerk, was to become principal of the Delhi College.[73]

The contrast between the *nouveaux pauvres* Muslim aristocrats and the rich Muslim merchants who lived near them was as striking as that between the former and the rich Hindu *banias*. The numerous Punjabi Muslim *biradari* was particularly conspicuous in this respect. They had come to Delhi in the reign of Shah Alam II, and numbered some twenty thousand by the late nineteenth century. They had lived near Kabul Gate and in the Punjabi Katra before 1857, but had subsequently moved to Kishenganj, Baradari Nawab Wazir, Katra Ghee. The Siddiqi family, which began by investing its profits from the shoe business in eight or ten houses in Chamdewalan, and later in Churiwalan, bought land in the Sadar Bazaar area in the 1880s. They owned printing presses, and their sons in the twentieth century became doctors, *vakils* and administrators, though the family wealth remained solidly based on their shoe trade with Bombay, Calcutta and Punjab. They were by religion Hanafi, and generously financed mosques and *madarsas* in the same way as their *khatri* and Jain counterparts financed *dharmsalas* and *pathsalas*.[74]

The Fatehpuri Masjid became increasingly a focal point which was a rival to the Jama Masjid. Till 1877, it remained the property of Lala Chunna Mal, who had bought it in 1860 for Rs 39,650. It was returned to the Muslims in a deliberately calculated gesture by Lytton in 1877, and thereafter it became an arena for religious debate in a way that the Jama Masjid, controlled by officialdom, could not hope to become. It formed a link between the city and the suburbs, because it was patronized by the Punjabis within the walled city and in the Sadar Bazaar.

On the fringes of the walled city were 'those separate territories, assigned to poverty'[75]—Mori Gate, Farashkhana, Ajmeri Gate, Turkman Gate and Delhi Gate. Mori Gate had always been inhabited by the poor, and after 1857 it became even more crowded,

chiefly with survivors from the Court. This area, and Delhi and
Ajmeri Gates, became the foci of missionary activity, because the
poorer classes who lived there were ready to accept Christianity
of a rough-and-ready kind, and its social organization in *bastis*.[76]
In the wards near Delhi Gate and Turkman Gate, the difference
as between the number of houses and flats was very little at the
end of the century. This indicated the poverty of the residents,
who could not build beyond their needs. They were the *kumhars*,
butchers, dyers of cloth, *chamars* (this caste was, alone in Delhi,
Muslim by religion) and *telis* (one of whom, the well-known
Nanvateli, was described as very *sharif*, and as being superior to
the average *teli*).[77] The only open space in this area by the end
of the century was Hauz Qazi. This area became even more
congested in the years after Partition, and led to serious discussion
on ways of 'decongesting' it, and ultimately to the tragedy of
April 1976, when so many people whose families had lived there
for over two centuries were moved out to the barren desert of a
'resettlement colony' and their houses and property bulldozed.
Delhi has died so many deaths.

The wall on the south-western side, unlike that in the west and
north, marked a real barrier, until parts of it were demolished in
the 1820s. As late as the early twentieth century Farashkhana was
called *Jangal-baahar*.[78] The wall of the city rose sheer and beautiful against the verdure of the vegetable fields, and the Jats and
Gujars just beyond the wall spoke Braj, a language quite different from the polished Urdu of the city. Only the rituals of pleasure
or of grief took people beyond the walls—in autumn, the Ramlila,
celebrated in the grounds near Shahji's tank outside Ajmeri Gate,
again in October, the *Gulfaroshan* in Mehrauli; the one-rupee
ekka ride which enabled visitors to see the ruins of the older
Delhis, the funeral processions of Muslims to the Mehndion ka
Mazhar outside Ajmeri Gate. The poor Muslims living along the
fringe of the wall had no incentive or wish to move beyond, and
the area was too far from the business and trade areas to tempt
the rich entrepreneurs to build there, so that till the 1920s, when
New Delhi started to be built to the south, there was a sharp
dividing-line between city and countryside. In the 1920s the area
beyond the wall from Ajmeri Gate to Delhi Gate was auctioned
as commercial plots and were bought up, because by then cheap
land in the west and north was no longer available.

When the railway had been originally proposed, it was expected that it would follow a line from south-east to north-west, through the cantonment on the Ridge. Bahadur Shah had been very upset at the prospect of this innovation which would shatter the tranquillity of his city, and begged that it be built even further north. But after the reconquest of the city, the officials proposed that the line should run through the city, since the army had been shifted within the walls. They could suggest this with impunity, since, as things stood, the dislodging of some hundreds of people posed no problems. The east–west alignment of the railway-line rudely distorted the concentric pattern of Shahjahanabad. The tourist's approach to the city is as instructive a point as any from which to observe the changes. Before 1857 Delhi was approached by river or from Ghaziabad by crossing the bridge of boats. Travellers in the early nineteenth century had described vividly the first view of the majestic minarets. But the traveller of the 1870s descended from the train and was confronted with the sight of the proud Queen's Road, and the British statements of faith—the neogothic railway station and the classical façade of the municipal town hall, a colonial copy of the standard 'centre' of cities in Victorian Britain. Because the railway station was the point at which trade coalesced and debouched, and because the Town Hall was the seat of local government and of formal gatherings, and was surrounded by a generous garden (the Company Bagh colloquially, the Queen's Gardens officially), this area provided a more prosaic substitute for the erstwhile city centre, the Palace and the eastern end of Chandni Chowk.

By driving straight roads (the Queen's and Hamilton Roads) through these crowded areas and by widening the road between Kashmeri Gate and Lothian Bridge, much forcible decongestion was carried through. Queen's Road, the prestigious highway, the British rival to Chandni Chowk, was bordered by public buildings, but Hamilton Road was edged by many private holdings. On Nicholson Road and near Kashmeri Gate, rich bankers like Lala Ram Chand, Lala Hardhyan Singh and Lala Sultan Singh in the 1890s bought up plots and houses to enlarge their properties. At Kashmeri Gate, the shops (chiefly owned by Europeans, as can still be seen in 'London Stores' and 'Spencers' and 'Carltons'), the colleges (St Stephen's and Hindu) and school buildings and the Church preserved the pattern of the early nineteenth century.

This was an open space where the affluent Indians and the Europeans converged. The triangular park here, which is still recognizable, was the venue, like the Pipal Park, for political meetings in the 1920s. It never became congested (as the areas around Chandni Chowk did by the beginning of this century), not even when the Temporary Capital was located in the Civil Lines (1911-31), and the white and brown sahibs used to 'take the air' at Kashmeri Gate in the late afternoons. When the number of Bengalis in Delhi increased, after the transfer of the capital, they set up their modest version of the European Club at Ludlow Castle—the 'Bengali Club' at Kashmeri Gate, with its Library and recreation facilities, which is still a very lively place.

The occupation of Daryaganj and the Fort by the military constituted a sudden change, but mainly of a political kind. The buildings and roads in Daryaganj retained the old pattern.

Within the walls of the Fort were built quarters for the military personnel—'a kind of howling desert of barracks, hideous, British and pretentious'.[79] These formed a new skyline that marred the view of the Fort from the river. (In 1979, it has been decided that the Fort will be transferred from the military authorities to the Archaeology Department, and that the barracks will be demolished.) The Fort itself became a European ghetto, in contrast to the settlement in the Civil Lines. A painting of 1868 shows English children gambolling self-consciously, with governesses in tow, against the incongruous background of the Red Fort buildings.[80] Curzon, who savagely criticized the barbarities of army occupation in the Fort, in 1903 used the Diwan-i-Khas for a ball. It was lit with electric lights, and Lady Curzon appeared wearing a robe covered with peacock embroidery. Indians could enter the Fort only by paying a fee; they were allowed to attend the *Gora Bazaars* held there (a parody of the Mughal *Meena Bazaar*). (In 1970, an army veteran asked me eagerly whether the vendors who had sold ham pies in the Red Fort were still plying their business!) The 'Parade Ground' in front of Esplanade Row remained *banjar* till 1920, when it was grassed over.

When Daryaganj was evacuated by the troops in 1908 (when the Cantonment was moved to the Ridge) there was little hope that its sale would bring in profits. It was described as 'a kind of backwater, away from the business centre'.[81] It remained a sparsely-built up area; in the 1920s there were still only the twenty-four 'kothis' which had been the officers' houses. Between Faiz Bazaar and the 'kothis' there was dense vegetation, and a small hill adjacent to Delhi Gate (which was later levelled to build the police station). Plots were allotted generously to schools, and houses and plots sold very cheaply to private individuals, mostly professionals (lawyers, doctors, college teachers). Some houses were constructed by these new owners, especially to meet the demands of the Durbar of 1911. Many *kayasths* and some Bengalis (like Dr B. C. Sen and the lawyer A. C. Bose) moved out from the crowded and expensive Chandni Chowk, particularly when rents soared after the end of the War. Dr M. A. Ansari, who came to Delhi in 1913, bought a large house in Daryaganj, and for some years shared with Dr H. C. Sen the distinction of being the only Indians in Delhi to own motor-cars. The outlines of the estates of the Nawabs of Jhajjar, Kishengarh and Ballabgarh continued to be discernible even after having been occupied by army officials, and then passed on to Indian families. The houses on the river-front were the most popular, especially after 1920, by which time the Bela (the swamp between the river and the Fort and Daryaganj) had been mostly cleared. When the Jamuna was in flood, it was possible to lower nets from the back windows of these houses and haul up a catch of fish!

An area which started out as exclusively occupied by Europeans (though the houses were chiefly the property of Indians living in the walled city) was the Civil Lines. This was located north of Qudsia and Nicholson Gardens. It was the obvious choice for a Civil Lines once it was decided that the Europeans should live away from the 'native city'. It was here that earlier Englishmen, Ludlow and Metcalfe, had built their houses; it was separated from the city by the *cordon sanitaire* of the gardens, and, above all, the Ridge was 'sanctified' by the memories of.1857. It is difficult to play down the special place the Ridge and the battle-scarred Kashmeri Gate occupied in the minds of those brought up on Newbolt and Tennyson. For the generation of Englishmen after 1857, it was unthinkable that they should live in the conquered city. It was equally appropriate that they should live as near as possible to the sacred Ridge.

The Qudsia Gardens were used by the Hindus of the city and of Sabzi Mandi on their way to the bathing-ghats in the morning, but the Europeans had it to themselves for tennis in the afternoon;

the rose-garden in the Qudsia and the bandstand in the Nicholson Gardens were the British superimpositions on these beautiful gardens, where many fruit trees had been summarily cut down during the siege operations of 1857. The British presence also thrust an arm into the Sabzi Mandi area—in the Roshanara Gardens, which became a British preserve now, though before 1857 this had been a picnic ground for the *jeunesse dorée* of the city, who went there during the monsoon to recite poems and eat *pakoras*.[82] Because the Roshanara was wedged in between 'Indian' areas, the English women in their carriages were subjected to the unavoidable nuisance of having to encounter Indians *en route*. They complained, but there was little that could be done about it.

The land in the Civil Lines was partly *nazul* (Chandrawal *mauza*) and partly private, by the sales and *maafi* gifts made after the Revolt. The landlords were *seths*, sheikhs and Punjab Rajas and Nawabs. The Meerut Settlement Report for 1865–70 commented on the fact that there had been a substanial change in the neighbourhood of Delhi City since the 1830s because many 'mahajans and tradespeople [had] invested capital in land'. In this respect, Delhi was different from Allahabad, where Indians were not allowed to own land in the Civil Lines. But an Indo-English upper-class suburban settlement did not develop here as in Madras, because the landlords preferred to live in the walled city.[83] They reaped windfalls during the Durbars, when the visiting Indian princes paid the absurd rents demanded (Rs 50,000 for two months in the case of a house the rent of which was ordinarily Rs 50 a month).[84] In the 1870s the area as far north as Underhill Road was dotted with small bungalows in vast compounds. Ludlow Castle became the Commissioner's House, and Metcalfe House was used as a hotel. It was a lonely life in the Civil Lines for the small civilian and missionary population. Work and recreation still took them to the city, in the 1870s and 1880s, for both municipal offices and European Club were in the Town Hall, and the superior European military staff lived in the Fort. In the sprawling wilderness of the Civil Lines (the Indians in the city never ceased to marvel at the taste of the Europeans who opted to live in this *ujar* region)[85] they were as much at the mercy of the Gujars of Chandrawal as Metcalfe had been in 1857. The Gujars made it clear from the beginning that the houses would be robbed unless their men were appointed as *chowkidars*, and a determined effort in 1908 to resist this blackmail was quite ineffective. The night after the Gujar *chowkidars* were dismissed, every house in the Civil Lines was efficiently robbed.[86]

In the 1890s the Civil Lines population became diluted with 'second-class' Europeans—those working in the railways and mills. The racial polarization became more marked. The Club was shifted from the city to Ludlow Castle in 1898, perhaps as a result of the 'plague scare'. A new crop of hotels were built, not within the city as earlier, but in the Civil Lines—Lauries Hotel, Maiden's Hotel (which started with a single storey in 1900 but did well enough to justify a second storey within seven years), and in the 1920s Hotel Suisse and Cecil Hotel. In 1908 the army moved to a new Cantonment on the Ridge, and the offices of the Deputy Commissioner and of the Commissioner shifted from Kashmeri Gate to the Civil Lines.

During the Durbar of 1903, and later because of the plague epidemic, the Indian owners of plots in the Civil Lines began to build houses and, during the years of the War, many of them started to live there. The ubiquitous syndrome of the rich was evident here too; the same bankers and traders who were also to be the first to set up factories in the western suburbs, were the landowners here—among others, Lala Ram Chand, Lala Sri Ram, Lala Basheshar Nath Goela, Sheikh Hafizullah and Sheikh Abdul Ghani. When this area was constituted into the Notified Area in 1912, building activity increased, and the inhabited area extended to beyond the Ridge. The temporary capital occupied buildings sprawling from the Ridge down to Metcalfe Estate. The World War gave an excuse to the landlords to push up rents further; this increase tapered off by the mid-1920s, when officials started to move to houses in the new capital in Raisina. Many buildings in the Civil Lines played different roles at different times—a telling example is that of Curzon House, a building constructed to house Civil officers at the time of the 1903 Durbar; for a few years in the 1920s it housed the offices of Delhi University; it then became the Hotel Suisse; now the name survives but not the building, on the site of which are the 'Swiss Apartments'.

In contrast to the lack of settlement south of the wall, and to the slow growth in the north, the western suburbs developed into an area which by the 1930s became larger than that of the walled city of which it was originally an appendage. Unlike the old Sadar

Bazaar which had existed at Khyber Pass and had served the Rajpur Cantonment (1828–57), this one did not decline when the
Cantonment was shifted into the city. The reason was that when
the railway line was built along the Grand Trunk route and the
octroi boundary was made contiguous with the city wall, the
Sadar became the best location for wholesale shops and depots.
Immigrants found land in the Sadar abundant and cheap or, often,
'free' because of the lack of official vigilance. From the mid-
nineteenth century till very recently, settlement in Delhi has been,
in some areas, on an illegal basis, on the principle of possession
being nine parts of the law.

By the end of the 1880s the number of men and women in
Sadar Bazaar was less disproportionate than earlier, implying that
the second stage of colonization was taking place, and families
were living there. In the 1880s and 1890s many of the 1858 settlers
were bought out by Punjabi Muslim wholesale merchants, who
then proceeded to consolidate their gains by encroachments on
nazul land.[87] By the end of the century these Sheikhs were a
numerous and powerful community, whose style of living was
pedestrian but whose fortune (in business connected with European goods, oil and cloth) ran into lakhs.[88] At that time the
population of this area also rose steeply, chiefly in terms of males,
a fact explained by the major railway construction of the 1890s.
Because of the congestion in the walled city, the railway boom
and the increase in mercantile business, the value of land in the
Sadar became suddenly high, though it was still low when compared to the prices in the centre of the city. It also led to a spurt
of building activity, both of dwellings and of shops and factories.

Paharganj, Kishenganj, and Pahari Dhiraj, which had been separate pockets of population before 1857, expanded and coalesced.
Pahari Dhiraj merged into the Sadar Bazaar. Paharganj and Kishenganj were different in that the male–female ratio was more even
there, and increased at a slower rate than that of the commercial
Sadar. A major change here was the forcible displacement of the
reghars and *chamars* of Paharganj to Karolbagh when a cholera
epidemic occurred there in 1871.[89] Paharganj remained a low-
income area, inhabited by *chamars*, tanners and dyers and by ivory
workers and silversmiths and by former *umara*. In the early years
of this century the staff quarters of the Great Indian Peninsula
Railway were constructed there. The development of the new

capital area made Paharganj strategically very important, particularly after it was decided to locate the New Delhi railway
station there.

Another major impetus to the growth of Sadar Bazaar and of
Sabzi Mandi was the development of mechanized industry. In the
early 1880s, there were no industrial establishments in Delhi to
which the Factory Act was applicable. The *karkhanas*, which
came nearest to the definition in the sense that they employed a
number of people in a particular job at one place, much as the
karkhanas of the Mughals and their nobles had done, varied in
size. Ten were listed in 1885, varying from a cotton machine at
Bara Hindu Rao, owned by a Mr Wilson, and employing two
hundred men, to an ice 'factory' in Kauria Pul with twelve.[90] But
within five years, in 1888, the cotton spinning and ginning and
the flour industries were beginning to be mechanized.[91] In this
respect, Delhi was similar to Ahmedabad, where the cotton textile
industry became mechanized thanks to the infrastructural benefits
created by British rule.[92] Delhi's advantage was her proximity
to the cotton and wheat producing areas, her disadvantage her
distance from the coal producing area. The factory industries
were financed by local bankers and landlords, though the managers
were chiefly Europeans. The Delhi Cloth Mills and the Delhi
Cotton and General Manufacturing Companies were the first
cotton mills, established in 1889, with a capital of seven and five
lakhs respectively. The supervisor of the former was the same
Mr Wilson who had earlier owned a cotton press. The Indian
shareholders were local *banias* and *khatris*, the chief contributor
being Lala Ram Kishen Das. The Bohra Haji Abu Ahmad of
Bombay tried to browbeat the D.C.M. into closing down, but
they did not succumb.[93] These mills began as spinning units and
later took to weaving. The sharp increase in the number of people
engaged in the cotton textile industry (mechanized and hand-
produced)—5,000 in 1891, 11,000 in 1901 and 23,000 in 1911—
was obviously due chiefly to the increase in factory production.[94]
This is borne out by the fact that there were ten cotton factories
by the end of the century. In 1900 there were more than 2,500
workers in the twenty mills in Delhi.[95] As in other industrial
towns, so in Delhi, the labour for these factories was not local but
imported. Mill owners complained that labour was scarce in Delhi,
and that Delhi men were 'idle'. Operators had to be 'enticed' to

Delhi by being paid their railway fare (from Kanpur in the case of cotton workers, from Rajasthan in the case of flour mill workers) and in turn were tempted away to better-paid jobs in Lahore.[96] Competition for labour appears to have existed as between parallel industries in different towns and not as between different types of employment opportunity in Delhi.

The Delhi factories were not developed at the expense of, nor were the mill workers drawn from, local hand-spinners and hand-weavers. The mill yarn was sold locally to handloom weavers. There is no causal connexion between the industries that were becoming mechanized and those that were declining, such as one would expect from the statement of the Deputy Commissioner of Delhi that the 1890s had been 'marked by the rapid growth of mill industries. Indigenous trades and manufactures have suffered proportionately.'[97] The decline in the number of cap-makers from the early years of this century can be explained by changing fashions among Muslims and *kayasths*, whereas the sharp decline in the number of leather workers (11,000 in 1891, only 2,000 in 1911)[98] was due not to any competition from mechanized industry and could have been due to European competition.

There was one industry which was badly hit by mechanization and by foreign competition. This was *kandlakashi*. Gold and silver continued to be a major part of Delhi's exports in this century, but there was an overall decrease in the number of people engaged in gold and silver crafts from the 1890s.[99] *Kandlakashi* work suffered in Delhi as in Lahore from competition from inferior but cheap German manufacture of wire and tinsel. This competition led not to large-scale unemployment but to underemployment, which itself was serious for these workers who were living on the breadline. There were a lakh of people in Delhi and nearby villages like Chiragh Delhi, Hindus in *kandla* workshops near Chandni Chowk, Muslim men working as *tarkashis* and weavers and their women as tinsel workers at home. The *karkhanas* employed twenty to sixty workers each. Most of the self-employed were so poor that the fall-off in *kandla* production was an index of distress conditions; during times of famine, the workers lacked the money to buy the metal which they manufactured into wire. In such a situation, the Islamic Lametta Company set up in 1899[100] (to manufacture wire by machinery) was an additional blow. It had a capital of one lakh (compared to the D.C.M.'s 5 lakhs). The combined effect of foreign competition, mechanization and famine explains the decrease in the number of employed women in Delhi, from 16,000 in 1901 to 11,000 in 1911.[101]

When additional railway lines were constructed in Delhi in the 1890s the number of factories multiplied. An added incentive was the introduction of electricity in 1902.[102] This was quickly taken advantage of not only by the new factories but also by many smaller flour mills and saw mills in Chandni Chowk and near Jama Masjid, residual industries which resisted contrifugal tendencies because they were near their local clientele. The flour from Delhi's mills was sold in markets as distant as Bengal and Assam.[103] The North-Western Railway initially benefited Delhi merchants and industrialists by opening up the Karachi route. But after 1905 when the railway carried raw cotton to Karachi and stimulated the development of the cotton industry there, Delhi's predominance in this industry in north India declined. Delhi mill owners in 1909 argued, with obvious self-interest, that a 14-hour day was necessary for factory hands, for only by working at such pressure could Delhi hold her own against the other cotton manufacturing towns.[104]

Delhi became the major railway junction in north India by the early years of this century and its commercial activity increased greatly. Lying as she did between Punjab, Rajasthan and the United Provinces, it was Delhi that took the largest share (in Punjab) of European cotton piecegoods (as earlier) and also European woollen piecegoods (for re-export to the United Provinces). She also imported much gold and bullion (partly as payment for grain exported from Punjab, and iron and steel manufactures from Karachi). She continued to export wheat, cotton and oilseeds—the products of the hinterland. But her trade had no connection with the needs of the city's inhabitants, and therefore the transfer of the capital did not increase the volume of trade; rather, trade fell off because of the rise in prices. Trade also came to be placed progressively lower on the list of priorities for investment.

Delhi became the commercial capital of north India in 1905, when the Punjab Chamber of Commerce established its headquarters there, with branches in Amritsar and Lahore. This Chamber was concerned with the trade and manufactures of the North-West Frontier Provinces and Kashmir as well as Punjab. Two other local organizations with branches elsewhere, and with more Indian members than the Chamber had, were the Delhi Piece Goods Association and the Hind Mercantile Association. In 1905 trading companies were third in order of importance as a sphere of investment in Delhi. The most popular form of investment was cotton mills and presses. Banking and insurance figured second.[105] After the capital was moved to Delhi, many joint-stock banks, British and nationalist Indian, established branches there. But both before and after 1912 the bulk of the banking business at Delhi was carried on in the indigenous fashion. There were two innovations worthy of note. One was the creation of a Kayasth Mercantile Bank in the 1880s, an attempt to break down the monopoly of the *khatris* and *banias*.[106] This was a symptom of the caste-conflict which in the Presidency towns took the form of competition for white-collar jobs. The other was the establishment of a Native Commercial Bank in 1898, with the purpose of lending money, buying and selling *hundis*, and undertaking insurance, an attempt to combine Indian and European banking methods.[107]

Around 1912, when Delhi became politically the most important city, its economic links were not with the immediate hinterland but with the whole of north India. The combination of this wider political and economic role led to a blurring of the boundaries that had hitherto marked off the urban area from the rural hinterland. By 1910 there was no village in Delhi District which was more than twelve miles from a railway station, and railways had replaced all forms of transport other than the cart traffic in the area around the city.[108] The railways and the factories had also changed the pattern of urban Delhi. The location of factories was determined by accessibility to the wholesale markets and the railway stations. Apart from one or two factories located inside the wall near Kashmeri Gate, they were all in the Sadar Bazaar or Sabzi Mandi area, where land, *nazul* and private, was available cheaply. The most obvious change was in Sabzi Mandi. Here, beyond the market, stretched many acres of gardens, belonging to the Government (chiefly enclosed in the Roshanara Bagh) and to private individuals, gifted to some of them before 1857 as *sardarakhti* estates or bought by them subsequently. In the 1890s this area became more heavily built-up, and large sections of land under trees were earmarked for railways and used or sold for factories. In 1902 this ward had the largest number of taxable

5

houses of all the wards in the city, and the volume of tax assessed bore out that the majority of the Mandi assessees were lower-middle-class shop or godown owners (9,000 houses assessed for Rs 5,794 as against 4,400 houses in Ward 6 assessed at Rs 17,585).[109] In the first quarter of this century, those who owned land there found it paying to sell, and those with money thought it useful to buy; some owners of plots constructed houses. As plague became, from a threatened epidemic in 1898, a reality in 1905, the prejudice against living in the suburbs decreased. Sadar Bazaar ceased to be inhabited only by workers, and both it and Sabzi Mandi (and the Civil Lines) saw much building activity. This was accelerated by the transfer of the capital, and the constitution of the northern suburbs into a temporary capital.

The political decision of 1912 led to a major morphological change. Just as the political decision about the route of the East India Railway in the 1860s had led to the Chandni Chowk core-pattern being modified by a ribbon development westward, so the need to link the temporary capital with the new Imperial Capital led to the road from Sabzi Mandi through Sadar Bazaar to Panchkuin becoming suddenly important. These developments brought the Jats of the rural neighbourhood into closer contact with the city and its influence, and in turn involved them in its politics. The development of the western suburbs now followed this artery, and when in the 1920s plots were auctioned on the Jhandewalan and the Idgah roads, these were snapped up by Marwari and Sheikh merchants respectively.

The first barrier to westward development, the city wall, having been crossed, the second barrier, a geographical one, the Ridge, was crossed in the second decade of this century. Karolbagh, hitherto inhabited by lower class-groups, now appeared attractive because of the soaring land prices in the walled city and Sadar Bazaar. The Tibbia College was the first major institution to buy land there. It was followed by other educational institutions and, later, by individuals. In comparison to the nineteenth century and to the development of the 1930s and 1940s, it was in the three decades of the mid-1890s to the mid-1920s that the rate of Delhi's urban sprawl was the most impressive, just as this was the period when her commercial development was most rapid.

NOTES

1. *Khutoot*, p. 423; M. A. Aarzu (ed.), *Ahwal-e-Ghalib* (Aligarh, 1953), p. 64.
2. *Nazul Lands Administered by Delhi Municipality* (pub. by Govt. of Punjab, Lahore, 1908), Table I.
3. Bashir-ud-din Ahmad, *Waqa'yat-e-dar-ul-Hukumat-e-Delhi* (Delhi, 1919), Vol. II, p. 508.
4. *Ahwal-e-Ghalib*, p. 62.
5. *Mof.*, 8 Sept. 1868.
6. Ashraf Subuhi, *Dilli Ke Chand Ajib Hastian* (Delhi, 1943), p. 67.
7. *Khutoot*, p. 287.
8. A. Harcourt, *New Guide to Delhi* (Allahabad, 1866), p. 21.
9. *Mof.*, 12 Sept. 1868.
10. Trade figures are given in the *Punjab Administration Reports*.
11. Roberts, *Forty-one Years in India*, Vol. I, p. 472.
12. Campbell to Saunders, 12 June 1858 (Saunders Papers, III, ii, p. 299).
13. *Khutoot*, p. 161.
14. Mrs Saunders to parents, 13 March 1858 (Saunders Papers, IV, i, p. 52).
15. *Mof.*, 2 Nov. 1867.
16. M. Mujeeb, *Indian Muslims*, p. 431.
17. B. Chunder, *Travels of a Hindoo*, p. 377.
18. Harcourt, *New Guide to Delhi*, p. 19.
19. Women's Letters from India (U.S.P.G.A.); Imdad Sabri, *Dilli Ke Yaadgar Hastian* (Delhi, 1972), p. 30.
20. J. Matheson, *England to Delhi* (London, 1870), p. 357.
21. I.O.R., India and Bengal Despatches, 16 April–26 May 1858, No. 533; N.A.I., Railway Despatches to India from Secy. of State, 1862–3, P.W.D. Rlys, No. 52 of 1862.
22. *Mof.*, 6 Feb. 1863.
23. N.A.I., Rly Despatches from Secy. of State, No. 11 of 1863.
24. *Mof.*, 11 Jan. 1867.
25. 'Aahni Sadak', *Khutoot*, p. 291.
26. *Mof.*, 3 July 1866; ibid., 11 May 1869.
27. D.D.R., Report on Operations of Western Jamuna Canal, 1860–1, H.R. Delhi, P.W.D., F.2.
28. B. Chunder, op. cit., p. 379; Mrs Tremlett to Miss Bullock, 25 June 1869 (Women's Letters from India, U.S.P.G.A.).
29. *R.N.P.*, 1877, *P.A.Rs*, passim.
30. B. Chunder, op. cit., p. 378.
31. Anon., *Brief History of the Family of Rai Chunna Mal* (Delhi, 1930).
32. *Punjab Municipal Progs.*, 31A/Oct. 1884.
33. *Report on Income Tax in Punjab*, 1869–70.
34. *D.G.*, 20 Aug. 1859.
35. *Punjab Gazetteer*, 1883–4, Delhi District, p. 124.
36 Ashish Bose, oral interview.
37. *Punjab Gazette*, Supplement, 30 Aug. 1877, p. 587.

38. *Friend of India*, 18 Mar. 1858, quoted in *Mof.*, 26 Mar. 1858.
39. *Census of India 1891*, General Report, p. 44.
40. *Report on the Working of the Income Tax in Punjab*, 1896–7.
41. *Punjab Gazette*, 17 Aug. 1876, Part I, p. 379; ibid., 1877, Supplement, pp. 59–62.
42. A. A. Roberts, *Report on 'Selections'*, *N.W.P.* (1849), I, p. 13; *Census of N.W.P.*, 1853, p. 66.
43. B. Chunder, op. cit., p. 371.
44. J. Wilson in *Journal of Royal Society of Arts*, 27 Dec. 1912, p. 145.
45. *Census of India 1901*, Vol. XVII A, Part II, pp. xi–xvii.
46. *Report of Settlement Operations*, Delhi District, 1910.
47. D.M.C. Progs., *passim*.
48. Contrast Calcutta. See S. N. Mukherjee in Leach and Mukherjee (eds.), *Elites in South Asia* (London, 1968), p. 45.
49. House Tax Assessments are given in *D.M.C. Report*, 1901–2, p. 24.
50. C. Foxley, 'The Chandni Chowk' (reproduced in *Delhi Mission News*, Vol. II, No. 4, Oct. 1898).
51. *D.M.C. Report*, 1901–2, p. 24.
52. Bradshaw, *Through Routes Overland : Guide to India* (London, 1890), p. 128; Bashir-ud-din Ahmad, op. cit., Vol. II, p. 246.
53. P. Wilmott and M. Young, *Family and Class in a London Suburb* (London, 1960), p. 127.
54. Sri Ram Mathur, 'Waqa-e-Sri Ram', MSS., Vol. I, fol. 19.
55. Ashraf Subuhi, op. cit., p. 105.
56. *Khutoot*, p. 222.
57. Oral evidence, the late Prof. M. M. Begg.
58. G. C. Narang, *Karkhandari Dialect of Delhi Urdu* (Delhi, 1961).
59. Ashraf Subuhi, op. cit., p. 107.
60. Interview, Prof. Mohammad Hasan.
61. Ahmed Ali, *Twilight in Delhi* (Delhi, 1973), for an evocative picture of Delhi in the first two decades of this century.
62. *Khutoot*, p. 105.
63. Ibid., p. 367.
64. C. Foxley, op. cit.
65. Louis Philippe, the Duc d'Orléans, cousin of the Bourbon rulers of France, had survived the French Revolution and subsequently claimed to be the legitimate successor to the throne. Ilahi Bux, cousin of Bahadur Shah, played a similar role.
66. Bashir-ud-din Ahmad, op. cit., Vol. II, p. 169.
67. J. A. Page (ed.), *List of Muhammadan and Hindu Monuments, Delhi Province* (London, 1913), Vol. I.
68. Bashir-ud-din Ahmad, op. cit., Vol. II, p. 188 ff.
69. Ibid., and *Khutoot*, *passim*.
70. Oral evidence, the late Dr B. N. Ganguli.
71. *R.N.P.*, 1868, p. 336.
72. C.C.O., Education, F. 98B/1914.
73. The late Prof. M. M. Begg, oral interview.

74. Imdad Sabri, *Dilli Ke Yaadgar Hastian*, p. 309 ff.
75. F. Engels, quoted in A. Briggs, *Victorian Cities* (London 1963), p. 26.
76. *Annual Reports*, U.S.P.G., *passim*.
77. Imdad Sabri, op. cit., p. 422.
78. Oral evidence, the late Lala Jagdish Prasad.
79. Val C. Prinsep, *Imperial India* (London, 1879), p. 24.
80. J. Fergusson, *India Ancient and Modern* (London, 1868), p. 67.
81. C.C.O., F.541/1906.
82. Sri Ram Mathur, op. cit., Vol. II, fol. 76.
83. S. J. Lewandowski, 'Urban Growth and Municipal Development in the Colonial City of Madras 1860–1900', *Journal of Asian Studies*, 34, February 1975.
84. I.O.R., MS., Austin Cook, 'Account of the Delhi Durbar of 1903'.
85. Ashraf Subuhi, op. cit., p. 26.
86. C.C.O., F.541/1906.
87. Whitehead, *Report on the Crown Lands at Delhi* (Lahore, 1910).
88. Bashir-ud-din Ahmad, op. cit., Vol. II, p. 254.
89. *P.A.R. 1871–2*, p. 198.
90. *P.H.P.* (Judicial), 4A/Aug. 1883.
91. *P.A.R.*, 1888–9, p. 108.
92. M. J. Mehta, 'Business Environment and Urbanization: Ahmedabad in the 19th Century' in J. S. Grewal and I. Banga (ed.), *Studies in Urban History* (Amritsar, 1981).
93. A. Joshi and Khushwant Singh, *Sri Ram* (Bombay, 1968), p. 32.
94. *Census 1891, 1901* and *1911; Report of Indian Factory Labour Commission*, 1908.
95. *P.H.P.* (General), 2A/Aug. 1899.
96. *Factory Labour Commission Report*, 1908, pp. 395, 398, 400.
97. *Census of India 1901*, Vol. XII, Ch. I, Pt. 2, p. 22.
98. *Census of India 1891*, Vol. XIX, Pt. II, Table 93; ibid., 1901, XIV, Pt. II, Table XV.
99. E. Burdon, *Monograph on the Wire and Tinsel Industry in the Punjab* (Lahore, 1909).
100. *P.H.P.* (General), 2A/1899; *Indian Industrial Commission Report 1916–17*, evidence of Lala Sultan Singh.
101. *Census of India 1901*, XVII a, table XV; ibid., 1911, XIV, Pt. II, table XV.
102. This was done in connection with the Durbar of 1903.
103. N.A.I.—Home (Municipalities), 8–9A/Jan. 1908.
104. *Factory Labour Commission Report*, 1908, pp. 397–400.
105. *P.A.R. 1905–6*, p. 36.
106. Oral evidence, Mr Maheshwar Dayal.
107. *P.H.P.* (Registration), 33A/June 1899.
108. *Military Report on the Country Around Delhi* (Lahore, 1907).
109. *D.M.C. Report*, 1901–2, p. 24.

3

RECOVERY AND REALIGNMENTS
(1858-76)

Delhi had to be built anew in the 1860s, in a physical and a psychological sense. What had been a royal capital was now a provincial town. The Court and the loyalty it had commanded had disappeared. The *kotwali* and the *mohulla* system had been abolished. Delhi College was closed. The Jamá Masjid was, till 1862, closed to worshippers, the Fatehpuri Masjid was sold to Lala Chunna Mal. Between 1857 and 1861 the vacuum was filled by the British army. But when the town was returned to the civilian authorities that year, both Indians and Europeans had to start contributing to the building of a new Delhi on the framework of a battered Shahjahanabad. The vacuum was sought to be filled by setting up a Municipality, a Jama Masjid Committee, and a Delhi Society.

It might have been possible to have set up a Municipality in the 1850s, as had been projected, at the initiative of the inhabitants and specifically for local welfare. But the Municipality which was inaugurated in 1863, like the fifty other Municipalities set up in the Punjab before 1864, had its basis in the exigencies of the Police Act of 1861. The Resolution of the Viceroy, Lord Lawrence, in August 1864 made this quite explicit.

> Municipalities shall raise (in any manner they decide) funds for the *police* and for *conservancy* and such other funds as the members may think fit to expend on works of improvement, education and other local objects; and the cost of the Municipal Police shall be a first charge on all such funds.[1]

The details of the police charges were specified by the Provincial Government. For its part, the nascent 'Municipal Commission' of Delhi worked out a very comprehensive set of bye-laws concerning the other functions it intended to discharge.[2] These were generalized for the whole province in the Punjab Municipal Act of 1867. They defined the area under municipal jurisdiction to be 'the city and suburbs', including the Cantonment. Fines would be imposed for encroaching on roads, unauthorized structures, and carrying on 'offensive trades'. Penalties for other 'offences' had been provided for in the Police Act of 1861. The taxes to be levied included two which had been collected before1857—watering and lighting rates charged on shops (which were discontinued after two years when the octroi revenue increased) and *tehbazari* on pedlars. The innovations were slaughter-house fees and, the major source of income, octroi on tobacco leaf, ghee, sugar, oil, hides, *kandla*, charcoal, and limestone. No member of the Municipality was to be allowed to take any contract granted by the Municipality. In 1865 all municipal accounts were being submitted to a sub-committee consisting of the Chairman (i.e. the Divisional Commissioner) or the Municipal Secretary, together with Lalas Chunna Mal and Mahesh Das, subsequently to be audited by three British officials.[3] The Municipal Commissioners also fulfilled the role of Honorary Magistrates. The Civil Lines came under the Municipality's jurisdiction and was not governed by a separate committee.

The British officials used the Municipality to encourage loyalists, and to create their own equivalent of the Nawabs of Jhajjar and Loharu and Rajas of Ballabgarh and Kishengarh. The common denominator was that the chosen men had been sifted out as supporters of the British in the uncertain days of 1857. Nearly all of them hailed from established families, often with a tradition of service with the East India Company or, alternatively, of apolitical mercantile respectability. For their careful act of choice in 1857 they won their reward many times over. They won it in the form of wealth and land by virtue of their shrewd investments in 1858–9, and in the form of *khillats*, titles and positions of honour in the 1860s. As soon as any of them died (in some cases even in their lifetime) their heirs were granted marks of recognition. Hence the phenomenon of teenagers becoming members of the Municipality and being noticed in the Gazetteer lists. This official policy was very similar to that being followed *vis-à-vis* the aristocracy in the 'native states'. 'The British effort to make themselves permanent rulers of India led them to an attempt to arrest by artificial means the normal process of evolution ... They sought

... to salvage the aristocrats at all costs, attempting to transform them into good natural leaders.'⁴

Five such dynasties can be distinguished among the Hindus and Jains in the 1860s and 1870s. They were *khatri* and Jain families who had, for some decades, enjoyed a reputation as bankers, and who in the 1860s were very rich. These were the Saligram and Girdhar Lal families, both Jain, and the Chunna Mal, Gurwala, and Naharwala families, all *khatri*. Lala Saligram, who had been Government Treasurer, had aided the British forces in 1857 and was rewarded with the gift of Wazirpur village, and places on the Municipal Commission for both his sons—for Ajodhya Pershad in the 1860s and for Dharm Das in the 1870s.⁵ Girdhar Lal was Government Treasurer in 1863–6 in return for his services in 1857, and his son Paras Das figured in the select list of five or six individuals cited in the 1884 *Gazetteer*. Lala Chunna Mal and Lala Mahesh Das had been the Rosencrantz and Guildenstern who supported the British side in 1857 and after the siege was lifted. Chunna Mal spent the capital which he had refused to lend to Bahadur Shah on buying jewels, houses in the city, plots of land in the city and suburbs, and the Fatehpuri Masjid. Subsequently he moved to large-scale commercial ventures. By 1869 Chunna Mal was reputed to be the 'richest man' in Delhi, whose house in Katra Nil was a mini-court, flooded with hundreds of visitors at Diwali, and gay with chandeliers and candelabra. He combined this display of private wealth with an equally impressive record of public charity, by putting a lakh of rupees into the Delhi Bank to be used for 'charity, education and serais', in giving the lead to other rich men in organizing massive outdoor relief during the famines of 1860, 1862 and 1869 (enabling government to cut down its own relief expenditure proportionately),⁶ and even in contributing for a building for the *zenana* teachers of the Society for the Propagation of the Gospel.⁷ On his death, his Municipal Commissionership passed to his heir Umrao Singh and subsequently to the latter's younger brother Ram Kishen Das.⁸ Narain Das Gurwala, a banker whose business contacts extended all over India, had helped the British in the Revolt and was given a place in the Municipality in 1870. His son Sri Kishen Das was to be a public figure in the 1880s, at a very young age. The individuals mentioned above, and Narain Das Naharwala, are first noticed as members of the committee set up in 1863 to urge the government not to divert the railway from Delhi. All of them were to be members of the Delhi Society when it was formed two years later.

Other Hindu members of the Municipality in these years were Lala Sahib Singh, Lala Baldev Singh, Lala Shiv Sahai Mal (all *kayasths*, with a record of 'loyalty'), Pandit Lachman Das, a *kayasth* school-teacher, and Lala Rammi Mal, the Saraogi Jain leader and at one time an octroi contractor.[9] Many of the Hindu alumni of Delhi College, who happened to be mostly *kayasths*, were happy to be members of the Delhi Society, just as in former days they had integrated into the cross-communal *musha'ara* culture. They included Munshi Jiwan Lal, Munshi Bihari Lal 'Mushtaq', Munshi Dina Nath, Rai Bansi Lal, Pandit Basheshar Nath, Master Bhairon Prasad, Rai Hukm Chand, Munshi Pyare Lal 'Ashoob', Pandit Moti Lal 'Bismil', Professor Ramchandra and Lala Wazir Singh. They were eager to seek professional employment with the government but were less concerned with occupying nominated positions in the Municipality.[10] The British officials honoured even earlier commitments, as for example when the family of the *khatri* Bhawani Shankar (*Namak-Haraam*) became destitute, and had to mortgage their house. His son Jai Singh (who died in 1862), grandson Balmukand and great-grandson Moolchand were all given stipends.[11]

In the years after 1857, when the Muslims in Delhi were demoralized and attenuated, the rivalry between Jains and Hindus, particularly between their respective leaders, Lala Rammi Mal and Lala Mahesh Das, both very rich bankers, became prominent. The correspondent of a Lucknow newspaper commented in 1868 that 'Wealth is the only thing that matters [sc. at Delhi]'.[12] The Saraogi Jains' *Rathjatra* procession was a religious ceremony that afforded an occasion to display the patrons' impressive wealth. An ornate procession which compared with earlier Mughal cavalcades, but dominated by idols instead of by royalty, would proceed through the walled city to a Jain shrine outside, in Jaisinghpura or Talkatora. The Vaishnavite Hindus objected to the procession. The Jains once said that 'the inhabitants of Delhi consider themselves more influential than our men'[13]—an indication that the Jains regarded themselves as relative newcomers in the city. At times of tension, the Vaishnavites would discourage marriages between their families and Saraogis, and deny the latter access to their temples.[14] The Saraogis in many towns managed to hold their procession, but in Delhi it had been held relatively infrequently —only twice, in 1816 and in 1834.[15] On both occasions, there had been disturbances in the city between their followers and the Hindus.

In the 1860s the *Rathjatra* was an issue which could be used to test the policy declared in the Queen's Proclamation of 1858. It also was an issue that caused perhaps undue perturbation among officials. There was always something about Indian crowds and processions that made Englishmen lose their cool. The legends of the French Revolution or the experience of Chartist demonstrations may have been the reason—or, more simply, the memory of 1857 might have given many of them an abiding fear of a crowd of Indians. In the 1860s and 1870s the Jains and Hindus at Delhi bombarded officials at all levels with petitions and counter-petitions—the Jains for holding the *Rathjatra*, the Hindus threatening to take out a counter procession. Commissioner Hamilton did not want any group to complain about discrimination. His solution, therefore, was to prohibit *all* ceremonies. He banned elaborate marriage processions. He refused the Shias permission to take out a *Mohurrum* procession. About the *Rathjatra*, he wrote, 'This is a *dangerous* attempt to revive an *obsolete* ceremony. Delhi, a commercial city, is already too much infested with processions and religious processions are peculiarly dangerous here.'[16] The Jains appealed over his head to the Viceroy; they failed there but succeeded with the Secretary of State, perhaps because they were clever enough to refer to the Royal Proclamation.

The Hindus, angry at the Jains' success in 1863, alleged that one of the Jain leaders, Lala Jankidas, had bribed the local magistrate.[17] The Deputy Commissioner in 1870 went to the trouble of visiting a Jain temple to see whether the Hindus' charge about obscene idols was true, and declared that it was not. Having achieved their procession once, the Jains repeated their appeal every subsequent year. In 1870 action was taken against the Police Superintendent, whose policemen had escorted a Jain *Rathjatra* which had been passed off as a marriage procession. The sanctity of the Cantonment was preserved by an official order which laid down that 'in Saraogi processions ... the word "Jai" is shouted up to Begum Samru's Bagh, and no further, and music is permitted only up to the ... Fort'. The next year three hundred Hindus met and submitted a new cause for objection—that the *Rathjatra* obstructed traffic in Chandni Chowk.

To some extent the conflict was also one between the political Ins and Outs. In 1868, 1872 and 1873 Lala Rammi Mal and Lala Janki Das (both prominent Saraogis and both outside the Municipality) protested against a Municipal order to kill stray dogs, which was being carried out brutally by soldiers. This was in consonance with their belief in non-violence, but could also have been an act of defiance against the local government. In 1873 their protest was expressed in a *hartal* by shopkeepers. This method was by no means new, but because it was the first organized protest against governmental authority after a long time, and the first since 1857, it was magnified in the reports of startled officials into an *émeute*. The Jains won their point and the Municipality modified its orders.[18]

In May 1877 Lieutenant-Governor Egerton lifted the ban on the Jain procession with the argument that the Hindus' *Ramlila* (which was celebrated outside Ajmeri Gate after a procession was taken through Chandni Chowk) was 'more objectionable as a violation of the peace' than the *Rathjatra*.[19] He proposed to threaten the Hindus with having their names struck off the Durbar lists—a measure that would have affected Rai Sahib Singh and Rai Umrao Singh. The next month the two sects convened a joint *panchayat* at the Town Hall, with T. W. Smyth, Deputy Commissioner, as 'Umpire'. The Hindus were represented by Kanwar Gopal Singh, Raja Dinanath, Lala Nanak Chand and Lala Sri Ram (the last named proudly wrote 'M.A.' after his name, being the first student from Delhi to have secured that degree). The Jain leaders were Lala Dharm Das, Lala Ajodhya Pershad, Lala Baldeo Singh, Pandit Mathura Das and Lala Sri Ram, a pleader. This *panchayat* did not discuss the question of processions at all, which suggests that this issue was only a cover for more serious differences. The matters which were discussed and settled concerned inter-marriage and inter-dining.[20] The Deputy Commissioner's presence made this different from the *dals* of Calcutta, which were 'beyond the control of the British administrators'.[21]

Egerton's comparison of the *Rathjatra* and the *Ramlila* was not tenable, because of the great difference in scale. In July 1877, after the *panchayat* settlement, the Jains planned a celebration in which they counted on 50,000 visitors from other districts. This would have necessitated deploying 500 policemen. Some Hindu shopkeepers had planned to celebrate the holiday by going to Kalkaji or to the Qutb, but the Commissioner induced them to keep their shops open, lest it should give the appearance of a *hartal*. This procession once again created tension, and the Hindus threatened a social boycott of Lala Rammi Lal. But the officials could not afford to displease Lala Meher Chand, one of the Jain leaders, who in 1878 wanted a procession to celebrate the completion of his father's temple in Dharmpura. Meher Chand had also donated liberally to the Dispensary, and a *quid pro quo* was called for.[22] After 1878, the tension abated, probably because the joint *panchayat* achieved a *modus vivendi* between the two factions.

The conflict was largely of the Montagu–Capulet variety, but as a result of the repeated clashes between the leaders there was a greater consciousness of separate identity as between the communities. People who earlier would not have bothered to describe themselves as non-Hindus began to do so. This is the only possible explanation for the fact that the census early in 1868 returned 1,000 Saraogis, but that later in the year it was claimed that they numbered 4,000.[23] The completion in the 1870s of the Jain Mandir at the entrance to Chandni Chowk was a significant index to the viability of the community in Delhi then, just as the use of the Fatehpuri Masjid was to be in the context of the Punjabi Sheikhs in the 1890s, and the enlargement of the Sisganj Gurdwara to the growth of the Sikh population in the 1930s.

The Muslim loyalists figured in the Municipality and the Jama Masjid Committee. There was one officially recognized 'royal' family—the collateral Mughal line, represented by Mirza Ilahi Bux. He was nominated Co-President of the Delhi Society and was a member of the Municipality. His son Mirza Suleiman Shah was also nominated to the Municipality. The stamp of recognition given to this family suggests that, while the British officials were determined not to have anything like a repetition of the 1857 Revolt, they wanted to retain one of the Mughals as a puppet-figure, so that the Delhi Muslims did not become totally alienated from their rule, as well as because 'it pays politically to recognize such support'[24] (i.e. support in 1857). In 1875, by which time the phobias of the post-1857 period had abated, the Punjab Government made enquiries as to the names of the educated members of the Royal Family, so that they might be provided with jobs. The answer was that they were too poor to even afford an education, and that it would be more useful to increase their pensions.[25]

In 1867 when Mirza Ilahi Bux presided over the Id celebrations at the Idgah, the *Zia-ul-Akbar*, a mouthpiece of the Loharu family, was quick to make an issue out of it. It insinuated that he had accepted *nazars* and *morchuls*, and was obviously trying to reassert a sovereign position; another local newspaper, the *Chiragh-Delhi*, was sceptical, doubting whether he, a government pensioner, would do anything so imprudent.[26] Nawab Ziauddin 'Nayar' of Loharu had much more self-assurance than the Mughals. This was probably because of his friendship with John Lawrence, which not only secured him a certificate of his own respectability but also enabled him to secure the release of Kotwal Muinuddin, arrested for complicity in the Revolt. When Viceroy Lawrence passed through Delhi in 1867, many loyalists went to pay their respects to him, and the *Zia-ul-Akbar*, reporting this, tabled the hierarchy acceptable to it, where Nawab Ziauddin headed the list, and mere merchants like Sheikh Mahbub Bux and Lala Chunna Mal (both Municipal Commissioners) were at the end.[27] Nawab Ziauddin was not above accepting a place on the Municipality the same year for his son Nawab Shahabuddin Khan. His grandson, Nawab Bashiruddin Ahmad Khan, was to marry the daughter of Nawab Baqar Ali, another of whose daughters married a Dr Zaid Ahmad, an Assamese surgeon at Delhi, whose marriage was arranged for him by the British officials. Their son, Fakhruddin Ali Ahmad, was later to be President of India.[28]

Two other survivors of the Mughal Court, for whom, as for Ziauddin, it had been a matter of touch-and-go as to whether they would be hanged or admitted to the ranks of respectability, were the Mughal Talleyrand, Mufti Sadruddin 'Azurda', and the royal physician, Hakim Ahsanullah Khan. Both of them were present at the meeting held in 1865 to protest against the threatened diversion of the railway. They both died a few years later, and played only a limited part in local affairs.

Nawab Hamid Ali Khan, the son of Nawab Fazl Ali Itmad-ud-daulah, had been spared in 1857 because of a letter from Hodson which guaranteed him his life because 'he has been a useful informer'.[29] As a result, he received compensation for his houses

on Nasirganj Road (near Kashmeri Gate) which were 'ruined' by
the army in 1858, and had his three houses in Daryaganj restored
to him. In 1911 Syed Murtaza Khan, the grandson of Saifuddaula
(who had been Bahadur Shah's *vakil* at his trial) appealed for the
restoration of his great-grandfather Nawab Ataullah's jagir, by
reminding the officials that the Nawab had helped Lake in 1803.[80]

The other Muslim loyalists were Nawab Mohammad Husain
Khan, Diwan Inamullah Khan, Hakim Ghulam Raza Khan, and
Hakim Zahiruddin (the last had a long innings in the Municipality, from 1874 to 1906), Mohammad Ikramullah Khan (also
with a record of service from 1875 to 1907), Hafiz Azizuddin (a
member of the Muslim Reform Association in 1875), Nizamuddin
Khan, Syed Safdar Husain, and Sheikhs Mahbub Bux and Wilayat
Husain Khan. It is instructive to find that of these only the last
two, who were merchants without any pretension to aristocratic
or upper class status, took the trouble to join the Delhi Society,
which was dominated by Hindus who were of the same class as
themselves. Among the Muslims the equivalent of the *kayasths*
among the Hindus were those *rais* who did not need the stamp of
official favour to enhance their status—the *Hakims,* the literati, and
the *maulvis* and *ulema.* Hakim Hisamuddin and Hakim Mahmud
Khan were physicians whose reputation was all-Indian, not merely
local. They were both offered lucrative posts by rulers of Punjab
after 1857, but they turned them down. Hakim Mahmud Khan
was a member of the Delhi Society. Maulvi Ziauddin was an
eminent Arabic and Urdu scholar, who had helped the British in
1857 and who, twenty years later, was to improvise the title
Kaiser-e-Hind for the Queen at the time of the Delhi Durbar.
In 1870 the Lieutenant-Governor received Maulvi Ziauddin 'with
every respect' because he was 'the grandson of the late Nawab of
Basai-Darapur and . . . a famous *rais* of Delhi and the best Oriental
scholar in India' but the more important reason was that stated by
the Delhi Commissioner in 1894, 'It *pays* politically to recognize
such support [i.e. the Maulvi's help in 1857] ungrudgingly . . .'[31]
Nawab Nabi Bux, Altaf Husain Hali, Nazir Ahmad and Mohammad Husain Azad were the literary figures who were young
enough and resilient enough to make a new beginning in literature
(which the authors of *Fugan-e-Delhi* could not); they were ready
to seek employment under the British regime.

Notable *ulema,* who disdained any contact with the British

officials other than the indirect one *via* the management committees of mosques, included Haji Kutbuddin (a Waha'bi and the President of the Muslim Reform Association in 1875), Maulana Mohammad Husain 'Faqir' (who helped Turkey during the Russo-Turkish War of 1877), Maulvi Mohammad Najmuddin, one of the founders of the Muslim Reform Association, and Maulvi Syed Nazir Husain, who was given the title *Shams-ul-Ulema* by the government.[32] Some of these *maulvis* crossed swords with the missionaries of the Society for the Propagation of the Gospel, though there was in these years no debate on the scale of the high drama of the Rahmatullah–Pfander debates of the 1850s.[33] In the 1870s even these esoteric and academic discussions ceased, because of an order by Commissioner Hamilton that no one was to argue with the missionaries on the subject of religion.

After the Revolt, officials at Delhi were not only anxious to strain out the loyalist element, but were also obsessed by a fear of the more anonymous poorer sections. A common stereotype in late nineteenth century *officialese* in Britain and in India was of the 'criminal and dangerous classes'. 'The presence of an unknown number of the casual poor, indistinguishable to many contemporaries from criminals, apparently divorced from all forms of established religion, ... inhabiting unknown cities within the capital constituted a disquieting alien presence in the midst of mid-Victorian plenty.'[34] This was said of London, but could well have been about mid-Victorian Delhi. This blanket term, 'the criminal classes' was used to explain any incidents of violence and tension, minor or large-scale. It afforded an explanation for the spate of petty crime in the city in these years, most noticeable between 1867 and 1874. The targets were the Chandni Chowk and Dariba shops, and bankers, merchants and pensioners. That the incidence of crime was fairly high is proved by the fact that it was noticed by newspapers outside Delhi, and was the subject of discussion in the local press and in the Delhi Society.

One major reason for this spate of crime was that the city gates were no longer always closed as they had been before 1857, and were often open all night and not adequately guarded. During the period when the railway line was being constructed, access to the city was very easy from the points of egress of the railway line. After 1857 the *kuchabandi* system of locking off one *mohulla* from another at night had been prohibited, and this also made for insecurity. The mildness of the legal punishment made crime attractive, while the paucity of policemen in many *mohullas* made things easy for pickpockets. Gambling and wrestling were blamed for causing brawls, and the journal of the staid Delhi Society suggested that the gymnasiums—*akharas*—be closed, because they were a 'source of vice'.[35] But these vices were not new, and were not peculiar to a particular period of time or to a particular class of society. The Gujars and Mewatis of the neighbourhood were in many cases made the scapegoats for the crimes, and were said to be in league with the city '*badmashes*'. One of the reasons undoubtedly was the 'shortage of grain'—something listed even by the Delhi Society, an association dominated by merchants.[36] There was great wealth in the hands of many wholesale merchants, who hoarded grain in the years of famine in order to enhance their profits later. 'The Delhi market has fallen on account of the great demand of corn from the eastern districts, where thousands of maunds of wheat, gram, *dal*, etc. are daily exported from the city by the Rail in 1866.'[37] This must have tempted the poorer sections of the inhabitants and the traditional marauders, to test and provoke the raw police force. There were grain-riots in the city in 1877.

The new police-force was heartily disliked by the inhabitants, and even by the Europeans and the loyalists. This prejudice was to continue for many decades. One reason for this was the novelty of the institution. Another very cogent one was that a very large percentage of the municipal income went to pay for their upkeep. (This was not peculiar to British India. It was also true of Birmingham.) In 1865 Rs 50,000 out of a total expenditure of Rs 66,000 was spent on the police. This seemed far more than was merited by the services they performed, to judge by discussions within the Municipality. 'The Municipal Commissioners' and Honorary Magistrates' meeting computed that less expense was incurred under the old *chowkidary* system than in that of the present police,' wrote the *Mofussilite* in 1866.[38] The attacks by the Urdu press must be treated with caution, for it is very possible that many local newspapers deliberately played up the incidents of anarchy to show the police in a poor light in comparison with the old *chowkidars*. One specific point of criticism was that the government was employing as policemen many Jats and Gujars

who were 'by profession thieves'.[39] The Gujars made a practice
of this till well into the present century. The Europeans living in
the Civil Lines had perforce to employ Gujars as *chowkidars*.[40]
They had other problems too. 'The servants are all crying out for
an increase of wages,' Reverend Winter wrote to Miss Bullock in
October 1868.[41]

If thieving was the illicit manifestation of distress, begging was
the open one. 'As a rule everybody in Delhi seems very poor' was
the impression of a newcomer in 1869.[42] The local English newspaper urged the Municipality to 'remove' the *chamar* and Jat
women beggars.[43] This would have involved initially removing
the acute grain shortage and high prices. One abjectly poor community, largely women, who did not display their distress, partly
out of a sense of pride and partly from a deep-rooted fear of the
British, were the Mughals. When the S.P.G. Missionaries began
their work of educating girls in 1867, they made some headway
with the Muslims of the Delhi Gate area and the Mughal prin-
cesses living in the 'nests of native hovels' near Mori Gate.[44]
'Thousands of poor have been thrown on their own resources
by the fall of the sham royalty of Delhi. The men deserve their
fate ... Our sympathy is for the women who cannot be accused
of participating in the Mutiny. It is well known that they spin
gota for a living. We have not introduced sewing machines or
looms. We should do so.' This plea came from the *Mofussilite*,
which went on to plead that the local government should establish a poor house, to which the rich merchants could subscribe.[45]
Within three years of this request, in 1870, the Municipality did
set up a poor house.

In 1861 the situation was grim. Eight thousand people queued
for meals daily at the Idgah 'asylum'. At Delhi Gate four thousand
women, half of them widows, were given rations. That Lala
Mahesh Das contributed generously was vouched for even by an
English newspaper of a particularly self-righteous hue.[46] Another
English newspaper, writing at the time of the next famine in 1868,
said, 'Among the native gentlemen of Delhi we anticipate little
liberality with one or two exceptions.'[47] This forecast was belied
by the official report. 'Delhi District (by contrast to Karnal and
Gurgaon) has hardly any need for assistance from without.' The
Municipality, it went on to say, contributed Rs 2,000, the inhabitants Rs 5,000. Lalas Chunna Mal and Mahesh Das, Sahib Singh,

Rammi Mal, and Khan Mahbub Bux made donations, and devoted
much time to supervising relief operations personally.[48]

Famine years were a bonus to the missionaries. The poor Muslim
chamars and the equally poor Mughals, who formed, ironically,
the two ends of the social spectrum, were the first victims of the
renewed zeal of the S.P.G. and the Baptist Mission. In the 1860s
Christian *busties* mushroomed in Paharganj, Sadar Bazaar, Mori
Gate and Delhi Gate.[49] These conversions were in many cases
purely nominal. 'It was in Padri Winter's time,' recalled one of the
converts many years later, 'there was a famine, he gave us a bribe
and we all became Christians.'[50] The missionaries were secretly
chagrined at the lack of response from the middle classes. 'In
Delhi the difficulties are social, not religious,' said Canon Crowfoot, resignedly.[51] Reverend Winter made an analysis of the
Christian population of Delhi, which showed 82 to be converts
from the weaver and *chamar* castes, 13 middle-class Muslims, and
27 'high-caste' Hindus. *Zenana* work was among 'people of middle
orders'—Mughal families, some Bengali and some local Hindu
families.[52]

An anecdote related how in 1867 when a heavy shower led to
the collapse of a house occupied by some poor Muslims, they
abused the owner roundly and called down on his head the
vengeance not of Allah but of the Municipal Commissioners![53]
A Municipal decree the same year empowered the Commissioners
to destroy dilapidated houses, but they do not appear to have
taken any steps towards this. Earlier a municipal order had prohibited thatched roofs within the walled city as a safeguard against
fires. When it came to repairing or building drains and roads,
many of the back roads of the city were attended to. But one of
the essential facilities in a crowded and commercial city was
neglected. The thoroughfares which had been brightly lit by
kerosene lamps before the Mutiny were now lit dimly by oil
lamps.[54] Delhi was a dark city. This must have been a major
contributory factor in the rising incidence of thefts and the general
sense of insecurity. 'We would suggest reducing the police establishment and replacing them with as many lamp-posts as policemen,' wrote the incorrigible *Mofussilite*. Shopkeepers put up their
shutters at dusk. In 1870 the Municipal Report claimed that all
roads were lit by kerosene, but a local Urdu newspaper in 1876
said that only the main roads were well-lit, and that the Munici-

pality was being guided 'not by the convenience of the people at large but only their own comfort'.[55] The dichotomy between the interests of the loyalists and that of the people at large appeared very real to many people.

An average Indian Municipality in the later nineteenth century spent 20–25 per cent of its income on the police, and 15–20 per cent each on conservancy and road maintenance.[56] In the 1860s Delhi Municipality's expenditure on the police amounted to 75 per cent of its income. The remaining 25 per cent had to be spread very thinly over a large surface. The volume of octroi fell sharply in 1868 after the Government of India drastically reduced the number of items on which octroi could be levied. Following complaints in Punjab, the tax was reimposed. Earlier, in 1866, the *Mofussilite* had said that the introduction of octroi had caused a rise in prices, and it had urged that 'true public opinion' should be elicited—'NOT [*sic*] the opinion of Municipal Commissioners and *mohulladars*'.[57] No such public poll was taken but in the absence of complaints it might be assumed that the inhabitants were prepared to accept the octroi. The mercantile interest dominating Delhi Municipality ensured that the exemption for grain and piecegoods was retained. The octroi revenue was used for contributions towards local institutions and for the maintenance of roads and public health facilities, and on occasion for public works. But most of the public works in this period were carried out by Imperial and Provincial departments and financed partly by private subscriptions.

After 1871 the Municipality's structure became more rationalized. It secured a paid secretary, divided the city and suburbs into 15 wards (of which 12 were intramural, and corresponded roughly to the Mughal *thana* divisions) and put each of these under the charge of a non-official member. In 1871, also, Delhi was given the status of a first-class Municipality. This status was conferred on six other towns in Punjab, four hill-stations with largely European populations, Lahore and Amritsar. It was one of the three categories created by the 1867 Act. A first-class Municipality was to enjoy independence with regard to expenditure, subject only to a government audit. This made it possible to project ambitious plans for public works.

That favourite Victorian term 'improvements' was bound to

be part of the mental make-up of the British officials coming out
to India.[58] For Delhi, what did it amount to? Did it 'improve'
conditions for the inhabitants of the town generally, or did it
only concentrate on public works which were ancillary to the
development of British trade and the boosting of the British self-
image? Some, like the poor-house, would fall into the former
category, but public works chiefly concentrated on 'imperial'
improvements.

In British Delhi, there were two periods when much was done
by way of public works: in the 1860s and 1870s, and during the
building of the Temporary and Imperial Capitals after 1912. The
first public works stemmed as much from considerations of military exigency as from commercial and civil administrative needs.
The railway line was built through the city instead of outside
because this made for greater security in the event of a local rising.
Once Salimgarh and the Red Fort were occupied by the British
army, from a military point of view a railway line cutting into
the city between these two bastions was far more useful than one
which (as earlier planned) terminated at Ghaziabad on the east
bank of the Jamuna. In 1860 Fort William conveyed its sympathy
for the hardship caused to the 'Hindu population' of Delhi by
the new roads which were being built through the most densely
populated parts of the town, but did nothing to alleviate their
distress.[59] The 100 ft wide Queen's Road and Hamilton Road,
built as adjuncts to the railway line by the Imperial and Provincial
Departments, displaced many hundreds of people. No sooner had
Queen's Road become a boulevard worthy of its name than there
appeared the disadvantages of having it serve at once as a prestige
road and as a commercial highway. '*Ticca*' (*theka*) *gharries* made
grooves on the footpaths and *thelas* ('those terrible little four-
wheeled trucks which have come into general use since the railway
came to Delhi'[60]) cut tracks into the road and blocked traffic.

The railway station was followed by those other structures so
central to Victorian civic thinking—a Town Hall which would
double as an office for the Municipality and would also house the
Chamber of Commerce and a Literary Society and a Museum,
to 'improve' the local mind and 'to forward intercourse between
Europeans and Natives'. Cooper, the Commissioner, also wanted
the *Kotwali* to be located inside the Town Hall. This rather un-

imaginative suggestion was vetoed by the Judicial Commissioner of the Punjab, who said: 'It is not desirable to make Kotwalis the handsomest public buildings in India, and prominence should be given to the College and Museum.' This suggestion was 'hailed with delight' by the people of Delhi.[61]

The Town Hall had been planned before the Revolt, and was built in 1860–5, and was at first called the Lawrence Institute. It was built not as an imperial undertaking but with provincial funds and subscriptions from Hindu and Muslim loyalists. Over Rs 30,000 was contributed, of which Rs 25,000 had been donated by Lala Mahesh Das; the others who promised contributions were Lala Saligram, Lala Naharwala, Lala Gurwala, the Nawab of Dujana, Nawab Ziauddin and his son Aminuddin (against whose names, however, the sceptical Deputy Commissioner wrote 'Doubtful'), and Mirza Ilahi Bux, who excused himself later on the plea that his son's wedding was impending. (Similarly, in 1862 the people of Lahore raised subscriptions for the Ravi Canal.) By the time it was completed, the loyalists wanted it to be made over to the Municipality; the phrase they used was 'the people of Delhi'. 'The feeling is generally among Indians and Europeans,' said the *Mofussilite*, '[sc. that we should] return [sc. to the Educational Department] their Rs 10,000 [sc. out of a total cost of Rs 200,000] and let them pack up and be off ... The natives subscribed not only to the building but have been getting portraits of eminent men connected with the former history of Delhi. To deprive them of the building would be a gross breach of faith.'[62] In 1866 the Municipality by a special effort managed to buy the building for Rs. 135,457. They set aside rooms for a library and for a European Club. The Delhi College was the chief loser by the Education Department being edged out; they had also been deprived of the Ghaziuddin Madarsa.

The classical façade of the Town Hall was complemented by the castellated architecture of the station of the East India Railway Company, and the Italian-style buildings of the Punjab Railway, in a typical Victorian confection. The *Mofussilite* was not very enthusiastic about the Town Hall's architectural style. 'The public have a right to expect something better. An official said that the public gave only Rs 40,000, and therefore should not complain. This dichotomy between the government and the public is absurd.'[63] Before government became formalized, therefore, the local newspaper on occasion expressed the cross-communal sympathy of pre-1857 days.

In 1869 the Municipality constructed an imposing *serai* on Queen's Road, at a cost of Rs 100,000. This was variously called Hamilton, Queen's and, finally, in tribute to the gilded peacock on its roof, Mor Serai. It was also referred to as 'Chunna Mal Ki Serai', because he had donated generously to it. It was Mahesh Das's misfortune that the Town Hall was not named after him. Symbolizing the shift from Court to Town Hall and the need for a Western concept of time in place of that associated with the call of the *muezzin,* whose voice had been stilled since the British took over the Jama Masjid, was the Clock Tower in Chandni Chowk. (It did not achieve the purpose for which it was set up, for the pigeons sat on its hands so that it never showed the correct time.[64]) When Lord Northbrook visited Delhi, he disapproved of this structure and contributed from his own income towards another architectural piece of equally dubious aesthetic value, the Fountain in Chandni Chowk. The area between the new railway bridge (Lothian Bridge) and Kashmeri Gate was changed beyond recognition, when a Post and Telegraph Office and a Dak Bungalow were constructed on the site of the old Magazine. Thus these latter-day 'Mughals', remodelled two-thirds of Shahjahanabad in a different mould, complementing works of utility with those of ornament. Thus does a town become a palimpsest, where the aesthetic purity of one generation's achievement is overlaid by the tastes of a succeeding age. The impression of Bholanath Chunder in 1869 was that Delhi had 'all the features of a metropolis, but in comparison with Calcutta the latter [had] the advantage in general magnificence'.[65] But by 1870 the appearance of Delhi had become so 'respectable' that tourists were coming to see not only the sites of the fighting in 1857, but also the city itself. 'It is now the theme of a guidebook,' remarked a traveller in 1870.[66] British sentiment was given a safety-valve by the building of an imitation Albert Memorial, the Mutiny Memorial atop the Ridge.

The Municipality sometimes found it difficult to work with the Cantonment Committee, the local representative of another imperial department. The occasions for friction were also greater than in most other towns, because in Delhi the Cantonment was not a geographically separate area, but occupied one-third of the walled city. There was a static quality in the army's attitude on most issues, as was to be seen over the next half century. Problems arose because high policy decisions of the army sometimes clogged proposals made by the Municipality, or because of the ambivalence about their respective jurisdictions; the Cantonment had a separate administrative organization but was part of the municipal area. In 1867 the Municipality decided to demolish Mori Gate and Kabul Gate; all the members were unanimous on this point. They did this in defiance of the general military rules that the city wall was to be retained. The Rajputana Railway had made breaches in the wall on the west, and the army quartered in Daryaganj had demolished a great part of the wall on the river-front, without any objections from the Imperial Government. But when the Municipality sounded them about breaking down at least part of the northern wall, in the interests of public health, particularly of the European inhabitants, Viceroy Lawrence echoed the stand he had taken as Chief Commissioner five years previously. The wall was not to be breached, he said. Even its height was not to be lowered.[67] Till 1873 the area between Lothian Bridge and Kashmeri Gate was part of the Cantonment, and the Municipality had more than once to rap them sharply for the very insanitary state of the area. They said this was the cause of the renewed incidence of cholera, a disease unknown in the walled city before 1857.[68]

When the town revenues started to increase in 1871, the Cantonment Committee put in a demand for a larger share of it. The military authorities now asked that instead of a fixed sum they be given a fixed percentage of revenue, arguing that they consumed a large share of the goods which paid octroi and were therefore entitled to a proportionate income. The Municipality retorted that since the charges for which the revenue was contributed remained the same there was no justification for a varying sum. The Deputy Commissioner was a member of both the Cantonment Committee and the Municipality, but the maximum that the other members of the Municipality allowed him to do was to increase the monthly sum being given to the Cantonment from Rs 200 to Rs 250.[69]

In 1872 Delhi had an enterprising Commissioner—Colonel Cracroft. He wished to make Delhi more attractive and ecologically a more rational and well-planned city. He saw the wall as an anachronism, the *nazul* properties as capable of much development, the Municipality itself as apathetic and lacking a long-term perspective. He suggested detailed schemes to make Delhi more l.ealthy but most of these related to the Civil Lines only.[70] The Punjab Government was unable to accede to all of them because they impinged on their obsessive concern with 'the defences of Delhi'. After Lawrence retired, the obsession with the wall had abated somewhat, but the Franco-Prussian War of 1870 again convinced the Indian Government that fortified towns had their uses. The Municipal and Provincial Governments were not on the same wave-length—the Commissioner prefaced his suggestions with the phrase 'When Delhi was considered a fortified town ...', using the past tense for something that to the higher authorities was very much in the present tense. The Provincial Government permitted the ditch outside Ajmeri Gate to be filled up, but Cracroft's dream of 'sites for respectable buildings' to be made available by breaking the northern wall, and a 'people's garden' to be laid out by knocking down the wall between Kabul and Delhi Gates remained pipe-dreams. In 1881 the Supreme Government was to reprove the Municipality for having destroyed Mori and Kabul Gates without permission.[71]

In 1863 a special medical committee pronounced the Fort unhealthy for European troops and said that the site of the old Cantonment on the Ridge was more suitable.[72] The *Mofussilite* frequently complained that Delhi was unprotected because it was unhealthy, i.e. that because Europeans could not survive the Delhi climate long, the European soldiers were frequently changed and the city gates had to be manned by Indian policemen. The river and its miasma, the proximity of dirty Daryaganj, and the brackish well-water were the causes of ill-health generally and the 'Delhi Sore' specifically.

The city's water supply was also found to be inadequate. In 1867 the canal was flowing again, as in the 1820s, and was used by the inhabitants for bathing. But this did not solve the problem of procuring potable water. In 1867, as in 1846, three-quarters of the town's wells were found to be brackish. Sweet water could be got only at great expense from the springs on the Ridge and from distant Jhandewalan. In 1869 the Punjab Sanitary Commissioner suggested building a waterworks for tapping the Jamuna, and levying taxes to cover the cost. The *Mofussilite* wondered whether the inhabitants would agree to be taxed and whether the Hindus would accept Jamuna water if it flowed out of underground pipes. This scepticism was misplaced, for the scheme was accepted unanimously by the Municipality. 'In Delhi, the native inhabitants... entered heartily into the scheme, and [sc. were] ready to have additional taxation for sanitary improvement.' The 'traders and well-to-do gentlemen' were prepared to pay for private pipe-connections.[73] The question of how the waterworks were to be financed, however, was not to be settled as easily or unanimously.

In 1865 the Municipality planned to build a general hospital, a women's hospital and a branch dispensary. The main hospital, to replace the dispensary which had existed before 1857, was located in Chandni Chowk. It cost the Municipality Rs 70,000, and was intended to serve all the inhabitants; when in 1867 a special ward for Europeans was requested, this was not granted.[74] The response to medical facilities sponsored by the government was limited. Private treatment by *hakims* and *vaidyas* remained more popular. During the incidence of an epidemic the Municipality was unable to enforce its regulations fully, and during a major outbreak of small-pox in 1869 the Commissioners, lacking police powers, were powerless to prosecute those who left corpses by the riverbed.

In 1875, the unhealthiness of Delhi came to the notice of the Secretary of State, because the army authorities had sent him an alarmist report; and he too ordered the Punjab Government to take steps to improve it.[75] In the 1870s, apart from academic discussions on the proposed scheme for a water supply and the plans to improve drainage, some concrete measures were taken to rationalize policy on public health. The city was divided into *ilakas* for purposes of conservancy, each under a sub-committee of three municipal members. Lala Mahesh Das and other Delhi gentlemen raised subscriptions for a school for midwifery. Lala Narain Das and Lala Meher Chand contributed generously to the dispensary. The Cambridge Mission set up a women's medical branch, the first of its kind in India, and the S.P.G. and the Municipality jointly started a scheme in 1874 to train nurses. Smith of the Baptist Mission, who for some time was Municipal Secretary, was later to be credited with having driven cholera out of Delhi, a testimony important not so much for its accuracy as for showing that individuals achieved more than official agencies.[76]

Public works involved considerable initial investment, but intelligent policy could have made them profitable. In 1867 the *Mofussilite* deplored the lack of a market place in Delhi, like Calcutta's Dharamtolla. Ghalib had written that many bazaars and *qasbas* had been destroyed, and that the English did not know how to build bazaars.[77] In 1867 the Sadar Bazaar was inaugurated, formalizing the shops that had sprung up to cater to the needs of the army. Earlier, in 1865, the Municipality constructed a new wholesale vegetable market at the foot of the Ridge to replace the very old informal bazaar further north-west, because the latter became a busy cross-roads after the railway was built, and obstructed the traffic between the Roshanara Gardens and the new Civil Lines. The vendors and shop proprietors stubbornly refused to move into the new premises, and the Municipality handed it over to the police to be used for the time being as a *thana*.[78]

The Sabzi Mandi vendors were threatened with legal action for obstructing a major highway with their shacks. They were then shifted forcibly into the new premises, from which the police were evacuated. They petitioned the Punjab Government, complaining that the new market was too far from their homes, that their property was depreciating in value and that they had to pay a tax for the use of the new shops. Cracroft sympathized with them, and thought a conciliatory move was advisable since the *dalals* who were affected were Punjabi Muslims—an 'enterprising and laborious section of the people', and the gainers were Hindu market gardeners. In fact, those who stood to gain by the change were not the gardeners but the retailers in the walled city, since the new market was closer to them. Cracroft weakened his argument when he explained the mistakes in policy as having been caused by the absence of 'an experienced Commissioner' and by the Indian Municipal members having been overwhelmed by 'an English minority'. The Lieutenant-Governor regarded these arguments as special pleading, and the vendors failed to get the decision reconsidered.

The possibilities in another neglected source of income—the *nazul* properties—were first pointed out by the *Mofussilite*. These covered large parts of the western and northern suburbs, as well as pockets in the city. Richard Temple in the North-Western

Provinces had turned such property to profit and made them beautiful, whereas 'the garden and country-houses near Delhi are in a terrible state. Rank vegetation prevails, and the country-houses are pulled down for material.'[79] A European gardener, it suggested, would be the answer. Smith was put in charge of the gardens and as a result the Queen's, Roshanara and Qudsia Gardens regained some of their former beauty. The howler made by the local Christian convert who, asked by a missionary where Adam and Eve had lived, answered 'The Roshanara' indicates that to the average inhabitant it was perhaps the Mughal gardens that approximated most to Eden, not the creations of the Municipality![80] The *nazul* properties continued to exist in a very bad state of neglect. This was the great missed opportunity of the 1860s, when the Municipality failed to utilize the *embarras de richesses* it had inherited from the Mughals, landed assets far larger than most Indian Municipalities had. In the years immediately after 1857, much *nazul* land had also been sold for very small sums—1,800 sq. yards in Sabzi Mandi had been bought by Mahesh Das for Rs 550.

The Punjab Sanitary Commissioner criticized, in 1873, the vast extent of metalled roads in Delhi, because 'One bad effect of this ... is that the European community have been tempted to spread themselves over an immense area in a way which will soon prove inconvenient.'[81] The frequent changes of district officials had made any systematic survey or control impossible. When the Najafgarh Jheel Escape was constructed, the Karnal Road was cut off from the Rohtak Road. The health of the inhabitants of the 'Civil Lines', the communications between this area and the city, considerations of security, all furnished arguments for a survey of these properties, where municipal, district and provincial jurisdictions overlapped in great confusion. The Punjab Government sanctioned a special body of staff for a survey, and gave a special grant for the *nazul* gardens. Two years after the survey the Municipality was able to make out a convincing case for having the *nazul* properties made over to it and the extension of the municipal boundaries accordingly. This was a piece of luck which no other town in Punjab had. It gave the Municipality an elastic source of revenue for the future, and made possible a policy of planned expansion to the west and north. Forty years later, an official was to say that 'Government ... entrusted the Municipal

Committee with the management of *nazul* lands... with the
avowed object of furthering the prosperity of Delhi city.' Another
version, which appears nearer the truth, was that the Imperial
Government found it too much of a burden to manage these
properties, and the transfer helped the Municipality's finances.

European officials and Indian loyalists made mutual ritual genu-
flections. The *Mofussilite* praised Deputy Commissioner Cooper,
who left Delhi in 1864, for having 'pressed all the non-official
native and European talent in the city into useful employment'.[82]
When Lord Mark Kerr, the local Brigadier, left Delhi in 1864,
Nawab Ziauddin and Lala Chunna Mal joined the officials to say
that it had been through his exertions that 'a great part of the
city [sc. had] assumed an altogether new aspect... [sc. by] the
construction of the finest of roads, the laying out of new gardens
and the tasteful ornamentation of the grounds around historical
buildings'. The loyalists added obsequiously that they would
'remember with gratitude the courtesy of [sc. His] Lordship's
bearing towards them'.[83] Cooper had said that he would 'hold in
vivid recollection the remarkable public spirit of the leading
citizens'. The *Mofussilite*, however, said apropos of the 'improvements' in Qudsia Gardens that these had been carried through by
Hamilton alone. 'There is a sad want of public-spirited men in
Delhi.' In 1866 it used language that led to a libel charge, when
it described the Indian members of the Municipality as 'thoroughly
ignorant and illiterate upstarts' and contrasted them with the
'educated native gentlemen' who were appointed honorary magistrates in Calcutta. In 1869, when a vacancy occurred in the
Municipality, it expressed the hope that 'due respect will be
shown to worth, rank and respectability. There are many who
think that wealth is all that is necessary.'

It is a pity that there is no evidence of how the Indian loyalists
regarded their European colleagues, but the attitude of the British
civilians towards the Indians and towards the Municipality is
mirrored in the *Mofussilite*. Over the years its tone changed from
the patronizing to the irritable. In 1864, in its genial phase, it
enthused that there was 'no town in India with the amenities of
Delhi—a public garden that leaves Lahore nowhere... a choral
society, a museum, a library, a reading room, coffee shop, cricket
ground, racket court and railway'.[84] It criticized the snobbery

which banned the Indians from entering the public gardens. Thanks to its lobbying, and to the attitude of Commissioner Hamilton and Smith, the ban was lifted.

This attitude did not last long. The self-assurance of the *nouveaux riches* riled the British officials and visitors. As early as 1859 the openly blimpish *Delhi Gazette* took umbrage at the sight of 'the natives' 'rolling along in their carriages and sporting their Dacca muslins in Chandni Chowk'.[85] The *Mofussilite's* reaction came later but sharply. When a European was sent to prison at the instance of a local creditor, this was described as being 'opposed to all principles of law and precedent'. In the 1860s, when they had perforce to live in the city, the British residents were chagrined to find Indian landlords laying down their own terms. 'The natives have begun to behave as though the Europeans have left the country,' fumed the *Mofussilite*. 'One snob who owns half a dozen of the best houses has the insolence to ask me to keep the garden watered ... Another, a native million-aire, told me when I occupied a small house of his that it was the custom for the tenant to paint the ... house.' Again, 'those lucky enough to live in bungalows or pucca houses in the Anglo-Indian style find the landlords so independent that they will not do repairs'. The loyalists obviously were not as servile in their private capacity as in their public. The high rents charged by the Indian landlords exasperated the British but the officials could not do anything because these were the very men with whom they had forged an alliance. Gradually the newspaper began to sound as snobbish as the European 'conservatives' it had earlier criticized. 'The natives are going into the Queen's Gardens every day, instead of confining themselves to their days [i.e. Wednesdays and Saturdays]' and 'our station ladies will soon have no road open to them but the Roshanara Gardens'. By 1869 it was resigned to the situation: 'If the civil offices and station of Delhi were outside the city, we might expect to see the courts of law, as at Meerut, in the middle of an extensive plain, airy and neat; but being within an "Imperial" city, improvements are not likely.' Later, it complained that there were not enough houses for Euro-peans and that in the matter of public works, all attention was being paid to the intramural city and none to the new civil lines.

There was more in common between the Delhi Commissioners and the Calcutta magistrates than the *Mofussilite* realized. The

Calcutta gentlemen whom they had named were all of the conservative zamindar class, as also were the Delhi loyalists. How much 'public-spiritedness' were such men capable of? There were cases of municipal members misusing their office. When the land bordering Hamilton Road was being auctioned, an Indian municipal member purchased some at Rs 2–4 as. per square yard, whereas other bidders were made to pay at least Rs 8.[86] Lala Chunna Mal was reprimanded by the Deputy Commissioner for bailing out a man confined in the *kotwali*.[87] He and Lala Mahesh Das were guilty of encroaching on both sides of the Town Hall.[88] One individual, when offered the post of honorary magistrate, 'declined the honour for the reason that he would not dare to pass judgment on one of his own class if brought before him'.[89] Hindu and Jain members, so generous in private philanthropy, saw little need for a social welfare policy. When faced with the contradictions between individual interest and collective authority, they tended to regard the latter as something to be used to the advantage of the former. The British officials probably understood this. It was not, after all, very different from the situation in British municipalities before 1835. At a time when Joseph Chamberlain was just beginning to set the pace for civic 'improvements' in Birmingham,[90] one could not expect too much from his Indian counterparts.

NOTES

1. *Gazette of India Extraordinary*, 14 Sep. 1864, p. 13.
2. *Mof.*, 26 June 1863.
3. Ibid., 17 Jan. 1865.
4. F. G. Hutchins, *The Illusion of Permanence* (Princeton, 1967), p. 172.
5. *Settlement Report for Delhi*, 1882.
6. *Mof.*, 25 May 1866; B. Chunder, *Travels of a Hindoo*, p. 390.
7. *S.P.G. Report*, 1868, p. 18.
8. *Brief History of the Family of Rai Chunna Mal*.
9. Madho Pershad, *History of Delhi Municipality 1863–1921* (Delhi, 1921).
10. An exhaustive list of the *kayasth* families of Delhi is available in Sri Ram Mathur, 'Waqa-e-Sri Ram', Vol. II, fols. 25 ff.
11. D.C.O., F. 6/1862.
12. *R.N.P.*, 1868, p. 358.
13. D.C.O., F. 1/1863.
14. Ibid.

15. *Mof.*, 18 May 1863.
16. D.C.O., F. 1/1878.
17. *R.N.P.*, 1867, pp. 72-3.
18. *Mof.*, 11 June 1868; *P.H.P.*, 10A/Dec. 1872; ibid., 25A/July 1873.
19. *P.H.P.*, 27½A/May 1877.
20. D.C.O., F. 3/1877.
21. S. N. Mukerjee, 'Caste, Class and Politics in Calcutta, 1815-38' in E. Leach and S. N. Mukerjee (eds.), *Elites in South Asia* (London, 1970).
22. D.C.O., F. 3/1877.
23. *Mof.*, 11 July 1868 and 25 July 1868.
24. C.C.O., F. 14/1894, 'Maulvi Ziauddin's Pension Papers'.
25. *R.N.P.*, 1875, p. 277; ibid., 1876, pp. 174 and 513.
26. *R.N.P.*, 1867, pp. 112 and 115.
27. *R.N.P.*, 1867, p. 525.
28. Information kindly supplied by Hafiz-ur-Rahman 'Wasif'.
29. D.C.O., F. 14/1860.
30. D.C.O., F. 8/1858.
31. C.C.O., F. 14/1894.
32. Imdad Sabri, *Dilli Ke Yaadgar Hastian* (Delhi, 1972); Abdul Hai, *Safar Nama* (Delhi, 1894).
33. Imdad Sabri, *Asar-ur-Rahmat* (Delhi, 1967).
34. G. Stedman Jones, *Outcast London* (Oxford, 1971), p. 14.
35. *R.N.P.*, 1872, p. 244; ibid., 1873, p. 375.
36. *R.N.P.*, 1872, p. 244.
37. *Mof.*, 15 June 1866.
38. Ibid.
39. Ibid., 27 July 1866 and 3 Aug. 1866.
40. C.C.O., F. 541/1906, 'Delhi Cantonment Lands'.
41. Reverend Winter to Miss Bullock, 17 Oct. 1868 (Women's Letters from India, U.S.P.G.A.).
42. Miss Johnson to Miss Bullock, 2 July 1869 (ibid.).
43. *Mof.*, 13 Aug. 1867.
44. Reverend Skelton, *Delhi Mission News*, Oct. 1896, p. 11.
45. *Mof.*, 27 April 1866.
46. *Mof.*, 26 Feb. 1861.
47. *C.M.G.*, 26 Dec. 1868.
48. *Report on the Famine in Punjab, 1869-70* (Lahore, 1870).
49. U.S.P.G., *Annual Reports*.
50. Cambridge Mission to Delhi, *Twenty-fifth Report* (Cambridge, 1903).
51. Canon Crowfoot, in *Mission Life*, May 1872, quoted in *Delhi Mission News*, Vol. II, No. 1, 1898.
52. V. E. Hayward, *Church as Christian Community* (London, 1966), p. 34.
53. *Mof.*, 8 Aug. 1867.
54. Ibid., 28 March 1868.
55. *R.N.P.*, 1876, p. 328.
56. H. Tinker, *Foundations of Local Self-Government in India, Pakistan and Burma* (Delhi, 1967), p. 38.
57. *Mof.*, 24 Aug. 1866.

58. Asa Briggs, *Age of Improvement* (London, 1959), pp. 1–3, for definitions; E. P. Hennock, *Fit and Proper Persons* (London, 1973), for case-studies of Leeds and Birmingham.
59. N.A.I., Foreign Progs. (Political), 63A/7 Oct. 1859.
60. *Mof.*, 13 Mar. 1869.
61. D.C.O., F. 5/1863.
62. *Mof.*, 27 Jan. 1865.
63. Ibid., 3 July 1866.
64. Canon Crowfoot, op. cit.
65. B. Chunder, op. cit., p. 375.
66. J. Matheson, *England to Delhi* (London, 1870), p. 355.
67. C.C.O., F. 163/1863-7, 'Delhi City Walls'.
68. R. G. Wilberforce, *Unrecorded Chapter of the Indian Mutiny* (London, 1894), p. 123.
69. C.C.O., F. 553/1868.
70. C.C.O., F. 167/1872.
71. N.A.I., Home (Archaeol.) Progs., 10B/Nov. 1881; ibid., Military Progs., 8C/Nov. 1881.
72. *Mof.*, 11 Sep. 1866.
73. *P.A.R.*, 1869–70, p. 132.
74. *Mof.*, 21 Sep. 1867.
75. *P.H.P.*, 3A/June 1875.
76. Letter from Mrs Smith, 1898, Box IN/42 (Baptist Missionary Society Records).
77. *Khutoot*, p. 491.
78. C.C.O., F. 198/1876, 'Vegetable Market at Sabzi Mandi'.
79. *Mof.*, 24 Aug. 1867.
80. Miss Teesdale's Report, Nov. 1882 (Women's Letters from India, U.S.P.G.A.).
81. *P.H.P.*, 2A/Dec. 1873.
82. *Mof.*, 12 April 1864.
83. Ibid., 19 Jan. 1864.
84. Ibid., 19 Aug. 1864.
85. *D.G.*, 23 July 1859.
86. *Mof.*, 28 July 1868.
87. *R.N.P.*, 1867, p. 315.
88. *Mof.*, 27 Jan. 1865.
89. Ibid., 3 Aug. 1866.
90. A. Briggs, *History of Birmingham* (London, 1952), Vol. II, Ch. IV.

The traveller's first view of Delhi—the Palace seen from the Jamuna

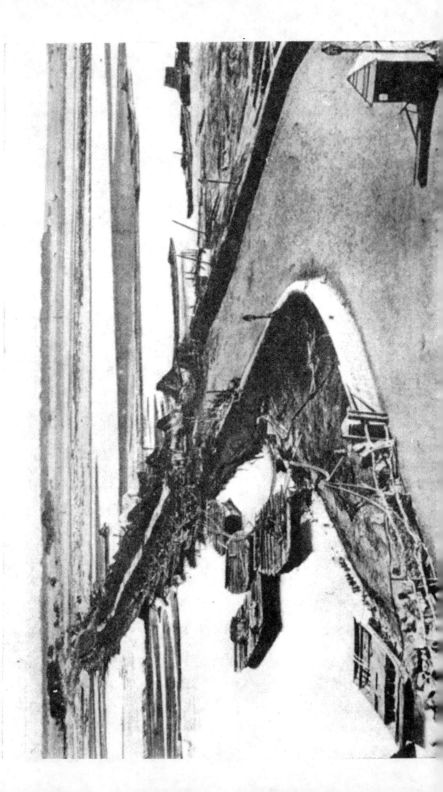

Contenders for Empire—Englishmen on horseback and Indian in palanquin in front of the Palace

Two supporting pillars of British hegemony: The Delhi Bank in Chandni
Chowk (*above*); St James's Church near Kashmeri Gate (*below*)

The poet laureate of the city—Ghalib

The growing racial distance: Delhi Club before 1857, south of the Palace (*above*);
Delhi Club after 1898, in Ludlow Castle (*below*)

Life in the City: Ornate facade of a house on Chandni Chowk (*above*);
the tranquillity of the inner courtyard (*below*)·

Beyond the City wall: Kashmeri Gate, sacred to the British (*above*);
Ram Lila, beyond Ajmeri Gate (*below*)

The Loyalists; Lala Chunna Mal (*a*); Lala Sheo Pershad (*b*):
Members of Delhi Municipality, 1873 (*c*)

'Improvements':
Town Hall and Clock
Tower (*above*)
St Stephen's Hospital (*below*)

Those spacious days: Chandni Chowk (*above*); Jama Masjid seen from the north (*below*)

Conformity and non-conformity: Jama Masjid (*above*); Fatehpuri Masjid (*below*)

The old college and the new: Delhi College (*above*); St Stephen's College (*below*)

a

The Hakims of Ballimaran:
Hakim Mahmud Khan (a)
Hakim Abdul Majid Khan (b)
Hakim Ajmal Khan (c)

The cardboard cities: The Durbar of 1877 (*above*); The Durbar of 1903 (*below*)

Two cavalcades: Before the Fort—the Princes' pageant during the Durbar of 1911 (*above*)
Behind the Fort—the People's pageant, celebrating the inauguration of New Delhi, 1931 (*bel*

4

PUBLIC OPINION: EDUCATION AND ELECTIONS
(1877-85)

'Nothing will remove prejudices from the native mind more than familiar intercourse with Europeans in debating societies and literary institutions,' the *Mofussilite* had written pompously in 1864. The educated Indian in Delhi would probably have interposed the words 'native' and 'European', recalling how 'Indianized' many of the Europeans at Delhi had become before 1857. In 1865 the Commissioner, Hamilton, inaugurated the Delhi Society. 'Delhi is not backward in schemes of social improvement,' he said, 'as seen by the success of the working of the municipal committee for the reduction of marriage expenses. The proposed Society will deal with matters not falling within the scope of these two... history and antiquity... trade, arts and manufactures.'[1] In the printed proceedings of the Society, the stated objectives were 'the advancement of knowledge and general welfare'—'*ba-is e tarakki uluum e rifae aam*'. In a later volume, the learned members were described as being concerned with 'the knowledge of sciences and the art of writing'—'*Society ke bazm e mualla ka zikr hai/Yani uluum e hikmaat o insha ka zikr hai.*'[2]

The first members of the Society were seventeen Englishmen and seventy-six Indians. Some of these, like Ghalib and Syed Ahmad Khan, were only nominal members. Ilahi Bux, the Mughal Prince, was Co-President along with Hamilton, and Lala Sahib Singh was Vice-President. The active members included Municipal Commissioners Chunna Mal, Mahesh Das, Nawab Shahabuddin Khan; Deputy Sheikh Wilayat Husain, Sheikh Mahbub Bux, and the Reverend Smith. The other *rais* who were members were Nawab Ziauddin, Maulvi Ziauddin, Pandit Basheshar Nath, Maulvi

7

Jafar Ali, Pandit Gopal Sahai, Lala Wazir Singh, Nawab Najaf
Khan and Hakim Mahmud Khan. That the loyalist element was
more vocal than the Delhiwala is shown by the fact that the
Society took exception to the Delhi College conducting its classes
in the Institute where the Society and the Municipality held
their meetings.

The Society's proceedings were conducted and printed in Urdu,
to this extent continuing the spirit of the modern Urdu renaissance of the 1840s in Delhi College, of which many of its members
were alumni. Thanks to the enthusiasm of its President, Hamilton,
and its Secretary, Pyare Lal 'Ashoob', it met frequently in the
1860s. This is evidenced by its publications (printed at the Akmal-
ul-Mataba), which ranged in size from fifty to one hundred and
fifty pages; from 1867 its proceedings were printed at the press
owned by Bihari Lal 'Mushtaq', a pupil of Ghalib. These were
referred to by the French scholar Garcin de Tassy (who translated
part of *Aasar-us-Sanaadid* into French) in his annual lectures
on the state of Urdu literature. Pyare Lal's persuasion brought
Ghalib as a guest to the second meeting of the Society, where he
read a letter describing the tragedy of 1857 and its aftermath,
with a reference to his latest *qasida* to the Queen.

The intellectuals soon lost the battle to the shopkeepers. Rai
Bansi Lal read a paper on different scripts, Nawab Shahabuddin
of Loharu spoke on ethics, his brother Nawab Alauddin on the
Urdu language, Rai Jiwan Lal on history, Lala Chandu Lal (a
Christian) on Devanagari. Bhairon Prasad read an article which
earned praise from Hali. The members agreed that learning was
more important than wealth, but listened to Rai Sahib Singh's
lecture on the *mahajani* system, that of Bishamber Nath on the
details of property transfers, of Sheikh Mahbub Bux on the
advancement of trade.[3] In July 1868, 'The Punjab Tenancy Rights
Bill was discussed by a heterogeneous lot of *banias* at Delhi Institute,' noticed the *Mofussilite*. 'The absence of the proprietary
element was conspicuous.'[4] The same year, however, the Society
had taken an interest in establishing a Sanskrit school, and had
suggested that the Punjab University be located in Delhi. Lala
Pyare Lal spoke on contacts between Indians and Europeans,
suggesting that Englishmen should settle in India, and abandon
racial prejudice.[5] The members agreed that if Indians were educated like Englishmen, there would be no distinction between

them, but Rai Mahesh Das in 1871 was not prepared to extend this logic further. He did not approve of education for *chamars* and other lower classes because 'the mean may pollute knowledge'. People as different as Lala Rammi Mal (who on the question of the Saraogi procession had been in the opposite camp from Mahesh Das) and Rai Hukm Chand (one of the most promising young students of Delhi College, who had that year completed his M.A.) agreed with him.[6]

The members of the Society were 'respectable' in the eyes of British officials. They aspired to maintain contact with them but not to assimilating a Western philosophy or political ideas. No wonder Bholanath Chunder, who in 1869 visited the Institute and admired its architecture, ignored the very existence of the Society. 'In an intellectual point of view, Delhi is yet far behind Calcutta,' he said disparagingly. 'It has scarcely made the progress to form an enlightened public opinion, to call public meetings, . . . to speak out its ideas through the press, to discuss questions of social reform, . . . to project political associations.'[7] A Meerut newspaper of 1871 criticized the Society for suffering from the same shortcomings as other similar societies, in having rich officials as members.[8] The Society had not 'done much good', said Canon Crowfoot in 1868. 'Most of the members are respectable old gentlemen who come to pay their "salaam" to the Commissioner.'[9] The Guidebook of 1874 did not mention the Society when describing the Town Hall.

The Society's first secretary, Pyare Lal, left for Lahore in 1868, and even the blimpish *Civil and Military Gazette* said no one would be able to equal his efficiency. To Canon Crowfoot the change was welcome because the new secretary was a Christian, Lala Chandu Lal, a teacher in the Mission School. Hitherto religion had been banned as a subject of discussion (this was in consonance with Hamilton's ban in 1868 on public debates between the local people and the missionaries). The missionaries hoped that Chandu Lal's election would make it possible to discuss religious subjects. Whether because of their pressure or otherwise, the Society by 1871 had bifurcated into the older Urdu-speaking section and a new English-speaking one. The latter included younger men like Pyare Lal's nephew, Sri Ram, the brilliant Urdu scholar and author of *Khumkhan-e-Javed*. He was interested in discussing religious and reformist subjects, perhaps because of his having studied in St Stephen's School. The Muslim members remained few, and participated only rarely.[10] From the mid-1870s the Society was to cease to be a sedate group of men uttering generalities and banalities, and become a forum for expressing the opinion of the intelligentsia on public matters.

The Delhi Society did not become a channel to transmit the spirit of the Vernacular Translation Society of the 1840s. One reason was that, with the ending of the Court and the introduction of English, the prospects for Urdu were discouraging. But the decline was not a death, and in the 1860s the enthusiasm of connoisseurs like William Muir and Hamilton (compared by Maulvi Ziauddin to Milton! and described by an Urdu newspaper as *nekzaat*)[11] saw to it that the Urdu writers in Delhi did not go unsung. Many of them received both official appreciation and monetary rewards—Ghalib, Maulana Husain Azad, Hali, Sarfaraz Khan (for *Ajaib-o-Gharaib*), Nawab Nabi Bux and Nazir Ahmad (for *Mirat-ul-Urus*). But with the Palace turned into a fort, and the College a police lines, the *musha'aras* of Delhi were now limited to the homes of Muslim, *kayasth* and *khatri* enthusiasts.[12] After 1857 there was no place left in Delhi where *ghazals* could be recited, complained Nasir Nazir Firaq, the author of *Dilli Ki Askhri Deedar*. The Delhi College Library had been destroyed in 1857, and the rich collections of manuscripts which had belonged to Ghalib, Jiwan Lal, Munshi Ziauddin and others were auctioned, instead of being collected and preserved at Delhi in the custody of a qualified *munshi* or *maulvi*. But Ghalib's esoteric and pungent debate in 1869 with Maulvi Aminuddin of Patiala on the *Burhan-e-Qata* excited interest not only among the *ulema* and the *rais*, but even among Anglo-Indian papers like the *Mofussilite*. The charge of defamation against Aminuddin reached the civil courts, where many prominent citizens were called upon to testify. It was ultimately settled out of court by the Delhi *rais*.[13]

In the 1860s, English newspapers in Delhi and Lahore were forthright, even pugnacious, in criticizing the Municipality and its individual members, usually by measuring their activities against European standards. This kind of criticism was not to recur in subsequent decades. The local Urdu newspapers became bold enough only by the 1870s. Their disapproval was to some extent caused by nostalgia for the age that was past, to some extent by the feeling that this new-fangled system of local government should show some dividends. In particular the revived *Urdu*

Akbar, now edited by Syed Hasan, made frequent and detailed suggestions for correcting many 'abuses and irregularities'. These included drainage, disposal of filth, checking adulteration and controlling noxious trades. In 1874 it echoed Cracroft's suggestions that plots of land be given to the local *rais*, and the land just beyond the wall be developed as gardens, as had been done a few years previously at Lahore.[14] The *Mayo Memorial Gazette* published by the Delhi Society after 1872 was also sharp in criticizing the inadequate measures for cleanliness and conservancy taken by the Municipality. All these meant either that Delhi had been a cleaner city during the Kotwal's regime, or that people's expectations were now higher, and they wanted a more positive policy from the loyalists and the British officials.

When inaugurating the Delhi Society, Hamilton had referred to another 'society' aimed at reform. This was an organization set up 'spontaneously' (though the Delhi Society falsely tried to claim credit for it in 1882) by some Hindus (Lala Jiwan Lal was a leading light) to effect savings in marriage expenses. The official report stated that 'forty-seven castes and tribes solemnly agreed, through their representatives, to certain reduced rates of expenditure'.[15] The *Mofussilite* was all praise. 'Marriage *panchayats* have done much good and despite grumbling by some older people ... a new day is dawning on this dark city.' It called itself the Association for the Suppression of Unnecessary Expenditure in Marriage, and had branches in Oudh and Agra. It circulated essays and speeches, with encouragement from the government. An attempt to set up a branch of the Arya Samaj at Delhi, a few years later, did not get much support locally.

The earliest Muslim 'reform' association was the Anjuman-i-Imani, founded in 1871 with the purpose of reforming Shia customs, and propagating widow-remarriage. This was founded by a teacher of the Delhi Normal School, Maulana Ulfat Husain, and had a dozen members.[16] In 1875 was founded a more enduring Muslim association—the Anjuman Islamia, with Hali, Hakim Abdul Majid and Hakim Zakiruddin among its members. The same year, 'to celebrate the arrival of Lord Northbrook' some Muslims founded the Anjuman-e-Rifaiat-e-Hind (Legal Reform Association for the Benefit of Indians), which echoed many of the statements of the Delhi Society; it undertook to hold lectures for the moral benefit of the people, and professed to eschew religious discussion; Shias and Sunnis were to be admitted equally as members. How this was to be possible is not clear, for the association was subdivided into two sections, one to discuss 'national' problems and the other Muslim theology. Among its leaders were Maulana Haji Ahrari (a *vakil*) and Haji Kutbuddin.[17] They were both Waha'bis but they seem to have fallen out and started bickering. This came into the open sharply in 1877, at the time of the Durbar, when it was known that Fatehpuri Masjid was to be restored to the Muslims. The Secretary of the Anjuman Islamia, Ahrari wrote anxiously to the officials that only Rashideen Muslims should be allowed to have charge of the Masjid. The Waha'bis were 'like the Saraogis among the Hindus—bigoted and anti-Muslim'. They were 'few, and of the lower classes'; and Kutbuddin, the Waha'bi, should be removed from the post of Chairman and replaced by Syed Khaji Nasir Wazir, the son-in-law of Nawab Ziauddin. The Deputy Commissioner suggested six names for the Fatehpuri Committee, all of them tried loyalists. The Commissioner added to these the name of Kutbuddin, as a 'wealthy gentleman'. He also added the name of Ilahi Bux, son of Suleiman Shah.[18]

The efflorescence in education was destroyed in 1857. When the city was returned to the civilian authorities in 1859, the old Delhi 'College' was noticed as 'a superior school'. After two years, it was supplemented by a *zillah* School, with Master Ram Chandra as Headmaster. In another two years there was a rapid mushrooming of girls' schools all over the city, after the Commissioner and Deputy Commissioner persuaded some of the *rais* (none of these was from among the loyalists in the Municipality) to sponsor these and to guarantee subscriptions and a minimum attendance. This gambit had been used in other Punjab towns too, but was most successful in Delhi. Lala Wazir Singh came in for special praise for his efforts; the others included Sahib Singh Chowdhury, Chowdhury Mathra Das, Shiv Prasad Sarkar, Nawab Hyder Hasan Khan, Maulvi Ziauddin, Maulvi Latif Husain, Raja Debi Singh, Rai Saligram and Rai Hukm Chand. The Commissioner said that Muslims were more responsive than Hindus, but there were more Hindu 'patrons' than Muslims.[19] These schools were supplemented by those run by the S.P.G. (distinct from their *zenana* teaching). Such a plethora of 'neighbourhood schools' suggests that the task was to create a demand rather than to meet one. In 1865 the Director of Public Instruction in the Punjab suggested that the duties and powers of the patrons of these schools should be defined, for the shared jurisdiction was unsatisfactory. If the Punjab Government were to provide matching grants, it should have greater control. The patrons were all equally emphatic in not wanting this. This dichotomy was to persist for decades.

In 1867 Holroyd, the Inspector of Education, expressed the wish that Arabic and Sanskrit should develop in Delhi along with English. The next year the Delhi Society discussed the question of establishing a Sanskrit School, and Lala Chunna Mal offered to finance it. An Arabic School was opened at the residence of Nawab Mohammad Aminulla of Loharu.[20] A less-publicized and smaller philanthropic effort of some significance was Mirza Ilahi Bux's opening of a school for the Mughal survivors at Arab Serai, near Nizamuddin. The educated women of the royal family also found employment as teachers in the new girls' schools. For the poorest classes the thirteen schools run by the energetic Smith of the Baptist Mission offered an opening. St Stephen's School, run by the S.P.G., had the largest number of students among schools in the Ambala Circle in 1866, and in the 1870s it had four branch schools in the town. Till 1874 the Municipality spent Rs 2,000 a year on grants to schools. From that year this sum was doubled, following the provision in the Municipal Act of 1873 that primary education should be the responsibility of the local governments and not of the provincial departments.

There was one exception to the general attitude of suspicion of government agencies on the part of private philanthropists. This was Hamid Ali Khan, the son-in-law of Nawab Itmaduddaula. He wanted the institution funded by his bequest to be directly under government control. The reason for his request was that he wanted the money to be used solely or largely for Shias, who were a minority community in Delhi.[21] He tried to make out that this had been the Nawab's own intention, a case weakened by the absence of any written evidence, and by the opposition from a large number of people in Delhi, Hindu and Muslim, Shia and Sunni—Mirza Ilahi Bux, Nawab Ziauddin and his son Shahabuddin, Vilayat Husain Khan, Raja Debi Singh, Mahesh Das and Jiwan Lal. Hamid Ali Khan, finding himself in a minority, appealed for sympathy to the Supreme Government (just as the Saraogis had done). Mayo responded favourably, and in 1872 an Anglo-Arabic School was set up, and part of the Itmaduddaula Fund was transferred to it from the Delhi College. Holroyd began the process of blurring the issues by saying that this school was being founded as 'a special gesture to the Muslims of Delhi', who had been the chief sufferers in 1857–8. After the passage of the Municipal Act of 1873, he wanted it to be made a government school, and was supported by Hamid Ali Khan, by Cracroft and by Nawab Ziauddin (the last-named had shifted his stand). Holroyd gave up when he saw the strong opposition of many local Muslims, including the parents of the students. But Hamid Ali Khan did not give up, and he was to find another ally in Leitner, the eccentric principal of Lahore College.

Delhi College remained a high school till 1864. It was considerably depleted in numbers, its library had been destroyed, and the Ghaziuddin Madarsa was occupied by the police. Commissioner Hamilton had been unhappy about this but neither he nor any of the officials or the loyalists was prepared to donate part of the new Town Hall to house the classes. These were held in a house in Gali Kasim Jan. Among the loyalists there were no alumni of the old Delhi School who might have protested against the *Mofussilite's* remarks about this 'miserable native school', which did not deserve a place within the fine Institute building. The increasing attendance and good results in the higher classes helped it to recover its former importance. College classes were started in 1864 (the same year that a college was opened at Lahore). When sanctioning the collegiate section the Viceroy, Lawrence, had said that the College 'had risen to a high order of excellence; not a few of our very best native officials were brought up there. Delhi's aristocracy and gentry will still supply a class of youths peculiarly well adapted for a high degree of mental training.'[22] Some of the *rais* instituted scholarships, which were particularly useful to many of the 'new poor' among the Muslims who could not afford the fees.[23]

A degree from Delhi College was sufficient qualification for government jobs in Lahore and elsewhere. Because Delhi was relegated to the status of a provincial town, most of the promising littérateurs in Delhi, who were also anxious to secure well-paid posts—Hali, Azad, Nazir Ahmad, Shiv Narain 'Aram', 'Bismil', Ram Chandra and 'Ashoob'—left Delhi. But the proliferation of

Urdu newspapers in Delhi, owned by Hindus as well as by Muslims, indicated that Urdu was still very much the popular language. Garcin de Tassy, in his annual lectures on the state of Urdu literature, frequently referred to Urdu newspapers being published from Delhi, including one edited by Sadasukh Lal.[24]

At the same time as Delhi College was re-establishing itself as a successful institution, Leitner of Lahore College kept up a running stream of disparagement of the College (even calling it 'plebeian' in contrast to 'patrician' Lahore!). This was more than off-set by the frequent praises it received from the Inspector of Education and from Lieutenant-Governors. In numbers and in results it compared very favourably with Lahore College. When the Punjab University College (overlapping with Lahore College) was opened in 1868, Leitner suggested that as a measure of economy the staff of Delhi College be transferred to Lahore. This proposal was hastily abandoned when it was seen how strongly the people of Delhi opposed it. McLeod, the Lieutenant-Governor, assured the Delhi Society that the College would not be truncated. The *Urdu Akbar* in 1872 wanted the proposed Anglo-Oriental College to be located in Delhi, and the Delhi Society suggested that a University be set up in Delhi to serve both the North-Western Provinces and Punjab. Neither of these suggestions was accepted. In 1874 the proposal to merge Delhi College's classes with those of Lahore College was brought up again. Egerton, the Lieutenant-Governor, vetoed it on the grounds that this would only strengthen the case for re-transferring Delhi city to the North-Western Provinces, for the Delhi students were more likely to go to Agra than to Lahore for their college education.

At this point Leitner found Hamid Ali Khan a convenient ally in his main aim of discrediting Delhi College and forcing its closure. He echoed the Nawab's argument that the Itmaduddaula Fund had been intended only for Shia boys, and not for Delhi College as a whole. The Fund could be administered by Punjab University and devoted entirely to Shia students; Delhi College, deprived of its main income, would therefore have to close, and its classes could be transferred to Lahore. At this point the question of Delhi College started to arouse interest not only in Delhi and Lahore, but elsewhere in India. The *Akbar-o-Anjuman Punjab* of Lahore, the *Delhi Gazette* of Agra and the *Times of India* of Bombay stated that any amalgamation would be a blow to the cause of higher education. The Delhi Society was highly agitated, but not the loyalists nor the Municipality. The matter was finally referred to a committee of Punjab College headed by Leitner. But even he could not convince the others and the committee was emphatically of the opinion that Delhi College should be retained.[25] This was in June 1876, and by the end of that year Delhi College was well set on the forward road, having reached a point where its all-India prestige made it a source of pride to the city's inhabitants. The *Oudh Akbar's* comment in an article entitled 'What is Civilization?' is worth quoting. 'Ask the Bengalis, and they will reply that the English are civilized; the Muslims at Lucknow . . . will say "Go to some Maulvi". In Delhi, they pointed to the School.'[26]

In February 1877, at the Delhi Durbar, the Lieutenant-Governor announced that Delhi College classes would be amalgamated with those at Lahore. This was an unexpected blow. The reason given now was that Delhi was developing as a commercial city and had 'long ceased to be a centre of literary activity'; there was a vague promise that if Lahore's resources proved inadequate, the College might be revived. The Durbar was criticized all over India as being in bad taste because it was held at a time of severe famine. To the people of Delhi the decision about their College appeared to be another example of bad timing. It cancelled out the good-will generated by the government's conciliatory gesture of restoring Fatehpuri Masjid to the Muslims.[27]

A possible explanation for this *volte-face* appears to have been missionary pressure. Sir Bartle Frere, who visited India in 1875, wrote home about the S.P.G.'s Delhi mission, that 'You [sc. will] have a larger Tinnevelly at Delhi in the course of a few years, but they want more money and more men'. In response to this a committee was organized at Cambridge to raise money to help the S.P.G. The 'special character of the work' was defined in their resolution as being 'in addition to evangelistic labours to afford the means for the higher education of young native Christians'. It added, 'There is no Christian school in all India for the sons of native gentlemen.'[28] It might have been the knowledge that such a college was being projected that made the Lieutenant-Governor and the Viceroy ignore the appeals of the citizens of Delhi to reconsider the decision. Meanwhile the Bishop of Lahore, French, campaigned in England for a college at Delhi which would combat the dangers of a secular education, as well as the possible threat of Jesuit or Arya Samaj indoctrination.[29]

In the paper-war that ensued, a memorial from 'the inhabitants of Delhi' put forward arguments to counter those of the government. They explained that the edge that the Lahore College had recently got in terms of numbers was due to the fact that it drew students from all over the Punjab, whereas Delhi College got students only from the city and its neighbourhood. The city of Lahore contributed nothing to its College, whereas Delhi College was financed largely by private subscriptions and by a grant from the Municipality. Their strongest argument was 'not on grounds of statistics, but on the claims of our city, and the history of our college'. They said what many others, officials and private individuals, were to say, that 'we feel the College to be one of our own institutions, . . . and not, like most other institutions in the country, the gift of the British government'.[30] A large meeting was convened at the Institute, presided over by Nawab Ziauddin. No officials appear to have been present. The vocal members included one Municipal Commissioner, Rai Sahib Singh, Rai Jiwan Lal, Lala Madan Gopal (younger brother of Pyare Lal 'Ashoob'), Babu Sri Ram, a pleader, Professor Ramchandra and Lala Mulraj, who was the secretary and was noted as having been a brilliant scholar, who held an M.A. degree. All of them were alumni of the College. A letter to the editor of the *Civil and Military Gazette* from 'A Member of the University Senate' (who was obviously Leitner) defended the abolition, and made out that this memorial had been issued by the Delhi Society, which was not a representative body. To this, Madan Gopal replied that the memorial had been issued by the participants at a massive meeting, not by the Society. With a dig at Leitner, he said that the Delhi Society was 'more independent than the Anjuman-i-Punjab, (founded by Leitner). Their memorial was supported by another from a hundred citizens of Lahore, led by Pandit Manphool (another former student), who added the argument that to abolish the College would 'remove the counteracting influences over the conservative and bigoted element in Delhi'.[31] Nawab Hamid Ali Khan's assertion that the Itmaduddaula endowment had been intended for the education of Shia boys alone was denied by the Anjuman Islamia of Delhi.[32] The local *Khair-Khwah-e-Alam*, owned by Syed Mir Hasan, lashed out in protest.

Delhi is a large city and even in its present decayed state it is inhabited not only by merchants and traders but by descendants of ancient families who have been very devoted to learning...No appreciable saving will accrue from the abolition of this college. If the retention of the college is impossible, a school of industry and art should be established at Delhi as at Lahore. But the government will not do this because it has the interests of the mercantile communities of Manchester and Glasgow at heart.[33]

Newspapers at Meerut, Kanpur, Amritsar and Lahore echoed the protest. The irony of a decision to establish a college for European girls at Simla, financed by donations from Indian princes, immediately after the decision to deprive Delhi of its college, was not lost on the *Khair-Khwah-e-Alam*.[34] The Lieutenant-Governor was impervious to all this criticism and dismissed the Delhi petition with the specious remark that 'there is no strong feeling in Delhi on the subject of the abolition of the college classes, except among a very small section of the community'.[35] The memorialists thereupon petitioned the Governor-General, but Lytton backed the Lieutenant-Governor. The argument now was that the decision had been taken because more funds were needed for primary as against higher education and because the Lahore College would be strengthened by adding on to it the staff of Delhi.

The citizens of Delhi gave up petitioning the Provincial and Supreme Governments, and planned instead to try and revive the College by their own efforts. A meeting was convened in December 1877, this time presided over by the Mughal prince Surayyah Jah, and attended by an assembly of two thousand people, including Syed Ahmad Khan and Maulvi Syed Fariduddin Ahmad Khan, a judge at Aligarh. It was estimated that five lakh rupees would be needed to re-establish the College. Syed Fariduddin lashed out at the policy of economizing on education and spending so lavishly on the police force. Syed Ahmad, speaking in more moderate tones, urged the people of Delhi to take the initiative, since providing education was not the duty of the government. Contributions adding up to Rs 18,000 were promised. A long-term drive to raise funds was planned by the College Memorial Committee, supported by the Director of Public Instruction, Holroyd, and by the Delhi College professors, Dick and Syme.[36]

The movement did not fizzle out. Nor did it dwindle into an issue of merely local importance. Surendranath Banerjea publicly denounced the government, which 'could not spend Rs 12,000 a year for the maintenance of an ancient and time-honoured seat of learning [when] the Delhi Assemblage cost 60 lacs'. He added, 'I am glad to be able to say that the people of Delhi will not allow themselves to fall asleep over the abolition. A fund is being raised and Rs 25,000 has already been subscribed ... Delhi will have a college of its own, this time depending no longer on the generosity of the Government but the ... outcome of native effort.'[37] When Lefroy came out to India in 1880 as part of the new Cambridge Mission, he said that 'The Delhi College ... is being reopened by a sort of joint movement of the chief natives, chief Englishmen, privately, and Government.' He added that the local people would welcome the Cambridge missionaries as lecturers in the college they proposed to set up, though from the Mission's point of view a separate college of their own was desirable.[38] Therefore for three years after the abolition, there was a possibility of the college being revived. The Municipality's report of 1879–80 spoke of increasing the sum spent on education 'when a college is re-established in Delhi'. In 1880 the D.P.I. pointed out to the Punjab Government that a college could be re-established 'without any expense to Government'. Rs 60,000 had been collected in the city, and the Municipality had promised help. His statements should have carried weight, for it was he who had initially suggested the amalgamation. He reminded the Lieutenant-Governor that he had promised to reconsider the question if there was a sufficiently strong demand. He assured him that it would be wrong 'to think that the government would stultify itself by reconsidering the question'. Very few students had gone from Delhi to Lahore, as had been hoped; the distance and the expense, and prejudice, militated against this. The Ambala Circle was suffering from a want of teachers, hitherto provided by Delhi graduates, because Punjab University students were unwilling to serve in south Punjab. Holroyd refuted Leitner's malicious statements about the Delhi students at Lahore being anti-social and creating tension.[39]

Two Secretaries of State, Salisbury and Cranbrook, sought at different times to reopen the issue, but they gave in before the opposition of the Lieutenant-Governor.[40] A meeting in January 1881, which was attended (unlike those of 1877) by the local officials, municipal members and even the missionaries, confidently asked for a grant from the provincial government 'under the usual conditions', proudly pointing out that contributions had been promised not only by the Delhi Municipality but by the District, and by many of the adjoining districts.[41] 'During my long residence in Delhi,' wrote Smith, 'I remember no subject on which the public mind had been so much excited, nor is there a boon the Local Government has in its power to grant which would be received with more joy and gratitude.'[42] The Lieutenant-Governor refused flatly. He said that he would 'not apply Local Funds for higher education till primary was well provided for', but in the same letter he went on to make enquiries about the Cambridge Mission which was at Delhi. 'The Lieutenant-Governor recognizes that the presence of highly-educated gentlemen such as those who form the Cambridge Mission would conduce greatly to the cause of high education, if they are disposed to provide higher education in accordance with the rules for Government-aided institutions.' The decision was communicated to the members of the College Committee, who agreed reluctantly to accept a mission college as a lesser evil than the prospect of having no college at all. The subscriptions were returned to the donors. The Cambridge Mission opened its F.A. class in March 1881, with a generous grant-in-aid from the Punjab Government, exactly what the Delhi College Committee had asked for.[43]

In 1882, even after St Stephen's College started functioning, the local *rais* had not abandoned all hope of resuscitating Delhi College. But the missionaries proved right in their calculation that it would be difficult to maintain the necessary 'prolonged effort and self-denial'.[44] Most of the Muslims kept away from the new St Stephen's College, but the Hindus came to accept it. The five-year crisis left its mark on Delhi. It cut short the building up of cosmopolitan harmony which had begun so well in the 1840s. It created a sense of bitterness and frustration. 'The almost universal belief is that the opportunity was designedly set aside in favour of a mission establishment,' said Smith.[45] In 1871 and 1882 the government had emphasized the virtue of self-help in finances, but this major effort towards realizing it had been scotched.

The abolition of Delhi College in 1877 and the introduction of 'local self-government' in 1884 was a combination of events which convinced the missionaries that 'the wisest course will be for mission schools to concentrate on improving higher and secondary

education'.[46] The options for Delhi students were to go into the
family business after completing school, to join St Stephen's
College, to go to Lahore or Aligarh, or to go abroad. The number
of students going to Lahore fell off rapidly from thirty-three
students in 1877 to six in 1880. Some students joined the Law
classes at the Lahore Oriental College. Leitner was not cordial to
the Delhi boys. He complained that their 'greater vivacity and
exuberance of speech' made them dangerous companions for the
more 'phlegmatic' Punjabis, and that many of them were 'in-
subordinate'.[47] In 1884 he suggested that a college of law be started
at Delhi so that students would not have to go to Lahore for this.
A similar suggestion was later made by Lefroy but nothing came
of it. The decrease in the number of students going to Lahore
indirectly brightened the chances of survival for St Stephen's
College. The number of undergraduates rose from one in 1882
to eighty in 1892. A conflict between Winter and Lefroy seemed
to threaten the continuance of the College in the late 1880s, but
Lefroy, younger and more ruthless and more 'British' (Winter
always held that Indians were as good as Europeans), won the
battle; henceforward the Cambridge Mission remained in exclu-
sive control of the school and college.[48] The College Committee
in 1894 included former students—Lala Ajodhya Prasad, Lala
Shiv Narain, Lala Bala Prasad, and Lala Amir Chand (the last
became *persona non grata* with the College authorities ten years
later because of his associations with the nationalist movement).
As the numbers increased, the College hoped to get the premises
of the Civil Hospital near the Jama Masjid, but instead of this, a
site near Kashmeri Gate was given to it by the Municipality, as a
gift. Rs 22,000 was subscribed for the new building by individuals; an additional Rs 10,000 was given from the Provincial
Government. The students were enthusiastic fund-raisers.[49] Ten
years earlier, funds had been equally generously subscribed for
Delhi College.

Lefroy had been apprehensive that the citizens of Delhi would
nurse their resentment and stay away from St Stephen's College.
But within a few years it became clear that at least the Hindu
students would rather attend a missionary college in Delhi than
go to Lahore, Agra or Aligarh. In terms of numbers, therefore,
the College fulfilled the missionaries' hopes. What they could not
foresee was that some of the students of their College would

become ardent adherents of the Arya Samaj movement in Delhi in the 1890s, and of the extremist nationalist movement in the early 1900s.

Primary education was not a subject which could elicit anything like the excitement generated by the Delhi College crusade. The Cambridge Mission report of 1885 commented on 'the combined indifference of the mass of the population to the extension of education, and of Municipal Boards, representing the wealth and intelligence of the upper classes, to the extension of education among the lower classes'.[50] The replies submitted to the Hunter Commission on Primary Education in 1882 tended to stray from the track, because they were more interested in college education. The sub-committee formed by the Delhi Society to consider the Commission's questions included people interested in financing education, and intellectuals. The former category included Lala Ram Kishen Das (of the Chunna Mal family), who was associated with the Anglo-Sanskrit School; Syed Sultan Mirza, representative of the Itmaduddaula family and associated with the Anglo-Arabic School; and Allnutt of the Cambridge Mission. The intellectuals included Maulvi Zakaullah, Munshi (Reverend) Tarachand, Lala Sri Ram, Lala Girdhari Lal, and Lala Madan Gopal.[51] All the Indian members were alumni of the Delhi College, which explains why their recommendations digressed. They wrote more about the Delhi College than about primary education. They, and the missionaries, were henceforward to be more interested in secondary and higher education, since this would not, like primary education, be controlled by the Municipality.

The Delhi Society Committee used the issue of primary education as a stalking-horse for another issue, which was then under discussion—local self-government. Unless more members of the intelligentsia formed part of the Municipality, they said, it would be dangerous to give it charge of education. 'Merchants and bankers in India are not as intelligent as in Europe or America,' they wrote, 'and it is unwise to entrust education to them.' They deplored the fact that the 'upper classes' were not interested in educating the lower, but they had no constructive suggestions for remedying this. Maulvi Ikramullah and Rai Sahib Singh also spoke of the 'old' and 'new' classes.[52] There was an impression that a new group existed which was distinct from the loyalists

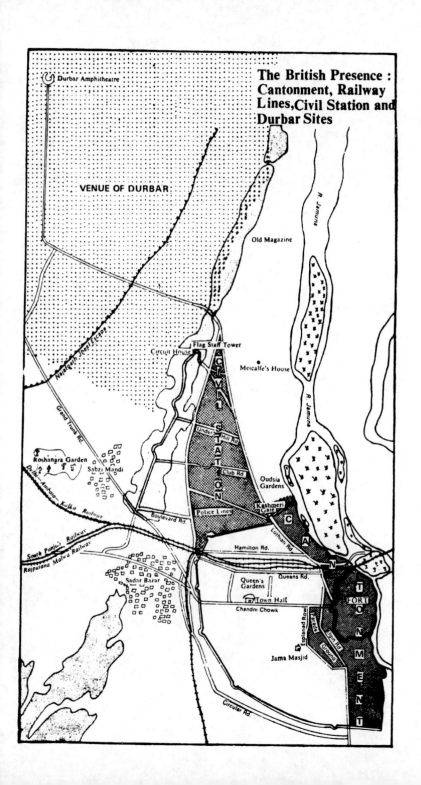

The British Presence :
Cantonment, Railway
Lines, Civil Station and
Durbar Sites

socially and in terms of objectives. This was perhaps a self-conscious imitation of phrases being used in Calcutta or Bombay. The missionaries made out all upper class Indians to be averse to extending education, but some of the Indians consulted were anxious to show that they were in favour of such expansion, and were being thwarted by others with less progressive views.

The missionaries at Delhi were a divided lot. The Baptist Mission regarded the Cambridge Mission as a rival, and in addition great bitterness developed between the Cambridge Mission and the older S.P.G., who were supposed to work as a team. The Baptist Mission could not expand its institutions, particularly in face of the unequal competition from the reinforced S.P.G. and Cambridge Mission. The latter, with their boys' schools, *zenana* teaching, medical mission and college, had a more impressive claim on government aid. St Stephen's School had 125 pupils in 1880 (of whom 112 were Hindu), which increased to 300 by 1889. In 1884, Allnutt said that 'the prestige of Government schools undoubtedly tends to draw boys of more wealthy classes to them'.[53] But by 1890, when St Stephen's School was the shortest route to higher education, they were able to report with satisfaction that they had as students 'the sons of gentlemen and shop-keepers'.[54] This had occasionally bizarre consequences, as in the case of an S.P.G. school dominated by sons of *banias* who induced the missionaries to give up the regular curriculum and teach the *mahajani* tables. 'The omnipotent word "rupee" is always to be heard in every question and answer,' reported the inspectors.[55] There was an element of schizophrenia among the missionaries—they wanted to give educational opportunities to the *chamars* and other 'lower classes' but at the same time were obviously highly gratified if their schools attracted boys from 'upper class' families.

Women's education under the S.P.G. was not subsidized by the Municipality after 1886 in the way the St Stephen's College was. Here the most important change was that the schools instituted by local philanthropists were now taken over by the missionaries, except for the school in Nizamuddin for Mughal women. There were many educated women in the city, especially among the aristocratic Muslims, but the Inspector of Education found their families reluctant to allow them to become school-teachers. The teachers were therefore chiefly Indian Christians, while the English missionary women concentrated on the *zenanas* in Muslim

8

and Hindu households. Some of their students had brothers educated in colleges in the Punjab or abroad, or trained in the legal profession.[56] In 1889 a representation was put up by the *Zenana* School Committee of Mori Gate that a vernacular language be allowed as an option to the classical stipulated as a requirement for the Punjab University Entrance examination.[57] The education of women in Delhi had progressed well beyond the desultory needle-work being taught in the 1870s.

The other aided and endowed schools were the Anglo-Sanskrit School, and four Muslim *Madarsas*. The Madarsa-t-ul-Quran, the Fatehpuri Masjid Madarsa, the Anglo-Arabic School and another Arabic school were the largest schools of their kind in the Punjab. In 1886 the Punjab Education Department ceased to give Delhi any of the special scholarships provided for Muslim boys, giving as its reason that in Delhi 'the Muslim boys hold their own'.[58] When Syed Ahmad Khan suggested that there should be a special committee to supervise Muslim educational trusts in the Punjab, the government could see no need for this, since the only trusts in the province were the Fatehpuri and the Anglo-Arabic *Madarsas*, both of which were viable.

The Managing Committee of the Anglo-Arabic School was sharply divided between its Sunni and Shia members and both, therefore, wanted to retain the official English members as a buffer. They opposed the idea of being under the Municipality, a mixed body of Europeans, Hindu and Muslims, not necessarily interested in the institution.[59] In 1890, rather than have a Muslim of either sect as headmaster, both groups asked Allnutt to be the headmaster.[60] The dispute stemmed from the question of whether the Shias should be given preferential treatment. The Sunnis, and the British officials, wanted scholarships to be given on the basis of need, not religion. In 1893, as a solution to keep both groups happy, all fees were scrapped. The argument continued intermittently into the next century. The teaching in the school did not suffer because of this feud. It had many good teachers, the most renowned being Altaf Husain Hali, one of the best-known Arabic and Urdu scholars, who lived in Delhi from 1874 to 1887. On its governing body were two other eminent writers and educationists, Maulvis Nazir Ahmad and Zakaullah. After Ghaziuddin Madarsa was given to the school it had more elbow-room than it had enjoyed earlier in Gali Rodgaran and in Sirkiwalan (in

Mohammad Ikramullah's house). In 1892 the Mohammedan Educational Conference held its annual meeting in Delhi, in Ghazi-uddin Madarsa.

When primary education was handed over to the Municipality in 1887, there were 2,000 boys attending schools in Delhi, i.e. 1.25 per cent of the total population, well below the 8,000 (i.e. 5 per cent) which was the government ideal. It was estimated that the 2,000 could be increased to 8,000 if the Municipality spent 10 per cent of its income on primary education, and subsidized the Muslim and missionary schools. Primary education suffered because it was neither provided for by the Provincial Government nor adequately subsidized by the Municipality. In 1889 the Municipality took charge of the Board School, housed in the premises of the old Residency, inside Kashmeri Gate. The income of government schools remained inelastic, since the bulk of municipal revenues was ploughed into police charges and for public health measures.

The Municipality was given charge of education as part of a more major change—the introduction of 'Local Self-Government'. This principle, first enunciated by Ripon at a meeting in Delhi in 1881, was typical of British Liberal free-trade imperialism. The Resolution of 1882 stressed the value of local self-government as a means of popular education. What was equally, if not more, important, was that this was emphasized so as to sweeten the fact that henceforward municipalities would not only have greater independence in disbursing their finances, but that they would have to fend for themselves to secure these. After 1884 the grants-in-aid from the Imperial and Provincial Governments were decreased. Ironically this was at about the same time as municipalities in England were reducing their taxes because the government was giving them more sizable grants-in-aid!

The Delhi College controversy had demonstrated that there was in the city a body of public opinion which straddled the older generation of loyalists and their sons (most of whom had received a more formal education than their fathers) and linked them to the literati, the Muslim aristocrats and the numerous alumni of the College. It had also shown that the Lieutenant-Governor could behave with unreasonable obstinacy and persist in his stand even when there was patently no justification for it, and when even the Imperial and Home Governments suggested that it be reconsidered. A section of the public opinion that had been mustered to fight for the College hoped for big things from local self-government. They were to be disappointed. Delhi was to be the last town in the Punjab where the Act became effective, and this too only in a qualified way. A visit to Delhi by the Punjab Chief Secretary was wrongly interpreted by an Anglo-Indian paper as having been undertaken 'to convince conservative merchants and the members of the Literary Society to accept the election of their own President as an advantage'.[61] In fact, it was not the Indians but the British officials who were reluctant to accept the principle of having an elected President for the Municipality. Their fear of Delhi as being still politically dangerous was echoed in some English newspapers. Elections, they said, were not advisable in Delhi because of the prevalence of communal tension.[62] This was a reference to a fracas in 1883 which was immortalized in official reports as a communal riot.

Delhi's Deputy Commissioner, Smyth, professed to be very anxious to balance the Hindu and Muslim communities just as, twenty years earlier, the local officials had been concerned to maintain a balance in the Municipality between nominated Indians and the British officials, and to keep the Muslims in a permanent minority.[63] Smyth proposed to achieve his end by two means— first, by making the Deputy Commissioner President of the Committee, with the power to dismiss members if they were unsatisfactory (this provision was incorporated into the Punjab Municipal Act of 1882 at his suggestion); secondly, by a generous franchise which would include all adult males with a monthly income of Rs 10 or who possessed property worth Rs 400. Otherwise the Municipal Committee might consist entirely of Hindus, communal riots would be a regular feature at elections, the income would fall and the Municipality would be corrupt and inefficient. He spoke vaguely and ominously of the 'criminal classes' in Delhi. These, he said, had been in evidence during Nadir Shah's invasion, the Revolt of 1857, the sweepers' strike of 1873, the grain riots at the time of the famine in 1877, and during the Jain–Vaishnav clashes at the Saraogi Mela of 1879. They would come into action again during municipal elections. Who he imagined these 'classes' to be is not clear, because at the same time he urged the enfranchisement of what he called 'the industrial classes'. Smyth elicited

the opinions of some local citizens in great detail, and then proceeded to distort them so as to make it appear as though the
majority wanted to keep the Deputy Commissioner as President
and favoured nomination rather than election, and that the Muslims wanted nomination and the Hindus election.[64]

If any generalization has to be made about the opinions elicited,
it is that preferences varied according to the individuals' occupational affiliations and economic interests, not communal loyalties.
Eight of the Muslim *rais* consulted wanted half the members of
the Municipality elected. The Muslim Principal of the Anglo-
Arabic School wanted a wholly elected committee, as did seven
of the ten Hindu educationists consulted. Lala Madan Gopal,
Secretary of the Delhi Society and earlier active in the Delhi
College movement, wanted extra votes for pleaders, jurors, graduates and Durbaris, and a wholly elected body. The Punjabi merchants who dealt in oilmen's stores, all Muslim, wanted two-thirds
of the Municipality to be elected, and the President to be an
Indian. The Marwari merchants and Hindu bankers, and the
manufacturers of jewellery, lace and embroidery, wanted half the
members to be elected.

A majority of nominated members was favoured by the European grain merchants, and a wholly nominated body by the
European manager of the Bank of Bengal, the Hindu wholesale
merchants, three Muslim *rais* and one Hindu, Rai Jiwan Lal, a
loyal *kayasth*. An iron merchant, Pyare Lal, wanted *mohulla*
representation and a vote for industrial workers. Some Hindu
bankers wanted a plurality of votes for some categories and a
high property-qualification as a floor. In short, the principle of
election was welcomed by Muslim and Hindu intellectuals and
professionals and some merchants, and nomination was favoured
by Europeans, by some loyalists and those mercantile groups who
were dependent on British trade.

When Smyth's views were published, local opinion was quick
to protest. The term 'classes' used by Smyth was now used by his
critics. Rai Hukm Chand protested against his populist approach
saying that, if it was implemented, it would make it difficult for
the 'aristocracy, the wealthy, trading and educated classes to
make the best possible contribution to local government. No really
respectable gentleman of at least the old class [sc. would] stand
for election.' Smyth's statement, in a different context, that the

municipal members dreaded the 'lower classes' appears to corro-
borate the impression created by Hukm Chand. The latter also
argued that to make the Deputy Commissioner President would
be fatal to the 'true liberty' of the Municipality, and an insult to
Delhi. Regarding the minimum qualifications necessary for a
voter, he thought it should be essential that he should be literate
in Urdu. His statement reached the level of the Punjab Government but was not taken into account.

The Delhi Society was also vehement in its opposition to
Smyth's proposals. It had by now a large number of younger
members and appeared different from the Society of the 'loyalist'-
dominated period. 'A Literary Society has recently been started
or, more correctly, resuscitated,' said Lefroy.[65] Its members did
not share Hukm Chand's veneration for the 'upper class'. In 1882
the Society had criticized the 'upper class' for its apathy towards
the lower and, in a tone reminiscent of the *Mofussilite* of 1866,
had criticized the nominated members of the Municipality as
being only slightly educated, and made a plea for admitting more
intelligent men as members.[66] Its protest against Smyth was set
out in a memorandum ably drafted by its secretary, Madan Gopal
(who had to his credit the fact that he had translated the Punjab
Municipal Act into Urdu). It expressed the Society's sharp sense
of disappointment, since its members had hoped that Delhi would
be the first town in the Punjab on which the gift of self-government would be conferred. It protested strongly against the insinua-
tion that there was communal tension in Delhi; it quoted the
Commissioner himself as having said that the riots had been the
work of the 'lower classes'. Logically, therefore, they said, the
franchise should be withheld from these 'classes', but local self-
government as such should not be denied to the rest. For president
they wanted an impartial outside official, not the Deputy Commissioner. Different trades and manufactures should enjoy special
representation. Their statement was couched in words identical
with those of Hukm Chand, suggesting that they had written in
concert.

These views were not publicized in the way that the protests
against the abolition of the College had been. (On the other hand,
the real or imagined fears of Smyth received publicity.) The
Delhi Gazette in June 1884 said that the introduction of local
self-government had been postponed in Delhi because of the state

of tension between Hindus and Muslims.[67] In September that year the Punjab Secretary, Tupper, reported Lieutenant-Governor Aitchison's views to the Supreme Government. 'If it is impossible in a place of such importance to introduce elections in a more thorough way, it is better to postpone the adoption of any new scheme for the present. The real obstacle is the state of feeling between the Muslims and Hindus of the city. And when there is good ground to hope that these classes are sufficiently prepared to lay aside party spirit ... and work impartially for the good of the city at large, the time will have come for a new departure.'[68] As in the Delhi College issue, Aitchison was sympathetic to the people of Delhi but unwilling to take a stand independent of his advisers.

In November 1884 special rules were framed for Delhi Municipality, modifying the elective principle. The Deputy Commissioner was to be the President of the Municipality. A candidate had to be a ratepayer who had lived three years in Delhi. A voter would also have to be a ratepayer, but possess property within his ward worth Rs 800 or be in receipt of an income of Rs 10 a month. The maximum number of members on any committee was to be twenty-four, half of whom had to be elected.[69]

The first elections held under these rules were significant mainly for the absence of any polarization between the two communities.[70] Contrary to the fears of the officials, more Muslims were elected than Hindus. There was a majority of Hindus among the voters, but six Muslims were elected as against five Hindus. This was a contrast to Lahore, where a Hindu minority secured more seats than the Muslims, who lacked 'any machinery for municipal organization'.[71] In Delhi, the only organization that was active during elections was the Anjuman Islamia, which sought to ensure that poorer Muslims did not get omitted from the voters' lists.[72] The *Delhi Gazette* in 1885 commented that 'The Muslim section of the community are straining every nerve to secure a majority in the elections.' But, as in other towns, because of the open ballot system there were some who wished to have their names deleted from the lists, claiming that they had been over-assessed, rather than risk incurring enmities because of their choice of candidate.[73] The Delhi Society's fear of uneducated men being elected was belied. There were four such candidates, *malis* and *chaudhuris*, in Paharganj and Sadar Bazaar, but they polled very few votes.

Democracy could not be forced on people who believed municipal membership to be the prerogative of the leisured *rais*. The
men who challenged the old loyalists were the relatively *nouveaux-
riches* merchants and traders. The stricture passed by a Lucknow
paper on Delhi in 1867 that wealth was the only thing that seemed
to matter there still seemed to hold good. Lala Madan Gopal (who
had looked forward to the day the uneducated loyalists would
be replaced by 'men of intelligence') stood for election and was
defeated by a prosperous cloth merchant, Sheikh Hafizullah, who
was to have a long innings of sixteen years in the Municipality.
The defeat was decisive, for Madan Gopal left Delhi shortly after,
and made a career as a barrister in Lahore, and eventually reached
the distinguished position of being the first Indian member of
the Punjab Legislative Council. The other newcomers in the
Municipality were Lala Girdhari Lal, a pleader who became a
regular delegate to All-India Congress sessions, Lala Bala Pershad,
a banker, Lal Singh, a shopkeeper, Mir Akbar Ali, a retired local
official, and Nur Mohammad, a *zaildar*. Five members of the
Municipality stood for election and were returned.

The official report said that 'the leading people of the town
deplore the religious basis of the elections, and have expressed
the fear that the elections may have helped to accentuate differences already brewing between the Hindus and Muslims'.[74] It
said that voting in the intramural wards was on communal lines,
and in the suburbs non-communal. The truth of the latter is
borne out by the details given, which showed that voting was on
occupational and not communal lines, and that many Hindus in
Sabzi Mandi and Paharganj voted for Muslims. The statement
about the city, however, was not correct in two instances. In the
Mori Gate ward, which was predominantly Muslim, a Hindu
shopkeeper defeated a Muslim *rais*. In Ward 5, Girdhari Lal won
against three Hindu rivals. Ward 6 had a largely Hindu population, but the victorious Lala Sheo Sahai Mal (already acting as an
Honorary Magistrate) won by only a very narrow margin over
his rival Sheikh Mohammad Ismail, a merchant. The Deputy
Commissioner was forced to admit that 'Considering the successful nature of the elections, the powers of nomination need not be
exercised to the full extent to which the rules permit.' 'Successful'
meant that there was no Hindu majority as had been feared, and
'to the full extent' meant that all the nominated members did not

have to be Muslims. Those nominated were Hakim Zahiruddin
and Sheikh Mahbub Bux, both of whom had been members of the
Municipality for many years. The latter was said to have withdrawn from the elections in order 'not to split the Muslim vote
in Ward 3'; the Hakim did likewise in Ward 7. Also nominated
was Sri Kishen Das Gurwala, the twenty-two-year-old heir to a
large fortune, who, the Deputy Commissioner confidently asserted,
would be 'efficient and popular'.

The novelty of elections soon faded. After 1885, elections
remained largely formal, with few contests. The fact that a person
could be a candidate from two wards simultaneously meant that
if defeated in one ward he could still hope to be elected from
the other. Many seats became the informal prerogative of particular families—'*khandáni*' seats, which they contested regularly
even if their chances of winning a particular election were slight.
By and large, the membership of the Municipality remained self-
perpetuating. Between 1885 and 1895, there were only ten new
Hindu members and nine Muslim. Five Hindu bankers, five Muslim
aristocrats, three Muslim merchants, two Hindu and one Muslim
lawyer can be identified from among both nominated and elected
members. The only example in these years of an untypical candidate was Maulvi Anwar-ul-Haq—a government *munshi* and a
Congress supporter—who was defeated. Lefroy stood as a candidate for the Civil Lines ward in 1886, in the hope that 'it may be
a step towards establishing relations with a class of inhabitants in
the city . . . whom we have as yet . . . failed to reach'.[75] In 1892
there was a case of a European resigning his nominated seat in
order to contest the Civil Lines seat when an Indian stood as a
candidate, thus emphasizing that ward's racial exclusiveness, which
remained intact till the end of the 1890s.[76] Lefroy, whose racial
bias came out in other issues too, was convinced that 'What makes
natives in Delhi take an interest in the municipality, so that there
is canvassing at election times, and some of the best families are
on it, is the direct authority that they wield. They make bad use
of it, employ their authority to annoy their personal enemies,
use the staff of the municipality to carry out their private affairs,
etc.' The European model of political ethics resembles the Delhi
picture of this period. The average citizen, unfamiliar with the
notion of independent political action, and familiar with hierarchy
and authority, interpreted political and civic relations in terms of

personal obligations, and put personal loyalties above allegiance to an abstract code of law.[77]

In the 1890s the number of committees increased. The general meetings of the Municipality were seldom attended by officials but more regularly by non-officials. More and more work was delegated to small sub-committees of eight to ten members, the total number of whose meetings was over a hundred a year. This enabled individual members to concentrate on the area of municipal work for which they had a particular aptitude. By contrast to the first twenty years of the Municipality, the Indian members were now more vocal and more involved, perhaps because they were more numerous. 'The native members... attend meetings regularly. Some think that by doing so they have discharged their duties; a few, however, take an intelligent interest in municipal administration, suggest improvements, supervise the execution of works, and spend some time inspecting conservancy arrangements in their respective wards.'[78]

NOTES

1. *Mof.*, 4 Aug. 1865.
2. A. S. Siddiqi, 'Ghalib and the Delhi Society', in M. A. Aarzu (ed.), *Ahwal-e-Ghalib* (Aligarh, 1953), p. 176.
3. *R.N.P.*, 1867, p. 337.
4. *Mof.*, 28 July 1868.
5. *R.N.P.*, p. 35.
6. I.O.L., *Risala-e-Debating Club*, April 1871.
7. B. Chunder, *Travels of a Hindoo*, p. 386.
8. *R.N.P.*, 1871, p. 87.
9. Canon Crowfoot, in *Mission Life*, op. cit.
10. I.O.L., *Risala-Dehli-Society*, 1871.
11. *R.N.P.*, 1867, p. 41.
12. Sri Ram Mathur, 'Waqa-e-Sri Ram', 2 vols., for a nostalgia-filled description of Delhi's *musha'aras* before and after 1857.
13. *Mof.*, 3 March 1868; Abdul Haq in M. A. Aarzu (ed.), *Ahwal-e-Ghalib*, p. 150.
14. *R.N.P.*, 1871, pp. 372 and 446.
15. *P.A.R.*, 1864–5, p. 27.
16. *R.N.P.*, 1871, p. 151.
17. I.O.L., *Prospectus of Anjuman-i-Rifaya'at-e-Hind* (Delhi, 1875).
18. D.C.O., F. 1/1868.
19. P. Educ. Progs., 1862.

20. *C.M.G.*, 3 Dec. 1868.
21. C.C.O., Educ., F. 3A/Aug. 1917; S. C. Sanial, 'The Idmaduddaula Institution at Delhi', *Islamic Culture*, IV, April 1930.
22. N.A.I., Home Progs., 201/Jan. 1864.
23. *Report on Popular Education*, Punjab 1859–60, p. 9.
24. *Ahwal-e-Ghalib*, pp. 172 and 188.
25. *P.H.P.*, 22A/June 1876.
26. *R.N.P.*, 1871, p. 49.
27. C.C.O., F. 196/1876–8.
28. 'Cambridge Mission to India', *Mission Field*, 1 March 1877, Vol. XXII, no. 255, and envelope marked 1876–7, correspondence re: founding of Mission (U.S.P.G.A.).
29. Bishop of Lahore to Tucker, 4 Dec. 1878 (U.S.P.G.A.).
30. *P.H.P.*, 28A/May 1877.
31. *C.M.G.*, 14 March 1877 and 22 March 1877.
32. *P.H.P.*, 10A/Dec. 1877.
33. *R.N.P.*, 1877, p. 152.
34. Ibid., 1877, p. 212.
35. *P.H.P.*, 28A/May 1877.
36. *P.H.P.*, 2A/March 1881.
37. S. N. Banerjea, 'Lord Macaulay and Higher Education', 1878, reprinted in *Nineteenth Century Studies*, 1974, no. 5, 'Old Calcutta'.
38. H. H. Montgomery, *Life and Letters of G. A. Lefroy* (London, 1920), p. 23. Also Lefroy to mother, 28 July 1880 (U.S.P.G.A.).
39. *P.H.P.*, 13A/Jan. 1881.
40. *P.H.P.*, 21A/April 1878 and ibid., 9A/Nov. 1878.
41. *P.H.P.*, 2A/March 1881 and ibid., 2A/July 1881.
42. Hunter Commission on Education 1882, *Punjab Provincial Committee's Report*, p. 446.
43. C.M.D., *4th Report*, 1882.
44. Letter from Allnutt, Appendix to *5th Report*, C.M.D., 1883.
45. Hunter Commission, *Punjab Provincial Committee's Report*, p. 446.
46. C.M.D., *5th Report*, 1882.
47. *P.H.P.*, 13A/Jan. 1881.
48. Bickersteth to Carlyon, 18 Oct. 1882, and letters of Westcott, Allnutt, Winter, 1888 (U.S.P.G.A.).
49. Most of the information in this paragraph has been obtained from the annual reports of the Cambridge Mission to Delhi.
50. C.M.D., *7th Report*, 1889.
51. N.A.I., Educ. Progs., 22A/Feb. 1882.
52. Hunter Commission, *Punjab Provincial Committee's Report*, p. 286 ff.
53. Ibid., p. 130.
54. Kelley, 'My First Two Years at Delhi', 1889, Occasional Papers, C.M.D. (U.S.P.G.A.).
55. *S.P.G. Report*, 1880, Appendix III.
56. Women's Letters from India (MSS., U.S.P.G.A.).
57. *P. Educ. Progs.*, 7A/Aug. 1889.
58. *P.A.R.*, 1886–7, p. 147.

59. *P.H.P.*, 4A/July 1883.
60. C.M.D., *13th Report*, 1890.
61. *C.M.G.*, 28 Sep. 1883.
62. *P. Mun. P.*, 35A/Sep. 1884.
63. Madho Pershad, *History of Delhi Municipality* (Delhi, 1921).
64. *P. Mun.'P.*, 31A/Oct, 1884. The next three paragraphs are based on this.
65. Lefroy, 'Review of Work, 1881-90', *C.M.D.* (U.S.P.G. Library).
66. N.A.I., Educ. Progs., 22A/Feb. 1882.
67. *D.G.*, 2 June 1884.
68. *P. Mun. P.*, 35A/Sep. 1884.
69. *P. Mun. P.*, 19A/Dec. 1884, *Punjab Gazette*, 6 Nov. 1884, Pt. I, no. 810.
70. *P. Mun. P.*, 9A/June 1885.
71. H. Tinker, op. cit., p. 49.
72. *D.G.*, 21 Feb. 1883.
73. *P. Mun. P.*, 9A/June 1885.
74. Ibid.
75. M. Pershad, op. cit.
76. Indians were not formally debarred from living in the Civil Lines, but few of them did so until the present century.
77. Hennock, *Fit and Proper Persons*, Appendix.
78. *A.M.R.*, 1881-2, p. 20.

5

CONFRONTATIONS: CITIZENS AND GOVERNMENT
(1883-1908)

The quarter-century after the introduction of 'local self-government' was the golden age of the Deputy Commissioner. The Imperial Government's pressure had been removed, and the local officials' authority was not yet circumscribed by popular opposition born of political consciousness. Officials in Delhi as elsewhere created or revived stereotypes to simplify matters. 'Communalism' became a favourite one, and this got free play in a city like Delhi with its Mughal past and its balance of population as between Hindu and Muslim. They fell back on stereotypes as short-cuts to understanding Indians because the social contact between Indians and Europeans was decreasing. The Victorian fetish about cleanliness drove the Europeans into the healthy isolation of the Civil Lines. The belief in godliness led them to zealously keep alive the myths of 1857, and to nurse their fastidious distaste for 'degenerate' Muslims and Hindus. To still their fears of a recurrence of the nightmare, they convinced themselves that the Hindus and Muslims would kill each other off before they could unite against the British.

One very likely explanation of the panic in the British parlour was that the Delhi Muslims had by the 1880s shaken off the quietude that had gripped them after 1857, and they were again interested in things temporarily forgotten. The unique combination of interests characteristic of the cultured man in Delhi—in literature, journalism, *unani* medicine, humanitarian reform—was now seen in individuals who belonged to old-established families as well as in some more recent immigrants. At this time, involvement in or even interest in large political issues was limited.

When the 'Hindi–Urdu controversy' became a matter of general discussion in north India, the Delhi Society discussed it. (This was one of the last significant discussions by the Society. After Madan Gopal left for Lahore in 1885, it declined as a. forum of public opinion.) That same year, 1884, three separate statements were issued from Delhi supporting Urdu as against Hindi. One of these had a majority of Hindu signatories, another largely Muslim, while the third, the 'Popular Language Advocates Committee', claimed to have ten thousand signatures, obviously including people from outside the city.[1] The local newspapers all supported Urdu. In the 1860s, there had been only half-a-dozen newspapers published from Delhi, all owned by loyalists or by individuals who were *en rapport* with the officials. The most enduring of these was the *Akmal-ul-Akbar*, published by the eminent *hakim*, Abdul Majid Khan. By the 1880s, there were more than twelve newspapers, many owned by individuals who were critical of the establishment. The large number of Muslim proprietors of presses and Muslim editors indicates that the statement that 'a Hindu influence was dominant in the Urdu press [sc. after 1882]'[2] did not hold good for Delhi.

The bond of the Urdu language was an old one in Delhi, and it revived easily in the 1880s; when Sri Ram Mathur wrote his reminiscences, he used a Muslim *taqallus*. There is undoubtedly a connection between this and the phenomenon of the decreasing number of members of the local Arya Samaj and Anjuman Islamia between the 1870s and 1890s. It also explains the absence of attraction for English. The Reverend Bickersteth drew the wrong inferences when he said in 1881 that 'the small progress of English education [sc. in Delhi] accounts . . . for the almost entire absence of the reformed element . . . There was an attempt by Dayananda in 1878 to form a branch of his society in Delhi, but with no results. Nor have I met with more than one Muslim who has approved of the liberal creed of Syed Ahmad Khan. As yet, too, there is no widespread fear of Christianity as in some other parts of India.'[3]

Though there was no 'widespread fear of Christianity', there was, as time went on, some alarm at the proliferation of missionary schools. In 1882 the Cambridge Mission reported that a local newspaper had criticized them for holding religious services in their schools and college. 'An influential Muslim' was said to have asked one of the students for information which could be used in an article attacking the Mission.[4] In 1892, three *hakims*, Ajmal Khan, Zahiruddin and Ghaziuddin, together with Mohammad Ikramullah and Ilahi Bux, organized the Anjuman-i-Muaiad-ul-Islam for educating Muslim children.[5] When the Anjuman set up its school, many boys left the missionary schools and many Sunni boys left the Anglo-Arabic School. There was at the same time a sharp drop in the size of the audiences at the lectures given by the missionaries. In the years immediately before this boycott, as many as twenty thousand people often listened to the debates between Lefroy and Sharf-ul-Haq in the Fatehpuri Masjid. (The *Ahl-e-Hadis* and the *Ahl-e-Fiqa* sects had in 1882 sworn an oath before the Commissioner undertaking not to hold debates in the mosques.[6] But this prohibition evidently did not operate against Christians.) Hakim Abdul Majid and Syed Sultan Mirza had been members of the audience at these debates. In 1885 Allnutt was asked to mediate in a debate between the followers of the Arya Samaj and those of the Varnashrama-dharma Sabha. In 1890 he was offered the principalship of the Anglo-Arabic School because of differences among its Muslim members.[7]

The control of and the rules of conduct in the two main mosques became public issues in the 1890s. The officials declared that 'all political interests [sc. had] died out' and that the Jama Masjid was no longer regarded as a symbol of Mughal rule. The 'only political danger' now was the disputes between the different sects of the Muslims; Hindus (referred to rather quaintly as 'non-Muslim Asiatics'!), under a special ruling made by the Deputy Commissioner in 1886, were prohibited from entering the mosque at all. The Lieutenant-Governor, Sir Charles Rivaz, was prepared to concede control of the mosque to a 'self-elected Muslim committee of management'. He was overruled by Curzon, who declared that the 'Government of India [sc. could] not ... divest itself of all responsibility for the custody of what is undoubtedly a great national monument'.[8] Europeans henceforward, he said, could show their respect for Muslim susceptibilities by wearing overshoes in the main part of the mosque, but they could not be compelled to do it. There was deep resentment over this 'shoe-question', which came suddenly to the surface during the Durbar of 1903, when some Muslim shoe-sellers pelted a group of British soldiers[9]—the first anti-British demonstration since 1857.

The question of controlling the mosques also caused a serious rift between the Muslim loyalists and their opponents; the former were by and large *Hanafi*, the latter *al-Hadis*. The Jama Masjid and Fatehpuri committees had overlapping memberships. They included Hakim Ajmal Khan, Ghulam Mohammad Husain Khan (a member of the Punjab University Senate and the secretary of the Anglo-Arabic School), Abdul Ahad (the owner of the Mujtabai Press and Secretary of the Anjuman Muaiad-ul-Islam), Mohammad Ikramullah Khan and Abdul Ghani (a prominent Punjabi Sheikh, a member of the Municipality and the brother of Fazl-ul-Rahman). The spirit of Haji Kutbuddin rode again when his son and grandson, Fazl-ul-Rahman and Zikr-ul-Rahman, together with Mirza Hairat, a Congress sympathizer and the editor of the *Curzon Gazette*, Abdul Wahab and Choudhry Mohammad Din, friends of Obeidullah Sindhi and themselves prominent members of the shoe-sellers' fraternity, united to accuse the Jama Masjid and Fatehpuri committees of various irregularities. They scoffed at them as being servile to the British, criticized them for allegedly prohibiting the recital of the Quran and accused them of embezzlement. There appears to have been no truth in the accusations, and the *al-Hadis* preachers were certainly not debarred from preaching, because a visitor in 1874 commented that they were very much in evidence in the Fatehpuri Masjid.[10]

The Jama Masjid appears to have been more 'loyalist' than the Fatehpuri, which was the venue of unorthodox religious sermons and animated politics, and was patronized generously by the prosperous Punjabi merchants of Sadar Bazaar. In 1893 the Deputy Commissioner tried to play off one community against the other. He warned Ajmal Khan and Karamullah Khan against the Punjabis. They replied, 'We have taken to heart your valuable advice as to the feared predominance of the Muslim Punjabi element in the Fatehpuri Mosque Committee', and suggested increasing the committee's strength from five to twelve to reduce their 'predominance'.[11] The Punjabi Muslims were becoming more numerous in this period, and increasingly conscious of their separate identity. Even the missionaries noticed their preponderance, for one of them said in 1912 that 'in Delhi, where the most advanced [sc. Muslim] class were the merchants, they were very wealthy, pushing and successful businessmen'.[12] When the Afghan Amir's

envoy visited Delhi in 1898, he was fêted not by the loyalists but
by Sheikhs Siraj-ud-Din and Mohammad Yaqub.[13] In 1902 Mirza
Hairat wanted the vacancy of Sheikh Hafizullah on the Municipality to be filled by a Punjabi, pointing out that this community
had already secured a special seat on the local bench.[14] The Mirza
opposed the Aligarh movement and the Mohammedan Educational
Conference, but hoped that the Nadwa-t-ul-Ulema would establish their college at Delhi. By contrast, Ajmal Khan did not show
much interest in the Nadwa movement. He, and Maulvis Zakaullah
and Nazir Ahmad (the last of whom once engaged in heated
discussions with Mirza Hairat about different translations of the
Quran)[15] were active supporters of the Mohammedan Educational
Conference. The 1902 session of the Conference was held at
Delhi, and presided over by the Aga Khan; the active members
of the local committee were Nazir Ahmad, Hakims Ajmal Khan
and Zahiruddin, Sheikh Ilahi Bux and Syed Sultan Mirza.[16]

The new confidence among the Muslims occasionally manifested itself in an aggressive attitude. In 1877 the Anjuman Islamia
petitioned the government to provide more jobs for Muslims.
Maulvi Nasir Ali, the son of Abul Mansur, a Shia who had been
one of the founders of the Anjuman Islamia, edited three newspapers—*Nusrat-ul-Akbar, Nusrat-ul-Islam,* and *Mihir-e-Darakh-
shan.* These were later described as having 'helped to create an
interest in current affairs among Muslims'.[17] But they did more—
in 1881 the *Nusrat-ul-Islam* proclaimed that the Muslims had the
right to expose beef for sale, and during the riots a few years
later it maintained this attitude. The background to this statement
appears to have been that after the Multan disturbances of 1881,
the question of cow-slaughter attracted attention from officials.
It was suggested that beef should not be exposed for sale in towns.
The Punjab Government replied to a query from the Imperial
Government by saying: 'The slaughter of cattle within the City
of Delhi has been prohibited for a long time, and about 1870 the
shops selling meat at Kashmeri and Mori Gates and at Phatak
Habash Khan were closed and transferred to the meat market
near Mor Serai. Besides this, there are beef shops in Muslim
quarters, though none in Hindu quarters. So far their existence
has created no bad feeling. The local officials therefore recom-
mend that there should be no change.'[18] In 1885 the local *Mufid-*

e-Hind criticized two Muslims for annoying Hindu shopkeepers by carrying beef through the streets, and apprehended 'a religious riot'.[19]

Sri Kishen Das Gurwala in 1885 gave up the practice by which the Muslims of the city, since the 1860s, had held their Tar Mela (following Id-ul-Fitr) in his garden, Bagh Mahaldar Khan.[20] He explained this on the grounds that he did not want beef cooked there—possibly a result of Arya Samaj influence. In 1887 Bulaqi Das reproduced in his newspaper, the *Safir-e-Hind*, the firman of Shah Alam which prohibited cow slaughter.[21] There were thus small groups of Muslims and Hindus who were taking a more rigorous attitude on matters connected with religious observance, such as had not happened before in Delhi.

The Arya Samaj became rapidly more influential in Delhi, at the turn of the century. This was most markedly to be seen in St Stephen's School and College[22] and among Punjabis. The orthodox Sanatan Dharm sect won the allegiance of people of an older generation. A mammoth Bharat Dharm Mahamandal was held at Delhi in 1908, where the local hosts included Lalas Hardhyan Singh and Pyare Lal, and Pandit Janki Nath; among the audience were many lawyers and government officials, including Englishmen.[23] The same Sri Ram Mathur who in 1884 had a Muslim *taqallus*, continued to write in Urdu, but in the second volume of his memoirs his pen-name was a Hindu one, and he eulogized Hindus generally and *kayasths* in particular. A counterpoise to St Stephen's College was Hindu College, founded in 1899 with weighty financial backing from Sri Kishen Das Gurwala. It began modestly, housed in a building in Kinari Bazaar. The fees were very low, and the College succeeded in drawing away many students from St Stephen's College. Lala Sultan Singh sold part of his property at Kashmeri Gate to the College, which thus became a neighbour of St Stephen's. As a result of the competition the attendance at St Stephen's decreased till 1902, but picked up again after 1903 (from 47 in 1902 to 79 in 1903). The explanation given for the increase was the 'lamentable university results' in Hindu College.[24] The latter began to do better after its finances became more secure, thanks to the generous donations of local businessmen.

The control of mosques and the pros and cons of cow-slaughter were not the only preoccupation of the Delhi Muslims. It was in these years that Hali produced most of his works. Maulvi Nazir Ahmad and Maulvi Zakaullah returned to Delhi after retiring from government service, and did much writing. Nazir Ahmad's vigorous novels scoffed at the 'westernized' Muslim (in *Ibn-ul-Waqt*—'The Time Server') and pleaded for a more humanitarian attitude to women (in *Mirat-ul-Urus*) as did Hali in his *Bewa-Ki-Munazat*. This book appears to have been read even by the officials; the Deputy Commissioner in 1903 commented, when Nawab Ataullah Khan's daughter applied for a life pension, that 'apparently she has read the story of "The Importunate Widow" ' and recommended that the case be dismissed.[25] On the practical side, Sheikh Karim Ahmad, a wealthy shoe-merchant and a friend of Zakaullah, who founded the Madarsa Karimia, also gave generous financial help to widows. The gentle Zakaullah, a friend of C. F. Andrews, wrote his elegant *Tariq-e-Hind*. The liberal humanist spirit of these men is seen in Nazir Ahmad's comment, 'If I had not studied in Delhi College, I would have been a *maulvi*, narrow and bigoted.'

The liberal spirit was not shared by everyone. In 1883, a fracas occurred about a cow being led to slaughter by a *maulvi*. The English *Delhi Gazette* laughed it off as 'a silly rumpus' and the local Urdu newspapers praised the police for restoring order quickly. Neither newspaper carried any slander against the Hindu or Muslim community.[26] But three years later a more serious clash occurred between a Hindu and a Muslim procession, the fallout from which remained in the air for some days. Riots also occurred that year in Ambala, Ludhiana, Itawah and Allahabad.[27] Smyth would have seen this as the outcome of increased communal separatism resulting from the introduction of local self-government. Others saw it as an accident which might have been averted by a more efficient police force.

The Deputy Commissioner in Delhi had two roles which could be conflicting. He was responsible for maintaining law and order and as President of the Municipality, he was expected to 'balance' the different classes and communities. In 1885 he had made arrangements, in consultation with local Hindus and Muslims, to avoid trouble the following year, when Mohurrum and Ram Lila would coincide. Local newspapers, both Hindu and Muslim, said that the Muslims were not satisfied with the arrangements.[28] Ultimately, they fell through because the date of the *tazia* procession was changed at the last minute, and coincided with the time when the Ram Lila festivities were at their height.[29] Before 1857 clashes had not occurred, because the Ram Lila route had been along the northern wall, well away from the Jama Masjid area. Once an 'impartial' officialdom permitted people of all religions to use the Chandni Chowk for processions, clashes were likely, just as, once they permitted cow-slaughter within the walls as well as at the slaughter-houses outside, the Hindus were likely to get irritated. The consideration that Smyth had thought necessary to show the Muslims at the time local self-government was introduced had been excessive. Similarly, the extra concessions granted them on questions which were only peripherally connected with religion were unwise, because they created occasions for tension in a heterogeneous society which otherwise coexisted in harmony.

In 1886 clashes occurred only in the heart of the city. The people of the poorer quarters—Delhi, Turkman and Kashmeri Gates—were not affected. Many *mohullas* in the area between Chandni Chowk and Jama Masjid improvised *kucha* gates during the early days of the Ram Lila procession, though this practice was prohibited by the government. When the Ram Lila procession was attacked by those participating in the *tazia* procession, the latter were accused of having indulged in 'large-scale plunder'; this was later watered down, and they were described as 'mostly hungry individuals helping themselves to sweets'. There was one instance of animosity being shown against a person, when some rioters attacked the *haveli* of Rai Ram Kishen Das.[30] This must have happened because Katra Neel was one of the most easily identifiable bastions of Hindu wealth, and was located on Chandni Chowk, the scene of the clashes. A Hindu temple in Sita Ram Bazaar was attacked and there was an act of desecration in the Jama Masjid, but the culprits were not found.

More serious than the riot was the fact that the British officials failed in their attempt to communicate with the people through the Indian municipal commissioners. The latter were reluctant to act, and some went underground. 'Can Local Self-Government be said to be a success in Delhi?' demanded the *Civil and Military Gazette*. 'If not, is it likely to be abolished? Should action be taken against Municipal Commissioners who shut themselves up

in their houses while rioting is going on? Should the city be forced
to have a more efficient and unpartisan police?' Local self-government had been introduced only partially in 1884 in Delhi because
Smyth had taken an alarmist view of the 'riot' of 1883. It now
appeared as though his fears had been justified. But what was
equally possible was that in order to prove his point Smyth now
exaggerated the gravity of this situation. The officials, having
failed to act through their municipal colleagues, sought to contact
the 'leaders' of the Hindu and Muslim communities. There was
no one who could be identified as 'leaders'. Ram Kishen Das was
summoned (earlier Smyth had said that he and two other Hindus
were the persons 'most hated by the Muslims', and therefore by
his own description he was not the most suitable representative).
The Muslims were to be represented by Mirza Suleiman Shah,
the Mughal descendant and the President of the Anjuman Islamia.
Smyth also sought out the *chaudhuries* of the gambling and wrestling fraternities, who must have participated in, even if they had
not initiated, the riot. To these, the *Civil and Military Gazette*
added another. 'If there is a turbulent class in Delhi, it is the
Muslim shoe-sellers.'

If in his Jekyll role Smyth was trying a pacifist approach, in
his role of Hyde he imposed a punitive police force on the 'disturbed areas' to chastise Delhi for having 'set an example of up-
roar to the whole of north India'.[31] This was essentially an admis-
sion that the local police had not been satisfactory. One reason
for the situation getting out of control had been the paucity of
policemen in Chandni Chowk. The *Civil and Military Gazette*
also made out that the police themselves had been partisan and
communal. Local opinion, already hostile to the expensive police
force, was bitter at the imposition of a posse of Punjabis, and the
extra cost this involved. The landlords of the Chandni Chowk
area were angry at having to pay. They argued that they had not
taken any part in the riot, whereas their tenants may well have
done, and that they should bear the cost. This was yet another
indication of the heightened class-consciousness of these years.
A very similar situation was to occur again in April 1919 (see
Chapter Seven). The officials complained, for their part, that the
imposition of the police force 'has encouraged those who are
bound to serve the Government and the city to shirk the less

agreeable portion of their duties, and to throw upon the Deputy Commissioner and the District Superintendent of Police the wear and tear [of] these recurring arrangements'.[32]

A significant sequel to the riot was a boycott of four Muslim piecegoods firms by their brokers and middlemen.[33] It is possible that this ostensibly communal act might have been instigated for economic reasons by older-established Hindu piecegoods wholesalers. Marwari merchants who imported drugs and perfumes in bulk from Bombay to sell to Muslim retailers ceased supplying them. Hindu landlords ejected Muslim vendors from the pavements they occupied near their houses (this must have been in retaliation against the stoning of their houses during the riot). The Muslims retorted by starting their own cobblers' shops, and sent for Muslim *halwais* from Lucknow in anticipation of the Hindu shopkeepers refusing to sell to them. This reciprocal boycott alarmed the Hindus. The lace and jewel merchants were afraid that their numerous employees, all Muslim, might migrate to Agra. '*Banyas* [saw] profitable business, the retail of articles of food in poor neighbourhoods, taken out of their hands. *Halwais* [had] to bewail the loss of customers. The Hindu pleaders will get no clients since the people arrested after the riot are largely Muslims.' The prophecy of the *Civil and Military Gazette* that 'whole classes of artisans' would be rendered jobless 'because they are Muslims' and that 'it will be a combination of Socialist and Belfast feeling' was exaggerated. The officials were alarmed by the paralysis of Delhi's most important line of trade—cotton piecegoods. In February 1887 a committee was formed, pledged to stop the boycott. It had four Hindus, four Muslims, one English official and Lefroy as members.

The constructive long-term measure adopted was that strict rules were laid down for the future. Processions in Chandni Chowk as well as music and the blowing of conches near the Jama Masjid, and cow-slaughter within the city, were banned. This created some sore feelings—the *Akmal-ul-Akbar* of Hakim Ajmal Khan complained that Muslims could no longer celebrate Id in a fitting manner—but it did mean that there were no more incidents of tension. In 1890 some Muslims sought to persuade the officials to permit intramural slaughter but without success. What the riot showed was that, as in the Saraogi–Vaishnav clashes earlier, the Hindu–Muslim tension was intensified by the different communities playing up the inconsistencies and prejudices of various officials. It also indicated that local self-government was not necessarily satisfactory in dealing with situations where the religious prejudices of the members were involved. It did not, however, have any repercussions on municipal politics, as had been predicted in 1883.

In 1886 the contingents of town police were increased in the Punjab. It was stipulated that the first-grade constables should be two-thirds of the total number of policemen in all towns, and in Delhi (and Peshawar) all constables were to be of the first grade. In addition, Delhi was punished for the riot by being saddled with the cost of a punitive police force consisting of Punjabis, to be paid by the inhabitants of those parts of the town which had been 'disturbed' during the riot. Similar measures were taken that year in Hoshiarpur, and were to be taken in Delhi in 1919, after the Rowlatt Satyagraha.

The people of Delhi had always had a hearty dislike for the police. In 1884 Smith had said that the Municipality might agree to taking over the cost of primary education 'if . . . relieved of the hated police charges'.[34] The general municipal body rejected the recommendations of the sub-committee which in 1886 prepared a list of the people to be taxed for the special police post. Lefroy suggested that a tactical device of putting the matter to the Municipality not as an order but as a request might help. The Municipality in fact was powerless in the matter, for it was made clear to its members that if they refused, the Provincial or Imperial Government would levy the tax.[35] The local newspapers complained that the tax was levied on mosques and temples, and on the owners of houses and landed property, 'so that all the bad characters, who were the chief cause of the riots, were exempted'.[36] In 1885 the *Sahifa-i-Qudsi* had written that the old *chowkidari* system and the *kuchabandi* pattern had been better safeguards than the police force. This popular conviction was strengthened after the riot of 1886, and at least one *mohulla* asked permission to revert to the *kuchabandi* system. Many improvised barriers were set up in different *mohullas*, a return to private and traditional means of self-defence. In 1890 the Municipality asserted that there were no *mohulladars* in Delhi any more but in 1877 the officials had compiled a list of *mohulladars*, who 'though they may not have a specific title are perfectly well-known'.[37] The people had no faith in the police, who carried swords and were drilled like soldiers.[38] 'If they form part of the army,' commented a local newspaper caustically, 'they should be kept in the cantonments and not employed for watch and ward.'[39] In 1890 the Municipality put up a proposal to reduce the police grant by Rs 5,000 per year. This was overruled by Deputy Commissioner Clarke, the only known case of the Deputy Commissioner using this power. But the Provincial Government compromised by reducing the cost by Rs 2,400.[40]

In 1889 when the Anglo-Arabic School won back the Ghazi-uddin Madarsa, the Provincial Police Reserves had to find some other accommodation. The army authorities refused to give them any of their buildings and they were therefore forced to build new police lines beyond the northern city wall in Tis Hazari. The Provincial Government asked the Municipality to bear the cost of this, but they refused. The government then tried to suggest that the 'community' buy the Madarsa. Clarke dismissed this as absurd, and registered his protest by signing the petition put up by the local Muslims. 'I do not know whether the government could really have supposed that there was sufficient wealth existing among the Muslims of Delhi for them to build the police lines in order to get back their *madarsa* which they probably consider to have been unjustly appropriated by the government,' he wrote cuttingly.[41]

Muslim and Hindu extremism, and any tendency to make capital out of street brawls, were briefly eclipsed in 1898. The years 1896–1900 were a period of exceptional distress in Delhi, comparable to the 1860s. A heavy burden was thrust on Delhi city at this time because of the massive influx of victims of famine from Rajasthan. In 1898 there occurred a panic in Delhi, similar to that in many other north Indian cities, when the local authorities announced the regulations which would operate if there was an outbreak of plague. These were announced in Delhi earlier than in Lahore, because Delhi, as a major railway junction and being nearer to Bombay, was in danger of being affected sooner. The regulations gave a large degree of control to civil officials, with the right to decide matters concerning segregation and treatment and the inspection of private premises.[42] In contrast, the regulations at Patna, which the editor of the local *Faiz-i-Am* wanted enforced in Delhi, permitted private segregation and allowed the option of treatment by *hakims* and *vaidyas*. These rules led to general uneasiness and added weight to the argument that Lahore was being given preferential treatment, an argument heard at the time the waterworks were constructed. The panic of February 1898 was general, but affected two groups in particular—the merchants and the poorer section. The wholesale market in Delhi was closed, and trade was paralysed. The Hindus were far more agitated than the Muslims. The Marwari merchants sent away their families and their goods; this exodus became brisker when the British Manager of the Delhi and London Bank offered to take into safe custody the property of any one wishing to leave the city. The two major commercial organizations—the Delhi Piece-Goods Association (which had European and Indian members) and the local branch of the Hindustani Mercantile Association (which was wholly Indian in membership) convened a meeting in the Town Hall, which was attended by more than 2,000 people, including representatives of all the European and Indian firms. A Vigilance Committee was appointed with James Currie as President, and thirteen Hindu, six British and three Muslim members.[43] The resolutions deplored the panic, and asked the local authorities to allay the fears of the people by announcing that there was no plague in the city. They accepted the rule which gave the Civil Surgeon special powers, on condition that the Surgeon, Dennys, who was very popular, should not be transferred from Delhi. This was supported by the local *Rozana Akbar*. Other meetings were convened by Ikramullah Khan, a magistrate, and by Babu Kedarnath, a *rais* and a pleader. Both were attended by a large number of Hindus and Muslims. Two Lahore newspapers, commenting on these events, reached opposite conclusions. The English *Civil and Military Gazette* said that the 'excellent example of trying to pacify the masses [i.e. that set by Ikramullah Khan] was being adopted by all those in authority'. The *Akbar-e-Am*, however, was convinced that 'no Municipal Commissioner has done anything to prevent the flight of people from the city', though it found it 'encouraging' that the Deputy Commissioner was 'doing his best to reassure the Delhi residents'. Robert Clarke, one of the most popular former local officials, was asked to address a public meeting. The stand adopted by the mercantile associations of keeping on the right side of government while suggesting a few concessions to soften the popular indignation was not backed by the people generally, and the possibility of an epidemic and of women having to be treated by the civil doctors kept the agitation simmering at a time when observers thought it had abated. Mohammad Mirza Khan's newspaper, the *Asbraf-ul-Akbar*, said that 'before the circulation of the plague notices in Delhi, [it was] under the impression that the reports which reached [it] regarding the oppression practised by the doctors in Bombay were exaggerated'. The news and rumours about the Bombay riots reaching the local Marwari merchants through private telegrams kept the market in a depressed state in March.[44] A Lahore newspaper estimated that one-fifth of the town's population had left. The month-long storm in a teacup showed that the Bombay riots affected Delhi only insofar as the Marwaris, who were in Delhi but not of it, were afraid for their property. The inhabitants were upset in the same way as they had been earlier about the vaccination rules, but did not think of leaving the city.

'The real key to success in carrying through the plague policy is to work through the people themselves and to keep the police absolutely aloof from it,' Fanshawe was to say in 1900, wise after the event.[45] The truth of this was borne out in 1898. Clarke thought that there would be 'more opposition to a "strong" policy in Lahore, Amritsar or Multan, as the inhabitants of these cities are less generally intelligent than the people of Delhi and less amenable to authority'. But the same Clarke, during the panic, had believed that 'we should have to count on the strongest opposition from the ignorant classes, and . . . we should not receive much assistance of any value from the persons who pose as the leaders of native society'. Both the Deputy Commissioner and he, however, were all praise for the help rendered by the Imam of Jama Masjid and Hakim Abdul Majid ('the most influential man in the city', a *rais* of eminence and a physician of great repute) in allaying the panic.[46] (Twenty years later, the brother of Abdul Majid, Hakim Ajmal Khan, was to perform a similar task of softening public anger; the Imam's successors, likewise, were to be involved with public issues in 1919 and in 1977.)

A *grande peur* was triggered off among the officials in 1898 because of the obvious fraternization that developed between Hindus and Muslims. This was something that provoked comment from newspapers as well as from officials—'The most remarkable

feature of the scare was the reunion of Hindus and Muslims as in
the time of Akbar', commented the Lahore *Akbar-i-Am*. A similar
phenomenon occurred in some towns in the North-Western Provinces also. In Delhi the initiative came from the Hindus. They
greeted the Muslims as they came out of the Jama Masjid after
the Id prayers. Once again Sri Kishen Das's garden was thrown
open for the Tar Mela. The Muslims reciprocated by participating
in the Holi celebrations. 'Grave *maulvis*' submitted to having their
faces smeared with Holi colour. Some Muslims tried to persuade
others that cow-slaughter was not a necessary part of celebrating
Id.[47] All this generated an alarm among the officials which, for
absurdity, was on a par with that of the Marwaris shortly before.
The paranoia of the Europeans described by Forster in *A Passage
to India* was seen in Delhi. Even a man as Delhiphil as Clarke was
apprehensive of a coalition against 'constituted authority' and a
possible attack on the local English residents. A scribbled notice
on the Clock Tower declared that 1857 had recurred; the Europeans behaved as though this was a reality. The horrific possibility
of a rioting mob blowing up the Jamuna bridge and attacking the
Europeans in the suburbs were discussed seriously. Myths are
often more real than facts, and the image of Delhi's 'inflammable
population' was very real to the British. That, and Delhi's strategic
position were adduced as arguments to back the demand for tight-
ening up the city's defences and for reorganizing the positions
occupied by the troops, so as to avert the grim prospect of European refugees from the Civil Lines having to flee to the Fort and
being intercepted by an angry mob at Kashmeri Gate. Fanshawe
wrote: 'As Delhi is still the centre of India, so is the old Mughal
Palace . . . the centre of Delhi—and it is very important that the
people of Delhi should see our garrison in the Fort and know that
the city is at the mercy of the guns in front of Lahore Gate.'[48]
There were demands that the European garrison be increased.
Clarke supported the Commissioner, and said that the need for
defending the city was even more imperative than it had been in
1889. One point of interest was that, while the fears about Delhi's
dangerous inhabitants were unchanged, the reason given for Delhi's
strategic importance had changed with the times. In 1857 Delhi
had been a frontier town, now its importance was because it was
the junction of five major railway lines, the centre of many industries and a commercial entrepôt.

The intercommunal camaraderie was seen when Hindus and Muslims united to protest against an official order during Mohurrum in 1898. The police banned the display of the *bajra* (a Delhi variation in the Mohurrum celebration, significant because the *bajra* was displayed by a Hindu *barbhunja*); the reason given was that the *bajra* contained fireworks and would be dangerous in a congested area. To show their displeasure, the Muslim *tazia-wallahs* abandoned the procession.[49] Alienation from the government was seen the same year when sympathy for Turkey was expressed by publicizing the Graeco-Turkish War to such an extent that it caused a significant drop in the number of Muslims attending government hospitals and schools in Delhi.[50]

An incident of 1901 showed that class was a more divisive force than religion. The Muslim and Christian *chamars* united to protest against Muslim shoe-merchants, who got support from Hindu moneylenders. The merchants declared a 'lock-out', to which the *chamars* retorted by going on strike. This paralysed the shoe-trade in Delhi and therefore in the whole of north India. A settlement was arrived at, but it was evident that as long as the monopoly of the rich Muslim merchants was not challenged, the *chamars* would be at their mercy.[51]

A much more long-drawn-out agitation was that against the levy of a house-tax. When it was proposed that the drainage scheme be extended to the suburbs, it 'took all the arguments of the enlightened few in the Municipal Committee' to accept it.[52] This was because some new tax had to be levied. The Municipality said that 'rather than risk interfering with prosperity by taxing food or piecegoods, we have decided on a moderate house-tax to meet the cost of the drainage scheme'.[53] There had been a house-tax imposed on Lucknow since 1868. When such a tax had been proposed in Delhi in 1878, the loyalist proprietors had rejected it. In 1902 these proprietors were not so adamant, because the burden would now fall not so much on them as on their tenants. (The population increase of the 1890s had led to a great increase in the number of tenants.) The officials knew that the tax would be unpopular, and hoped that 'the more enlightened Municipal Commissioners' would be able to persuade the public of its necessity;[54] but their efforts could not check the tide of popular opposition.

Similar taxes were being levied in Calcutta, Bombay, Poona and Karachi, but in the Punjab, Delhi was the first large town to impose it.[55]

A large cross-section of people cutting across communal and class divisions united to protest. Mirza Hairat, consistently anti-loyalist, blamed the Indian municipal commissioners for having 'proved unequal to the task' since it was not from them but from a European colleague that the Deputy Commissioner had learned that the tax was unpopular.[56] When an estimate was made and it was seen that more than half the amount of the tax would be realized from houses with a rental value between Rs 12 and Rs 60, the Commissioner decided that 'poor Muslims' should be exempted. Three categories were therefore relieved from payment—'persons owning large houses but in impoverished circumstances', poor widows who paid Rs 5 or less as rent, and the squatters who had erected huts in Sadar Bazaar and Teliwara on municipal property. When the general opposition to the tax continued, the rate was lowered from 5 per cent to 3½ per cent.[57]

These concessions did not end the agitation. The *Curzon Gazette* and the *Delhi Gazette*, which had very different viewpoints on most issues, were united in their criticism of the tax. They both said that many people, particularly the poor agriculturists of Sabzi Mandi, were leaving Delhi because they could not cope with this extra burden at a time when they were still suffering from the after-effects of the famine. There were nostalgic references to Akbar, as had been heard earlier at the height of the famine; it was asserted that he would never have taxed people at a time of distress. The Municipality made a further concession, and assured the inhabitants of the western suburbs that the revenue from the house-tax collected from them would be earmarked exclusively for the drainage works in those wards. This did not mollify the agitators, who were questioning the utility of the drainage scheme itself.

The house-tax agitation continued for some years. It became a more sustained movement than that of the 1870s against the closure of Delhi College because it became part of the armoury of those who wished to challenge the monopoly of a small number of loyalist families in the Municipality. In Delhi, 'local self-government' had not edged out any of them; this was in marked contrast to at least one other Indian town, Allahabad.[58] It was also remarkable that municipal elections had not led to any communal polarization, which in turn explains why the opposition to the loyalists was sometimes on a general and occasionally at a personal level, but never on a religious basis. Delhi had been the only town in the Punjab which was denied a full measure of self-government in 1884 on the pretext that communal differences were very strong there, but it was in the other towns that separate representation for different religious groups was conceded—in Lahore in 1891, in Amritsar in 1895, in Multan in 1899 and in Ambala in 1906.[59] The Deputy Commissioner of Delhi had suggested in 1896 that occasional vacancies in the Municipality be filled by individuals of the same religion as the earlier incumbent; from an experience of Delhi of over ten years, the Commissioner, Clarke, thought this quite unnecessary. He informed the Viceroy that 'religion has never been an issue in municipal politics in Delhi'.[60]

The loyalists had tried, in the 1890s, to perpetuate their monopoly by introducing a higher level of minimum qualifications for candidates. In 1892, the Deputy Commissioner said that 'public opinion, where it exists at all', which he defined as the 'collective sense of the Municipality as a whole and that of its members individually', favoured a higher property basis for candidates. The suggestion was for Rs 5,000 in property, or an income of Rs 100 a month, or an income-tax rating of Rs 28 a year. If the candidate was a graduate, a lower property qualification was sufficient. The practice by which a man's income was treated as entitling his son to a vote was criticized. These strongly-held views led to a revision of the 1884 provisions.[61] A candidate henceforward needed to have at least a monthly income of Rs 50, together with a certificate of the Entrance examination or in a classical language. These, in fact, had been the suggestions of Madan Gopal and the Literary Society in 1883. In 1892, also, advocates and pleaders were declared eligible even if they did not fulfil the property qualifications.[62] This concession agitated the local British officials so much that they decided in 1900 to revise the qualifications. Unlike 1884 and 1891, this revision was not supported by any Indian. The Deputy Commissioner wanted the minimum property qualification for candidates for election to be raised to twice the amount hitherto stipulated. The Commissioner was satisfied with less, but he wanted to raise the qualification for voters because most of the workers earning Rs 10 a month were only temporary residents. Both agreed that the rental qualifications should not be the same for all wards.[63] The bogey was no longer the Hindus generally but the educated middle class. With a degree of alarmism that could be paralleled for absurdity with that of Clarke during the plague scare of 1898, they said that 'the cases in which a person [had] such [i.e. educational] attainments but [was] not in receipt of Rs 50/100 per month would probably be few and far between, but they might of course be the most mischievous cases of all'.[64] In 1901 therefore the qualifications both for voters and for candidates were raised above the 1892 level. Voters needed an income-tax rating of Rs 35 (as against Rs 20), or land revenue of Rs 50 (as against Rs 30), or property worth Rs 7,500 (as against Rs 5,000), or a B.A. degree together with a salary of Rs 100 per month (as against an Entrance qualification and a salary of Rs 50 per month). But till 1906 the bankers' and merchants' monopoly in the Municipality was not threatened by the professional class. The reasons were that the latter were not very numerous in Delhi until after the establishment of New Delhi and that most of the lawyers were members of the loyalists' families. What rivalry there was in the Municipality was between established families and the merchants who had come to Delhi as immigrants after the 1860s. The generalization made by a contemporary British official, H. T. S. Forrest, about Indian municipalities did not therefore hold good for Delhi: 'The legal profession is always represented more fully than its stake in the fortunes of the town warrants. Landowners, bankers, merchants . . . hold aloof.'[65]

In 1902 these two grievances, against the house-tax and against the franchise qualifications, became the basis for forming a Ratepayers' Association. (In Bombay, a similar association had been formed in 1872.) The *Akbar-e-Am* commented that 'the disappointing result of the agitation has led to the establishment of a Ratepayers' Association . . . to relieve the people of the burden of unnecessary [municipal] taxation'. Mirza Hairat had earlier complained about the house-tax, but he did not support the Association. 'Some educated persons are still trying to induce the people to submit a memorial asking for [sc. the tax's] abolition . . . Some of the local pleaders have formed a Ratepayers' Association to safeguard the interests of the people and to keep an eye on the Municipal Committee's doings . . . This object can be better gained by electing responsible men as Municipal Commissioners.' He even went to the extent of changing his point of view, and saying that the house-tax was necessary, and was less burdensome than taxes in other towns. 'How else can sanitary arrangements be made?' The Ratepayers described themselves as 'comprising not less than one hundred and seventy-five members and having among them some of the most intelligent citizens of Delhi' and asked that they should 'be allowed to have their say and not treated as a body of no importance'.[66] Their secretary in 1903 was Munshi Mohammad Karamulla Khan of Fatehpuri (a teacher in a *madarsa*) and in 1905 Sardar Ram Singh. The Municipal Sub-Committee dismissed the argument of Karamulla Khan's lawyer that the house-tax was illegal and not according to the 1891 Municipal Act. The house-tax issue afforded these professional men a means of contact with the poorer sections through the medium of collecting petitions from inhabitants of crowded and impoverished areas of the walled city, protesting against the new drains. They complained of the burden of taxation—the wheel tax, cattle tax, heavy octroi duties and now the house-tax. They passed resolutions criticizing the work of the Public Works Department as wasteful and unintelligent, and as being based mechanically on western experience and unsuited to India. The new drains had little sanitary value, and merely narrowed the roads. The Municipality could earn revenue by using the Queen's Gardens for building sites. (This last would imply that the members were not men of much property, and hoped for the advantage of new houses in the heart of the city.) They were able to quote the Punjab Municipal Act with effect, and to compare Shahjahanabad as a planned capital city to Washington, while making the point that the Shahjahani drains were superior to the new-fangled open ones. They knew which arguments would carry weight with the government, as when they cannily pointed out that by ruining the people by heavy taxes, trade and railways would be ruined. They suggested that the canal be closed, because its water was not conducive to health; if this were done, it would 'produce healthier and wiser people, the most fitting candidates for the membership of the Municipal Committee'.[67]

By 1906 the agitation against the house-tax had abated, but the

Association did not as a result lose its *raison d'être*. That year there were three associations in Delhi with overlapping membership, and drawn chiefly from members of the legal profession and from St Stephen's College. These were the Ratepayers' Association, which now called itself the Citizens' Union, the District Association and the Sanat-o-Hirfat Anjuman.[68] These Associations sought to build up public opinion on matters of all-India interest, but public opinion generally remained preoccupied with local issues. The Ratepayers became more militant in their attacks on the Municipality. They demanded that the Municipality be suspended. 'The majority, are elected and appointed illegally and are ignorant of the true principles of local self-government. Some are illiterate, and few know anything of Engineering, Sanitation and Economics.'[69] Madan Gopal's generation in the 1880s had criticized the Commissioners for their ignorance; to this was now added the implication not only of incompetence but of venality.[70] In 1905 the election of Lala Jawahar Lal (who had been elected on four occasions earlier) was challenged by his rival Lala Chandu Lal Chawalwala (a merchant who was a member of the Citizens' Union and a sympathizer of the extremist Congress group) on the grounds that Jawahar Lal had been guilty of embezzlement some twenty years earlier. The Deputy Commissioner, Parsons, turned down the complaint. Parsons had also, in 1904, used the power that Smyth in 1883 had secured for the Deputy Commissioner, when he cancelled the nomination of Lala Shimbhu Nath (municipal member 1890–1903) and nominated instead Nathu Ram, a contractor and a house-owner in the Civil Lines who had helped with the house-tax collection, 'a self-made man, and according to Hindu caste theories, a man of somewhat inferior position'.[71] In 1907 two local newspapers and the Delhi District Association protested against the appointment of Mr Addison, an I.C.S. official, as Secretary to the Municipality, accusing him of embezzlement. They were successful, and the Punjab Government debarred Addison from trying cases where the Municipality was concerned.[72]

Once the tactics of protest had been used by a heterogeneous group with a common grievance, it was copied by sectional groups, by Muslim butchers protesting against Municipal bye-laws, and then by upper-class Hindus against a tax on cows. The Municipality passed bye-laws in 1906 giving itself control over

10

the sale of meat, which had hitherto been under the jurisdiction of the Deputy Commissioner.[73] Until this time the Municipality had no power to prohibit meat shops being opened in any particular locality, even if it had a largely Hindu population. There was a case in 1904 when a member of a ward reported that there was 'the possibility of a riot if sanction were given'. To this the [Muslim] Vice-President of the Municipality had replied that even the Muslims did not want more meat shops but that the Municipality did not have the power to refuse permission.[74] After the bye-laws were enacted, the situation became different. Meat shops now came under the same rules as governed other shops. The British Civil Surgeon wanted a provision that the shops should be screened, but this was withdrawn when it was pointed out that the shops of Hindu *halwais* were equally unhygienic. There was a proposal to remove meat shops from crowded areas and to open a new slaughter-house near the Idgah instead of repairing the old one at Turkman Gate. The latter suggestion was acceptable to the butchers, but they objected to closing any shops. The butchers argued that the grain shops (owned by Hindus) bred plague and were thus even more insanitary than meat shops; the bye-laws were an interference with the cutoms prescribed by their religion, and were unjust, since a majority of Delhi's inhabitants were meat-eaters. Using the language of those who complained about the house-tax, they said that the rules would harm trade and reduce municipal income.[75]

This agitation received attention from newspapers in other towns in Punjab. Abdul Qadir, a lawyer of Delhi, wrote to the Amritsar newspaper, the *Vakil*, that the proposed bye-laws had nothing to do with sanitary requirements and were a concession to Hindu prejudice. When the butchers achieved their object, and the bye-laws were abrogated, the Lahore *Observer* drew the moral: 'We warn the Muslims of other places in India to be on their guard. The Hindus in other Municipalities might do things against Muslims if the Muslims are not careful.' Prominent at a protest meeting called at the Idgah in 1907 were Fazl-ul-Rahman and his son, who were of a different social class from the butchers and who gave a communal and political tinge to an otherwise valid objection.[76]

The counterpart to the butchers' agitation was a protest against an enhancement of the tax on milch cattle. When this had been first levied in 1889, it had been opposed by the *gwalas*. In 1908 the protest came from a different class, self-styled 'well-off persons', who kept cows 'on Hindu religious principles, to get unadulterated milk' and from 'middle-state persons' who would find it hard to pay the tax. They suggested that only draught animals and the cattle belonging to *gwalas* should be taxed, and not cows 'kept on religious principles'.[77] Tilak's veneration of the cow was finding expression in Delhi just as the agitation in other north Indian towns for unrestricted kine-slaughter was also being echoed here. Neither of these sectional viewpoints was represented in the Citizens' Union or the District Association. These two expressions of protest were by tradition against change, whereas the Associations were composed of individuals seeking to challenge the loyalist monopoly of urban governmental office.

The Municipality had described itself somewhat deprecatingly, in an address to the Lieutenant-Governor in 1897, as an essentially mercantile body with no interest in politics.[78] This in fact was its most serious shortcoming, for as a result its members tended to pass on the burden of taxation to other classes. But this tradition of sparing the mercantile interests was sought to be modified in 1908, when the Municipality contemplated enhancing the octroi rates.[79] The officials admitted that things had changed a great deal in nine years. Far from being the 'most lightly taxed municipality of the plains', now 'in the multiplicity of taxes ... Delhi [sc. had] clearly reached the limit if not overstepped it'.[80] The owners of the local mills were alarmed when the Municipality proposed to levy octroi on grain, and to increase the rate on coal, oil, and gunny bags. If grain were taxed, they stated simply but effectively, dealers would cease importing wheat into Delhi and unload it at Hapur, Deoband or Muzaffarnagar, to avoid the tax and the freight. Delhi would also suffer because of competition from Lahore, Ambala and Amritsar. The European-dominated Punjab Chamber of Commerce, which had established its headquarters at Delhi in 1905, also protested. The Chamber had made a bid in 1907 to secure a special seat on the Municipality for its own representative as had been done in Amritsar, but without success. The Citizens' Union also objected to the threatened increase in the price of essentials. At a meeting attended by merchants, lawyers (including an Englishman), the Civil Surgeon and Amir Chand, they suggested that 'a committee of a few respectable citizens from every ward should be elected to arrange for a representation of grievances to the Delhi Municipality'. All the mills and factories which had sprung up in the previous twenty years bought cloth and grain locally. This explains why the officials, local and provincial, opposed the tax on cloth. The Punjab Government suggested an alternative, that the (low) 'standard rate' be retained on imported goods, and the octroi on Indian articles be increased by four to six per cent. This meant that British cotton piecegoods would continue to enjoy favourable treatment, while grain was to become more expensive. They added, however, with apprehension born of the lesson learned during the house-tax agitation, that an unpopular tax was inadvisable in Delhi, which contained 'so many elements for a conflagration'.

Apart from grievances against specific acts of the Municipality, vocal public opinion in Delhi was also evincing interest in municipal reform as such. This took different forms with different people. Mirza Hairat's dislike of the local establishment led him to exhort the people of Delhi to unite and abolish the Municipality so that the city's administration could be controlled by the government. The most effective criticism of the Municipality's wrong policies would be to 'elect no members for any ward, so that the structure of so-called self-government will tumble down'.[81] The officials were, for their part, already alarmed because in the elections of 1906 as many as three lawyers had been elected to the Municipality, apart from the traditional quota of bankers (six) and one merchant. This break in the loyalists' dominance could have been the reason why that year the official review of municipalities in the Punjab, traditionally warm in praise of Delhi, said that the electoral principle, while suited to central Punjab, in Delhi 'militated against municipal interests'.[82] Ibbetson, the Lieutenant-Governor, who earlier in his career had been Deputy Commissioner in Delhi, described Delhi Municipality in a letter to Minto as 'a large and troublesome one'.[83] At the popular level, there was a threat in 1906 to deface the statue of Nicholson which Minto, with that art of bad timing in which the British excelled, planned to install at Delhi.[84] The *Tribune* was dismayed at Minto supporting this 'imperialistic freak of his erratic predecessor'.[85]

When the composition of the Imperial Advisory Council was

being discussed in Delhi, only one lawyer was included along with the *rais*, the Indian and British mercantile groups and the officials who were consulted. They were all unanimous in criticizing the scheme for not providing special representation for 'commerce, industry, capital, and learning'. Syed Haidar Raza, a teacher at St Stephen's College who was becoming involved in the *Swadeshi* agitation, compared the proposed Councils to the French Assembly of Notables of 1788![86] The Hindu and Muslim merchants and bankers wanted the electorates to comprise 'respectable persons', not municipalities and district boards. The major difference between the opinions expressed now and those of 1883 was that most Hindus wanted joint electorates and the Muslims weighted or separate ones.[87] Ajmal Khan was in favour of separate electorates, as he had said to Keir Hardie the previous year. This was to be expected from him as a founder-member of the Muslim League in 1906. His premise that Muslims would otherwise be swamped in areas with Hindu majorities was probably strengthened by the fact that in 1906 the electoral pattern in Delhi had changed, and the Hindus had secured for the first time a majority of the elected posts. He used rather strong terms when speaking to Keir Hardie, saying that it was impossible to make common cause with the Hindus. The Muslims were well represented in the Municipality, but this was only because the Hindus in those particular wards were uneducated and unable to press their claims. Municipal government survived in Delhi, he said, only because the Deputy Commissioner was the President.[88]

The local grievances in Delhi were exploited by a few individuals and linked to bigger political issues, with the result that for a short period, from 1906 to 1908, Delhi witnessed some degree of nationalist political activity. The contingent from the city to the Indian National Congress was irregular and small in number. It was an extremist who initiated Delhi citizens into the language of the nationalist movement. Syed Haidar Raza was an angry young man from Rewari, who had been educated at St Stephen's College and for a few months had been a lecturer there. He gave publicity to the butchers' protest in Delhi, seeing it not as a victory of Muslims over Hindus but of public opinion against the Municipality. He quoted its example when he urged that 'Hindus and Muslims should unite and refuse to pay' the house-tax.[89] The next year, when a platform tax was proposed, he urged the hawkers to remove their platforms. It would not matter if one or two people were imprisoned, he said, so long as there was a united front. He and Lala Amir Chand, who had been a teacher in St Stephen's School, were active in the Ratepayers' Association, the Citizens' Union and the District Association, which had as members teachers, lawyers, some *maulvis* and some merchants. One professional group, the Punjabi lawyers, had a separate association of their own, the Anjuman Vakil-e-Qaum-Punjabian. This Anjuman, along with the Punjab Chamber of Commerce and the Hindustani Mercantile Association, was consulted by the Punjab Government in 1910 when a loan for financing the drainage scheme was under consideration.[90]

Raza's and Amir Chand's achievement was to bring these various groups together for a short period. To draw in a wider audience, they made frequent use of myths, which were also part of the stock-in-trade of Lajpat Rai and Tilak. They built up Bahadur Shah as the tragic hero of Delhi, and made nostalgic references to Akbar.[91] Raza's newspaper, the *Aftab*, and another which was similar in tone, the *Akash* of Ganeshi Lal, reached a wide audience and were regarded with much uneasiness by the government. Raza himself was *persona non grata* with the Muslim League and he had many Hindu supporters.

Raza and Amir Chand had a large following in St Stephen's School and College. In their enthusiasm, the students often dragged Raza's carriage to the meetings. Hibbert-Ware and C. F. Andrews, who were on the staff of the College, also developed strong bonds of sympathy with the nationalists. The Reverend Western, writing in 1921, recalled the 'strong prejudice in some English circles in India against the College as being seditious' that had developed between 1907 and 1911.[92] This was the time when Har Dayal, the most brilliant student of 1904 in the College and in Punjab University, had launched into his political career. This was also the time that Lefroy (by then Bishop of Lahore), was fighting fiercely to prevent Sushil Rudra becoming Principal of St Stephen's College. He failed in his crusade and later, in 1908, remarked unblushingly, 'How splendidly the bold experiment of making a native Christian the head of St Stephen's College has succeeded.'[93] For those in Delhi who were involved in the meetings, subscription-drives and the debates that were the stuff of national politics, there was something of the exhilaration of the 1840s as well as the cross-communal and, to a limited extent, cross-racial camaraderie of those days.

The *Swadeshi* Movement in Delhi had only a limited success, but its supporters included Muslims (though Mirza Hairat and Abdul Qadir warned the Muslims against this Hindu-dominated movement)[94] and prominent bankers and industrialists like Lala Sultan Singh and Ram Kishen Das. The Sanat-o-Hirfat Anjuman was pledged to promote *swadeshi*. Had this movement caught on in a big way, it could have been expressed with paralysing effect by the boycott of European piecegoods, the mainstay of Delhi's trade. But in fact the only *swadeshi* gesture in Delhi which was effective was Raza's organization of a boycott of the British-owned tramway.[95] This was a good target, because there was no section of the people who would really suffer if the trams did not ply. The most enthusiastic supporters of the boycott were the *tongawalas*, who were suffering because of competition from the trams. The meetings held to propagate the *swadeshi* cause were attended by audiences of a few hundreds. Raza lashed out at both the rulers and the loyalists. 'These *raises* are the enemies of the people. If the titles of Rai Bahadur and Khan Bahadur could be obtained by presenting the heads of a few Indians to the Deputy Commissioner, they would probably cut off the heads of a hundred Indians.'[96]

The threat of an impending crackdown by the government on Raza, his rift with Amir Chand and his escape to England in 1908 led to the collapse of the nationalists' control over the Citizens' Union. As far as the inhabitants of Delhi generally were concerned, their awareness and involvement had been very slight. There had been a massive turnout to welcome Lajpat Rai,[97] and funds had been collected for the defence of Aurobindo Ghose, but on the other hand the *swadeshi* boycott had not been spectacular, and attempts to build up public opinion about India's parlous economic condition or about the condition of Indians in the Transvaal had ended in failure.[98] Audiences of only a few hundreds attended lectures on political subjects. As against this, many thousands would flock to attend meetings to discuss matters of local interest. Raza's polemical *Aftab* had a very poor sale locally unless it was carrying on some campaign against the Municipality. The Delhiwala, of whom observers have said, generation after generation, that he is uninterested in anything outside his city, behaved true to type. With the exception of the students, the lawyers, the Punjabi merchants and a few individual bankers and other professionals, politicization had not touched the city. But the shadow cast by the national movement was seen in a more assertive attitude *vis-à-vis* the government authorities on the part of many groups. The decade after 1898 was a troubled one for the local authorities.

There were many individuals who had supported Raza and Amir Chand but none of them was prepared to don their mantle. The vacuum created by the collapse of the nationalist agitation in 1908 was filled by the extremist factions among the two communities, who had been in evidence only occasionally earlier; the Christian missionaries joined in when it suited them. The Aryas put up the backs of the Muslims by observing *'chhut'*.[99] To this the Muslim shoe-merchants retaliated with spirit. Mohammad Din exhorted Muslims to regard 'trade' and not 'service' as the goal of education.[100]

In 1909 Maulvi Abdul Haq (brother of Abdul Wahab) issued a *fatwa* bidding Muslims to co-operate with Christians against the Aryas.[101] The following year, at a meeting in the Idgah attended by an estimated eight thousand Muslims, and addressed by Muslim preachers and by a Christian convert, a memorial was drafted to protest against the preaching of the Aryas. This was organized by the Punjabi Sheikhs. A contemporary newspaper commented that the 'other party' of Delhi Muslims disapproved of the meeting.[102] It was again the Punjabi Muslims (led by the lawyer Abdul Aziz and the merchant Abdul Ghani) who held a meeting at the Jama Masjid in 1911, to demand separate electorates for Muslims and an equal number of seats for each community in the Municipality. This was also deplored by other Delhi Muslims.[103] In theory Ajmal Khan believed that Muslims needed special representation and reserved seats, but his dislike of polemic and of public haranguing made it impossible for him to join forces with the Punjabi Muslims who in language and culture and vocation were different from him. The other point of view, deploring separate electorates, was put in 1909 to an audience of five hundred people by Wazir Singh and Moti Sagar, well-known local lawyers.[104]

Though the nationalist activity in Delhi had been so far short-lived, it had given the inhabitants the experience of holding public meetings to discuss political issues; in the nineteenth century gatherings had been for cultural and literary interchanges or for religious debates. This political début prepared Delhi for the process of suddenly being transformed from a provincial town into the seat of the Imperial Government establishment. In the train of the 1911 Durbar came a Muslim Conference, a Hindu Conference and a Cow-Protection Conference. National and communal politics would be thrust upon Delhi after 1912. The *Tribune*, like Bholanath Chunder forty years earlier, was supercilious about the lack of public opinion at Delhi. It had to be seen whether the popular protests against local government and against the loyalists made in the first ten years of this century were to be the last of their kind, or only a curtain-raiser for more spectacular developments.

The rich Punjabi merchants, who transformed Sadar Bazaar into a residential area, competed for municipal office against the loyalists. In their political and religious attitudes, they found sympathy among the shoe-merchants of the city, who were also Punjabi but of older vintage. They were to be the earliest supporters of the Ali Brothers when they came to Delhi in 1911. The ground for the Pan-Islamism of Mohammad Ali was already prepared by 'Faqir', Nusrat Ali, Mohammad Din and Obeidullah. The Arya–Sanatan rivalry, a conflict between generations as well as between provincial groups, was less linked with political issues than was Muslim factionalism. The loyalist and the nationalist Hindus were not as clearly distinguished from each other as were the loyalist and the nationalist Muslims. Though the communities were by no means becoming polarized into monolithic groups, the sense of community in the city was becoming eroded as a result of its expansion and of the ending of its isolation from the rest of the country.

NOTES

1. Hunter Commission, *Punjab Provincial Committee's Report*, pp. 393 and 569. Also *R.N.P.*, 1882, p. 420.
2. R. Zakaria, *Rise of Muslims in Indian Politics* (Bombay, 1970), p. 219.
3. Bickersteth to Westcott, 1881, C.M.D. (U.S.P.G.A.).
4. C.M.D., *Fifth Report*, 1882, p. 4.

5. Imdad Sabri, *Dilli Ke Yaadgar Hastian*, p. 110; *P. Educ. Report*, 1890–1, Ch. VII, p. 185.
6. *R.N.P.*, 1882, p. 719.
7. Letter by Allnutt, Occasional Papers, C.M.D., 1886, p. 3.
8. C.C.O., F. 238/Vol. III/1895; N.A.I., Home Public Progs., 11–12A/1899.
9. D.C.O., MI(10)/46–General.
10. Abdul Hai, *Safar Nama* (Delhi, 1894), p. 19.
11. D.C.O., F. 1/1868.
12. *Church Times* (London), 17 May 1912 (U.S.P.G.A.).
13. *R.N.P.*, 1898, p. 815.
14. *R.N.P.*, 1902, p. 215.
15. *R.N.P.*, 1902, p. 361.
16. *R.N.P.*, 1902, p. 118.
17. R. Zakaria, op. cit., p. 219.
18. N.A.I., Home Progs., 233–234A/April 1882.
19. *R.N.P.*, 1885, p. 871.
20. *P.H.P.*, 12A/Jan. 1887. The Gurwala family had acquired this garden in the sales of 1858.
21. *R.N.P.*, 1887, p. 592.
22. *Report*, C.M.D., 1897–98, p. 32.
23. *R.N.P.*, 1900, p. 453; Sri Ram Mathur, 'Waqa-e-Sri Ram', Vol. II, fols. 240–43.
24. F. F. Monk, *A History of St Stephen's College* (Calcutta, 1935), p. 95.
25. D.C.O., 8/1858.
26. *D.G.*, 22 Oct. 1883.
27. *R.N.P.*, 1886, p. 759.
28. Bulaqi Das (ed.), *Safir-e-Hind*; Mirza Khan (ed.), *Ashraf-ul-Akbar*; *R.N.P.*, 1885, p. 728.
29. *P.H.P.*, 12A/Jan. 1887.
30. Ibid.
31. C.C.O., F. 27/1886.
32. C.C.O., F. 30/1890–General.
33. *C.M.G.*, 9 Nov. 1886; Montgomery, *Life and Letters of Lefroy*, p. 107; *The Times*, 29 Nov. 1886, quoted in Zakaria, op. cit., p. 281.
34. Enclosure to Hunter Commission, *Report of Punjab Provincial Committee*, p. 445.
35. D.M.C. Progs., 19 April 1887, n.p.
36. *R.N.P.*, 1887, pp. 537 and 550.
37. C.C.O., F. 30/1890–General; D.M.C. Progs., 1890, n.p.
38. This practice was given up in the 1920s.
39. *R.N.P.*, 1885, p. 870.
40. *P. Mun. P.*, 2A/April 1890 and 31A/Jan. 1891.
41. *P.H.P.* (General), 23A/Feb. 1889.
42. C.C.O., F. 31, 49-E(3)/1898.
43. *C.M.G.*, 18 Feb. 1898.
44. Ibid., 15 Feb. 1898.
45. C.C.O., F. 31, 49-E(3)/1898.
46. *P.H.P.*, 473-493B/April 1898.

47. *R.N.P.*, 1899, p. 303.
48. C.C.O., F. 24/1906.
49. C.C.O., F. 88-A/1899.
50. *Delhi Mission News*, July 1897, p. 11.
51. Ibid., Jan. 1902, p. 55.
52. C.C.O., F. 112, Vol. I, S-2/1892.
53. *A.M.R.*, 1902–3, address to Lieutenant-Governor, n.p.
54. C.C.O., F. 12/1902.
55. Ibid. H. Tinker is wrong in stating that in 1908 'indirect taxes formed the whole of the municipal income in the Punjab' (op. cit., p. 75).
56. *R.N.P.*, 1902, p. 147.
57. Ibid., and C.C.O., F. 12/1902.
58. C. A. Bayly, *Local Roots of Indian Politics: Allahabad 1880–1920* (Oxford, 1973).
59. H. Tinker, op cit., p. 49.
60. C.C.O., F. 78/1896.
61. *P. Mun. P.*, 82A/Aug. 1892.
62. *P. Mun. P.*, 1A/July 1892.
63. C.C.O., F. 15, Vol. I/1903.
64. C.C.O., F. 78/1896.
65. H. T. S. Forrest, *The Indian Municipality* (Calcutta, 1909), p. 1.
66. C.C.O., Bundle 131/1903.
67. Ibid.
68. N.A.I. Home Poll., 36–43B/May 1908.
69. C.C.O., Bundle 131/1903.
70. *R.N.P.*, 1907, p. 524.
71. C.C.O., F. 15, Vol. I/1903.
72. N.A.I., Home (Munys.) Progs., 11–20A/May 1907.
73. C.C.O., Case B.32/1897.
74. D.M.C. Progs., 23 Aug. 1904.
75. C.C.O., Case B.32/1897.
76. D.C.O., M.I(10)/46-General.
77. N.A.I., Home Progs., 22–23A/July 1908.
78. D.M.C. Progs., 22 Nov. 1897.
79. *Punjab Boards and Committees Progs.*, 12–18A/Nov. 1907.
80. N.A.I., Home (Munys.) 8–9A/Jan. 1908.
81. *R.N.P.*, 1907, p. 224.
82. *Punjab Boards and Committees Progs.*, 1A/Jan. 1906.
83. Ibbetson to Minto, 30 Sep. 1907 (N.A.I., Minto Papers, Microfilm Reel 2, 101).
84. Minto to Punjab Chief Secy., 11 March 1906 (ibid.).
85. *R.N.P.*, 1906, p. 93.
86. *R.N.P.*, 1907, p. 506.
87. *P. Legis. Progs.*, 119A/1907.
88. N.A.I., Home Poll., 50–63A/Feb. 1908.
89. *R.N.P.*, 1907, p. 524.
90. *Punjab Boards and Committees Progs.*, 2A/Feb. 1910.
91. N.A.I., Home Poll., 40–49B/Oct. 1907.

92. Western, 'Confidential Memorandum on the Ideals and Outlook of the Cambridge Mission, 5 Feb. 1921' (U.S.P.G.A.).
93. Lefroy, 'The Indian Unrest', *Church Times*, 29 May 1908, press-cutting in U.S.P.G.A.
94. *R.N.P.*, 1906, p. 8; ibid., 1907, p. 149.
95. N.A.I., Home Poll., 49–58B/Sep. 1908.
96. *R.N.P.*, 1908, p. 395.
97. N.A.I., Home Poll., 115–124B/June 1909.
98. N.A.I., Home Poll., 105–112B/Feb. 1908.
99. *R.N.P.*, 1910, p. 609; N.A.I., Home Poll., 1–8B/Oct. 1910.
100. *R.N.P.*, 1910, p. 609.
101. N.A.I., Home Poll., 115–124B/June 1909.
102. Ibid., 1–8B/Oct. 1910.
103. *R.N.P.*, 1911, p. 766.
104. N.A.I., Home Poll., 108–114B/June 1909.

6

THE STRAINS OF URBAN EXPANSION
(1892-1912)

The swelling population of Delhi in the 1890s was a result of the city becoming the commercial capital of the Punjab. In 1911 it was to become the neighbour of the new political capital of British India. Both the commercial status which she achieved naturally, and the political greatness that was thrust upon her, sharpened social tensions and also put a very heavy strain on the resources and services provided by the local government. Underlying explosive issues like the house-tax controversy was the fact that the city was bursting at the seams.

The diffidence shown by the Municipality with regard to taxation was not because the city was poor. From the 1870s Delhi was becoming more prosperous, with a sharp interruption for three years as a result of the famine of 1877. 'After three years of pinching want, there has been a sudden return to prosperity. There has been a bumper harvest, and trade has been restored to its usual activity,' commented Smith, the Baptist missionary, in 1880. But, he added ruefully, because lean years brought him a bumper crop of converts, 'The poor have tended to rush into worldly callings to the neglect of [sc. the spiritual].'[1] Octroi receipts increased by 20 per cent between 1878 and 1881. But this was far from adequate for the drainage and waterworks schemes planned since 1869.

A lack of insight and a deliberate bias meant that the increasing mercantile prosperity of Delhi was not tapped for municipal revenue, though the Imperial and Provincial Governments benefited by levying an income-tax from 1886. Any innovations in local revenue had to be approved by the Provincial Government, which meant that 'self-government' in finances was very much circumscribed. The Punjab Government was concerned about the heavy incidence of octroi, and in 1877 the Government of India, echoing the Secretary of State, warned that octroi would be abolished if it became a duty on transit goods. The Punjab Government suggested that octroi be reduced and revenue raised from direct taxes. The examples of other provinces were cited—the tax on professions and trades in the North-Western Provinces, Bengal and Bombay, the 'compound' tax in Allahabad, the taxes on property, conservancy and vehicles in different provinces.

In Delhi, the incidence of taxation was no higher than in other big towns in the plains, and the exemption of wheat and piecegoods and, after 1886, of oilseeds, made Delhi's octroi schedule the shortest in the province. Before the Punjab Government's concern about octroi was expressed, the Municipality had considered levying octroi on piecegoods to raise revenue for the waterworks. This was strongly opposed by the Provincial Government, by local piecegoods merchants and by the Anjuman Islamia, who were all agreed that this would ruin Delhi's trade, as had happened at Amritsar and Farrukhabad.[2] The wholesale traders in grain, spices and tobacco also forecast ruin if octroi were levied. These objections carried weight with the Municipality, which was dominated by traders. Thus the unholy 'alliance' of British imperial trade interests and Indian merchants who dealt in British piecegoods and British tobacco scotched these suggestions. In 1888 octroi was increased on betel-leaf, which led, as predicted, to the wholesale market at Katra Baryan moving out to Ghaziabad, as earlier the metals *mandi* had moved out of Delhi when metals had been taxed. One generous gesture by the Municipality was to reject the proposal to tax fuel, which would hit the poorer classes, and accept a tax on *ghee* and sugar, which would be borne by the well-to-do. When this was levied in 1887 it was cavilled at by a local newspaper on the specious grounds that it would 'tell against trade, which has already declined, and against the poorer classes'[3] —an instance of how the fashionable arguments of this period were those which professed concern for trade and for the poorer sections. In 1887 this tax and some others were suggested, which would increase municipal revenue by a lakh annually. The largest part would come from an octroi duty on fruit and vegetables. This sum, Rs 35,000, was to be realized by a heavy duty of one anna on every rupee (contrast this with the very light tax of one anna on every box of merchandise proposed by the sub-committee that had recommended octroi on piecegoods and which had been vetoed). It was admitted that this would be a tax on 'a necessity of life' and it was argued that 'unless a necessity of life is included, it is impossible to raise any considerable income'.[4] The priorities were clear—trade was not to be injured, but taxes which would hit the poorer people were permissible.

After 1888, octroi was lifted from materials imported to be manufactured into goods for export. This was first done with regard to *kandla* (which was imported from a distance or from the hinterland for manufacture into gold wire) at the instance of the Provincial Government. Later, in 1895, this exemption was extended to all articles imported for manufacture, this time upon orders from the Government of India.[5] The case of *kandla* was a special one. The Municipality continued the tradition of the Mughals of charging a fee from *kandla* workers in order to protect their guild and to maintain a basic standard. The Punjab Government chose to declare this illegal (though both the workers and the Municipality were satisfied with it). The tax was re-levied under a different name. But the guild was split, and some members refused to pay the fee, saying it was illegal. 'Something like a panic pervaded the guild and the general impression was that the trade would be ruined and widespread distress would be the result.'[6]

In respect of direct taxation, the class-character of the Municipality was apparent. A house-tax had been mooted in 1877, and again in 1885. But the Commissioners made out that this tax would be difficult to collect. When direct taxation was introduced for the first time in 1887, it was from *tehbazari* and from a tax on draught animals and milch cattle. The object of the latter was described by Deputy Commissioner Clarke as 'entirely sanitary, and not the raising of an income for the Municipality'.[7] He wanted the tax to be levied only on cows kept within the walls, in order to induce the *gwalas* to move their cows out to healthier surroundings. In 1893 free plots were made available in the area beyond the wall between Delhi Gate and Turkman Gate for *gwalas* in the city. This satisfied the *gwalas* in Gali Shahtara and Kashmeri Gate who had pleaded poverty, by giving them the option to move to the free plots, and also would have made the city's milk supply more hygienic by shifting the cattle from the crowded city lanes. The nature of the taxes imposed in 1887-9 (in contrast to those proposed in 1877) is remarkable for having pressed hardest on the poorer sections. In Delhi, at any rate, the stricture of the Lieutenant-Governor in 1889 that the richest groups in the province were being too lightly taxed was well-deserved. 'No doubt the class which would be most affected by a tax on buildings and lands is that which naturally possesses most weight in Municipalities and from which the majority of the members of Municipal Committees is usually drawn.' He concluded with the hope that 'the good sense and public spirit of the members of Municipalities will prevail'.[8]

A third method of raising revenue, other than increasing octroi and levying direct taxes, was to float a loan. In 1876 the Municipality was offered a loan of ten lakhs by an individual in the city, but the interest it was prepared to pay was too low. The Municipality then turned to the Imperial and Provincial Governments, but they were chary of giving a loan unless the army could be shown to benefit directly. When Ripon was in Delhi in 1881, he aired his proposals for local self-government, and the Municipality hopefully asked him for a loan. They were disappointed when he replied by lecturing them on India's indebtedness. When the Punjab Government also turned down a similar request, the Commissioner of Delhi, MacNabb, urged that 'If it [sc. was] impossible to grant [sc. the loan] without an Act of Parliament or the Secretary of State's orders, such sanction should be applied for in the interests not only of Delhi but of all municipalities in the country.'[9] In 1889 the Provincial Government gave Delhi a loan under the provisions of the new Provincial Account Code.

The waterworks were begun when the loan was given, twenty years after the scheme had been projected, and twelve years after the Lahore waterworks scheme had been completed. This was proof, in the eyes of the people of Delhi, that Lahore was being given preferential treatment. Delhi Municipality had been the first one in the Punjab to plan a water supply project, but they had 'been completely outdistanced by their rivals at Lahore'.[10] When the project was sanctioned, Mrs Winter, the wife of the S.P.G. missionary, considered it something worth writing home about.[11] It was obviously a local event, not merely an administrative innovation.

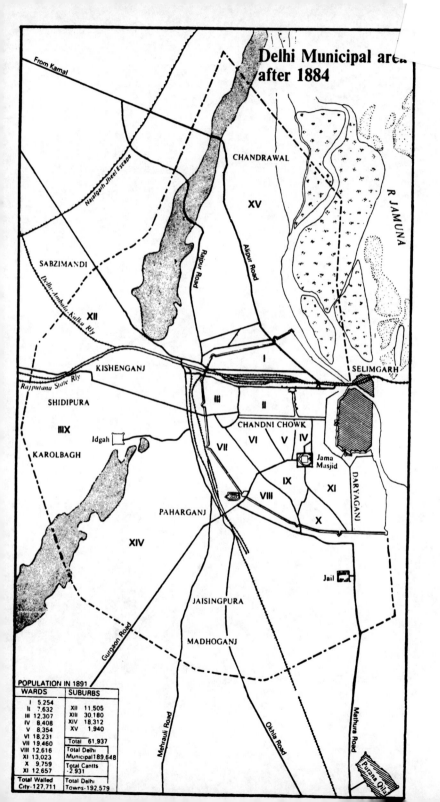

Delhi Municipal area after 1884

From Karnal

CHANDRAWAL

XV

R JAMUNA

Najafgarh Jheel Escape

Rajpur Road

Alipur Road

SABZIMANDI

Delhi-Ambala-Kalka Rly

XII

KISHENGANJ

SELIMGARH

Rajputana State Rly

SHIDIPURA

I

III

II

CHANDNI CHOWK

XIII

Idgah

VII

VI

V

IV

KAROLBAGH

Jama Masjid

IX

XI

DARYAGANJ

VIII

PAHARGANJ

X

XIV

Jail

JAISINGPURA

Gurgaon Road

MADHOGANJ

Mehrauli Road

Okhla Road

Mathura Road

Purana Qila

POPULATION IN 1891		
WARDS	**SUBURBS**	
I 5,254		
II 7,632	XII 11,505	
III 12,307	XIII 30,180	
IV 8,408	XIV 18,312	
V 8,354	XV 1,940	
VI 18,231	Total 61,937	
VII 19,460	Total Delhi Municipal 189,648	
VIII 12,616		
XI 13,023	Total Cantts 2,931	
X 9,759		
XI 12,657		
Total Walled City-127,711	**Total Delhi Towns-192,579**	

The water supply wells were located at Chandrawal, a village on the banks of the Jamuna. Its inhabitants were shifted out. The heavy cost, aggravated by the absence of any contribution from the Provincial Government, meant that the project was carried out in stages. The walled city was to be supplied first, followed by the western suburbs and then the Civil Lines—where the houses, spread out over a large area, unlike the crowded city, were adequately supplied with water from the canal. Shahjahanabad came first, because it included the Cantonment, and the project had originally been put forward as necessary for the health of the garrison. The Municipality got its own back on the superior Governments which had been so obstreperous when asked for aid, by charging the Fort and Daryaganj the same rates as private consumers. The military authorities fumed, but to no avail.

Many Hindus still preferred to use the Jamuna for bathing. One of the inhabitants was to write nostalgically that water flowing from pipes did not provide the same *raunaq* as the canal had done.[12] But many looked forward to the advantages of a supply of pure water, because the canal's supply to the city was becoming scanty and erratic. There were many applications for private connections, which gave the lie to the malicious statements of the military authorities that 'every native', even the potential 'rich consumers', would draw water from the free public standposts.[13] An incident of 1892 showed that the Indians in the Municipality were very much men of their class. They banned chamars from drawing water at the standposts. Commissioner Clarke made enquiries and found that the municipalities of Nagpur, Agra, Calcutta and Lahore practised no such discrimination; he persuaded the Municipality to revoke the resolution.[14]

The drainage and conservancy arrangements were linked with the water supply project and, therefore, though the blueprint was ready in 1881, work on these began only after the intramural water supply system was complete. But it had become clear that modern notions of drainage and conservancy would have to face general opposition, from the citizens and from the sweepers. The Municipality's attempt to take the conservancy arrangements into its own hands in 1876 was countered by a strike by the sweepers' guild. The officials had to admit defeat and allow the sweepers to retain their monopoly, and did not enrol them as paid servants of the Municipality. As early as 1879, well before the

11

local self-government scheme was spelt out, the Municipality had formed its first sub-committee, in charge of conservancy; by 1887 Delhi was spending more on conservancy than was Lahore or Amritsar. The sub-committee was commended by British officials for keeping clean the streets of the city, which were 'more frequented by Europeans, and wider and with more traffic than any other city in the Punjab'.[15] To an Indian inhabitant writing in 1886, Delhi's streets appeared not only clean, but aesthetically pleasing.[16] The *mohulla* sweepers went on strike again in 1889. But this time there was a difference. They were not supported by the inhabitants, who had begun to appeal frequently for municipal action against the sweepers. What gave the sweepers confidence this time was the fact that there was no bye-law under which they could be punished, and 'as education [sc. was] becoming more general and lawyers were plentiful' they were aware of this. The Municipality gave itself the responsibility for removing nuisances, but this bye-law was overruled by the Provincial Government as being illegal; they held that the onus should remain with house-owners.[17]

Just as the water supply scheme substituted purified river water for the traditional supply from the canal and the wells, the drainage scheme was planned to replace the Shahjahani drains, built for a limited population, by open drains. Local opinion, which included that of some members of the Municipality, was sceptical as to whether the proposed change would be an improvement. The details of the project illustrated a significant discrimination. The Fort and the area north of the railway line, which had a predominantly European population, were to be linked to a drain flowing out at Salimgarh. The rest of the city and the Daryaganj infantry barracks, which added up to a much larger proportion of the population, were to be served by a separate drain at Delhi Gate. 'No drainage from any native quarter will be allowed to enter Salimgarh channel.'[18] The same discrimination which dictated a *cordon sanitaire* between the 'native city' and the 'civil lines' was at work here. Since the scheme did not involve any extra taxation, as the waterworks had (and the second stage of the drainage works was to) there was no major protest against the drainage scheme in these years.

The apathy and occasional hostility encountered in connexion with conservancy were seen also with regard to vaccination. The

Indian municipal members were very reluctant to accept vaccination. The British Commissioner said in 1879 that compulsory vaccination was inadvisable, because the vaccinators, who were 'of the lower classes', might report those against whom they had a grudge. Among those who were known to be opposed to compulsory vaccination were Girdhar Lal, an elected municipal member, a pleader and member of a Hindu Reform Society, another person referred to as 'a nephew of a member of the Indian Council', Lala Sheo Sahai Mal, a co-opted member of the Municipality who was related to the Chunna Mal family, and some of the *rais* of Dharampura. They were very zealous in getting others' children vaccinated but helped their own families to escape the net. Some vaccinators were assaulted in one instance by an Indian Christian (which indicated that it was not just Hindus who opposed the measure). The *hakims* were hostile. The Punjabi Muslims were said to be the only group who accepted the innovation. Lala Sheo Sahai Mal became brave enough to accept vaccination later, and it was suggested that he be rewarded with a title. Some Hindu municipal commissioners warned against any official interference with the Seetla Devi temple in Gurgaon; if this were done, superstition would become religious feeling, and consequently more inflammable—they had learned the officials' language! Coming to terms with the popular prejudices, 'high caste' vaccinators were employed—one Syed and one Shahzada, a *kayasth* and a Brahman. In 1892 the Indian municipal members wanted the proposed compulsory vaccination to be limited to the northern wards (i.e. those north of the railway line with a largely European population) but in 1895 the other wards were also included.[19]

The Lieutenant-Governor shrugged off the burden of building a new dispensary by saying, 'If anywhere in the Punjab, then in Delhi subscriptions may be expected.' So, in 1884, Rs 70,000 was donated—Rs 24,000 by Rai Mela Ram of Lahore and the rest by local inhabitants. This was more than had been collected for the proposed Delhi College ('which the people were supposed to have nearest to their heart', the Commissioner could not refrain from gloating).[20] The Municipality and District authorities promised Rs 50,000 and a grant-in-aid was sanctioned. The Dufferin Hospital (as the new dispensary was called) was completed in 1892. It was located near Jama Masjid. The Municipality could not

agree on the question of the site. Nearly all the Indians wanted it
to be within the walls. 'One or two people of strong local influence' wanted a site beyond Lahore Gate. Smyth hoped for 'a large
hospital and one which would add to Delhi's public buildings an
enduring architectural ornament'.[21] The Jama Masjid site was
chosen because it was the cheapest. The year 1892, when the
Dufferin Hospital was completed, also saw the opening of the
S.P.G.'s *zenana* hospital in Chandni Chowk named after the late
Mrs Winter, who had spent most of her life in the missionary
cause. By 1895, it was three storeys high, and had over three
hundred patients. These hospitals touched only the fringe of
Delhi's needs. The *hakims* continued their practice, unperturbed
by any competition from the European hospitals.

In the lean years 1896-1900 the Arya Samaj, the two Christian
missions and private individuals took on the main burden of
famine relief. Despite objections by the Indian members to such
partisanship the Municipality gave a grant only to the S.P.G.
Hospital. In 1900 official relief was suspended except for 'respectable Muslims' (*sufed posh*) who, in the phrase of the officials,
'[were] a class of persons probably but seldom met with in any
other city—viz. those who cannot dig and for whom to beg is a
disgrace'. For the others little was done. 'It is difficult to persuade
the poor people that it would not be right for Government to
interfere in the market-rate of grain, to stop all export, and adopt
other artificial means as in the good old days of Akbar,' said the
missionaries sanctimoniously.

The Victoria Zenana Hospital, set up in 1901, was the tribute
of the Delhi millionaires (most notably Lala Ram Kishen Das)
to the Imperial Government. The Civil Surgeon hoped to attach
this to the Civil Hospital. Delhi, he said, was (unlike Lahore)
'very backward, and the word *Sarkar* [sc. was] still a name to
conjure with'; it lacked 'the facilities which exist in Lahore for
non-official control of a large hospital'.[22] But Ram Kishen Das had
the upper hand—he calmly threatened to withdraw his contribution unless the hospital was made *purdah-nashin* and independent
of the Civil Hospital. Mirza Hairat voiced Muslim opinion when
he hoped the Deputy Commissioner would take into account the
'wishes of the people', and locate the hospital in Lal Kuan, which
was convenient for Muslim women of the poorer sections. The
controversy took the form, as in the case of the Dufferin Hospital

earlier, of a debate on alternative sites. The Imperial Government objected to a site near the Jama Masjid, not on military grounds, but because it would mar the view of the Masjid and, as J. H. Marshall put it, be a 'memorial to the bad taste of those who allowed it to be set up'.[23] It was therefore built (in 1902) at a sufficient distance from the Masjid to ensure that this did not happen. Intended primarily for the *sufed posh* Muslim women of Delhi District, it attracted patients from as far off as Bikaner and Lahore, and came to serve the whole southern Punjab.[24] A separate ward was added for the families of the 'second-class Europeans'—the railway employees.

In the 1890s the number of Europeans in the city increased. No 'decent European' could go to the Civil Hospital, and the Municipality therefore suggested that a hospital be built in the Civil Lines, which would be financed by the Government and the railway companies since their personnel accounted for a majority of the Europeans in the city. By contrast to the Indians who had contributed so lavishly to the Zenana Hospital, the railway companies offered a niggardly Rs 200 a month as contribution, instead of the Rs 5,000 they had been asked for.[25] The scheme was therefore abandoned, as also that of an Infectious Diseases Hospital for Europeans. There was a case of a European victim of small-pox who had to be segregated by hiring a whole house. Less affluent Europeans went to the Civil Hospital. To some extent the needs of the Civil Lines population were met by the enlarged St Stephen's Hospital, which was shifted from Chandni Chowk to outside Mori Gate.

Another major venture was the expansion of the Tibbia College, founded in 1885. This was a centre for the medical educational system which Hakim Ajmal Khan, his father and his brother had been imparting. The Tibbia College Committee had as its president Thomas of the Baptist Mission, and as members Maulvi Zakaulla, Amba Prasad (the Jain secretary of the *pinjrapole* committee), Sri Kishen Das Gurwala (a prominent banker), Lala Sultan Singh (a rich industrialist) and the Nawab of Loharu. It passed a set of resolutions which reached the Viceroy's Council. These suggested that local governmental bodies be asked to aid *unani* and *ayurvedic* practitioners.[26] The Lieutenant-Governor was prepared to accept their suggestions. The cost of living had risen so much as to make some financial relief, by employing

Indian doctors on a part-time basis, very welcome. Thomas, a missionary who had lived many years in Delhi, said that the Government should not be regarded as being partisan, that it was 'essentially *swadeshi*', and that Indians should co-operate with it.

The pure water made available by the waterworks helped to reduce the death-rate and the incidence of typhoid, cholera and the 'Delhi boil'. But the swelling population and the increased density, the fall-off in the supply from wells and from the canal, the need to flush the new open drains in order to avert plague and to water the roads where increasing traffic threw up more and more dust, the needs of the new sewage farm, all made it imperative to secure more water, both of the potable and of the unfiltered variety. The consumption of water in 1904, with two thousand private connections, was more than double of what it had been in 1900.[27] By 1900 Delhi suffered because of the extension of the Western Jamuna Canal in different directions over the previous four years. The supply to the District was cut down to ten days per month, and even this was as a 'special consideration' because of the city gardens and the sugarcane fields in the District.[28] The wells were running dry, because they were supplied from the river, and the soil was acting like an overworked filter. When the water supply was reduced, the Civil Lines inhabitants used the Qudsia water-course for their domestic gardens. The waterworks were extended to cover the Civil Lines in 1911; the Delhi citizens saw this as one of the side-effects of the Durbar. The Deputy Commissioner confessed the difficulty he had when trying 'to impress on the Municipal Commissioners and through them on the citizens of Delhi that the extension of the waterworks and the increasing charges for water that the private consumer will in future be called upon to pay, are no mere incidents connected with, or attributable to the forthcoming Coronation Durbar, but that the expenditure is . . . inevitable whether the Durbar had taken place or not'.

The intramural drainage scheme was hampered by the lack of money, and by the obstreperous attitude of the people. Popular resistance took the form of improvising steps and platforms across the drains, and refusing to have houses connected with the new drains (often by the same individuals who had hastened to apply for private water connections).

The drainage project was further hastened in order to have it completed by the time of the Durbar, though on occasion the work was slowed down because the labourers preferred to move to the better-paid Durbar works. When it was completed, the officials claimed that it had transformed the unsightly Sadar Bazaar and Paharganj. The new drains were linked to the Bela, and this gave rise to some controversy. The officials wanted the Bela drained because they held that the chronic malaria in Delhi was caused by it. The Indian Commissioners, on the other hand, wanted to try to bring the river back to its original bank under the Fort wall, avowedly for sanitary reasons (though sentiment perhaps played an equal part—Sri Ram Mathur had written that the river had shown its displeasure in 1857 by moving away from the city wall).[29] They framed an appeal to the Lieutenant-Governor in 1897 to the effect that they wanted this engineering feat to be carried through. He scotched it on grounds of expense. In 1908 the then Lieutenant-Governor again urged on the Municipality the need to drain the Bela as a safeguard against malaria. The Municipality could not afford the expense; nevertheless, this was done for the Durbar, and the Badshahi Mela (translated unforgettably as 'Imperial People's Merry-making'[30]) was held there; there was an 'Imperial Darshan', with the Emperor and his wife, a twentieth-century 'Mughal' couple, looking on from the Red Fort's *jharokas*. Earlier, Curzon in one of his paranoid moments had wanted to install an elaborate Memorial to commemorate a commemoration—the 1903 Durbar. He wanted this structure to be on the river-front; the Lieutenant-Governor vetoed it, pointing out that the Bela was susceptible to flooding.[31]

Electricity, like the waterworks and the drainage scheme, came to Delhi in 1902 as a side-result of the Durbar. Fanshawe, discussing 'the subject of the introduction of electric lighting in the East[!]', dismissed it as an unnecessary extravagance. Using a cyclical argument, he said that in Delhi (unlike in Calcutta) business came to an end at dusk, and kerosene lighting was therefore adequate.[32] When electricity was introduced, a tramline network was also constructed. The trams first plied in the northern part of the walled city, then (in 1905) in Sabzi Mandi and Paharganj, and in 1907 to Sadar Bazaar and Ajmeri Gate. The sceptical Fanshawe was quick to point out that it was easier to reach Chandni Chowk by walking across Queen's Gardens than by taking a tram. The tramway was chiefly useful for linking the heart of the city to the suburbs, for travelling within the suburbs, and, for the side-line by which power was generated and supplied to the small-scale industries and factories. The result of the innovation which was most immediately obvious was a rise in the cost of maintaining roads. Their surface was cut by tracks, and this was aggravated by the damage done by *thelas*. The Municipality did not take sufficient warning from their engineer, who said gloomily in 1908, 'The *thelas* continue on their road-destroying careers with indifference to the fact that the Committee's income is not increasing in the same ratio as the commercial prosperity of the city, which results in putting more and more *thelas* on the road.'[33] In the early 1900s the traffic on Delhi roads was of a variety never seen before—the older carriages now competed with cycles, trams and even motor-cars. And as the number of motor-cars gradually increased, it became all the more important to provide good roads.

In providing the city with necessary facilities, the strain on the Municipality remained very great despite the help from private philanthropy. The Decentralization Commission was to criticize Punjab because 'the influence of departmentalism in converting the District Boards and Municipalities into mere paying agencies [sc. had] gone further . . . than in any other province'.[34] This was certainly true of Delhi, and the anomaly of the richest town in the province being unable to make local self-government meaningful because of its inadequate resources became increasingly obvious. The Provincial and Imperial Governments were reluctant to give grants because they could see that Delhi was 'the most lightly-taxed first-class municipality of the plains'. (The taxation per head in Delhi was Re 1–6–8, by contrast to Amritsar's Rs 2–1–4 and Lahore's Re 1–14–6.[35]) Curzon in a speech to the Municipality in 1899 praised it for its sense of knowing 'when to tax and when to spare'.[36] But to many inhabitants it appeared as if the municipal commissioners worked on the principle of taxing others and sparing themselves. The rich merchants, bankers and factory-owners paid income-tax but contributed little to local funds.[37] In 1899 the Municipality taxed them indirectly, by imposing a tax on carts and *thelas*. This was not done without a tussle. A newspaper report claimed that the tax was pushed through by the Deputy Commissioner in the face of strong opposition from the Indian members.[38] They were prepared to have public vehicles taxed, but not private. A year later, they were successful in reducing the rate of this tax, by resolving upon another—the house-tax. Even after this, the Municipality's resources remained inadequate for other services as long as it had to pay the police. Lahore was relieved of the police-charges early, but in Delhi this was not done, despite repeated requests, till after the transfer of the capital in 1911.

The increase of population which made the extension of municipal facilities so imperative was also seen in the pressure on the land. The encroachments on public land and roads, in the city and in the western suburbs, increased. But because land was still relatively cheap, the Government on occasion followed what was later realized to have been a short-sighted policy, of exchanging land for land—as when in 1877 the Fatehpuri Masjid was restored to the Muslims for worship, by exchanging for it four villages which were given to the heirs of Chunna Mal, who thus made a profit of 300 per cent (Chunna Mal had paid Rs 40,000 for the Masjid, and the four villages cost the government Rs 116,6,13).[39]

One remedy suggested both for overcrowding and for encroachments was that the land kept inviolate for reasons of military security be used for building. The Municipality often adopted an independent stand *vis-à-vis* the military authorities. In 1889 the Punjab Secretary asked the Municipality to specify in its building bye-laws the material of which buildings were being constructed, 'because the military needs information with regard to their influence on the defence capabilities of Delhi'. The Municipality took exception to this. All that was required for municipal purposes had been provided for, they stated tartly, 'and this committee will not introduce under the Municipal Act restrictions that are suggested by other than municipal considerations'.[40] But the military, in turn, was firm about retaining the clear radius around the Fort. The Dufferin Hospital was built on a site within the 500-yard limit, but the Cantonment did not permit a primary school to be built near the hospital. When the school was ultimately built in 1894, it was located in crowded Hauz Qazi.

In 1889 the Imperial Military Department complained that it was difficult to detect new building activity. 'In the crowded bazaar, it is impossible to find out such constructions till they reach a height above the adjoining buildings and even then it is sometimes impossible to catch sight of them.'[41] The Municipality also found it difficult to detect encroachments until they were far advanced. Girdhar Lal, an energetic member of the sub-committee concerned with the building bye-laws, wrote a memorandum which described the *modus operandi* of encroachers. A make-shift step was unobtrusively made into a *chabutra*: this in turn was protected by a wooden *saiban*, and then the *chabutra* was enclosed in the main building. Later a new *chabutra* was added and the whole process gone through 'till they render large and wide streets narrow enough for cart traffic'. To bribe the *jemadar* was easy, and often even the ward member connived with the offender. Rich and poor were equally guilty of violating the build-ing laws, just as they were all guilty of evading the conservancy regulations. In 1884 the Delhi Municipality sought and obtained exemption from the provisions of the Punjab Municipal Act relat-ing to the inspection of houses, and made their own bye-laws on the subject of building, but these were not very effective, because the discretion to take action lay with the ward member and the fines were very mild. Personal rivalries and animosities often dictated the degree of punishment.

Girdhar Lal suggested a frontage-tax on all projections, irres-pective of when they were constructed. This was to get round the dilemma the Municipality faced every time it tried to take penal action; when the defendant invariably took the matter to the civil courts, the latter always declared against the Munici-pality. This was seen notably in a classic case where it sought to prosecute for a notorious encroachment in Gali Batashan which occupied half the width of the street. The frontage-tax was vetoed by the Punjab Government, which regarded it as a tax on pro-perty[42]—another case of a municipal measure being frustrated in the name of abstract principles.

Robert Clarke, like Cracroft earlier, thought it very necessary to provide room for settlement just beyond the wall. In 1881 the Municipality made openings on either side of Lahore Gate, and wished to demolish Delhi Gate. The Commander-in-Chief ob-jected, though he admitted that the wall was no longer necessary from the military point of view; he wanted Kashmeri Gate and the adjacent walls to be preserved for historic reasons. Clarke suggested that Lahore Gate and the wall near it be demolished. This would link Sadar Bazaar with the main city, and also afford an outlet for the population within the walls. 'Building sites are not to be procured within the wall while the outer extremities are too far away for business purposes.' The Municipality approved his memorandum giving details of a residential suburb to be laid out on *nazul* land just beyond the canal outside the western wall. The Punjab Government approved the scheme, but refused to permit the destruction of the wall. The Indian members of the Municipality were at one with the Punjab and Imperial Governments on this, but their reasons were those of sentiment; the Europeans wanted demolition as desirable from a sanitary point of view. Clarke's plan to knock down the wall between Lahore and Ajmeri Gate and to use the money from the sale of the sites for the drainage works remained unfulfilled. So also his dream of a street from Chandni Chowk to Karol Bagh which 'would become a street without parallel in North India'.[43]

In 1892 the Municipality formally sanctioned the construction of a 'square' and the lease of building sites outside Lahore Gate. Between 1889 and 1892 the Indians' opposition to demolishing the wall was less strong. This may have happened because between 1889 and 1892 the construction of Delhi's first mills in Sadar Bazaar and Sabzi Mandi showed the rationale for linking Sadar Bazaar with Chandni Chowk. Of the sixteen members present at the general municipal meeting only three were reluctant to see Lahore Gate demolished, six wanted it removed when the *ganj* was built, and two, Sheikh Hafizullah and Posner, representing mercantile and industrial interests, wanted it removed at once. In 1892, the year this vote was taken, Deussen wrote: 'We went for a walk round the outskirts of the town, reverently admiring the lofty city walls, which... are in a good state of preservation.'[44] The Municipality decided that the land in the *ganj* would be sold by auction over the next ten years; in contrast to the casual policy of the 1870s, they were now aware that this area would appreciate in value, and that it would be in their interest not to sell it all at once. The plots in Clarkeganj were bought by prosperous mercantile families, some of whom were members of the Municipality.[45]

By 1900, when many shops, residences and factories were being built in Sadar Bazaar and Paharganj, the town was launched on the second stage of its railway history. In 1895, in anticipation of Delhi becoming the Charing Cross of north India, the Punjab railways department had asked the city authorities not to alienate

land within a radius of five miles of the Delhi station to any railway company without its sanction.[46] By 1906 it was commented
that the city had changed beyond recognition in the past twenty
years. The most noticeable change was that the fields beyond the
western wall had been in great part enclosed into plots by different railway companies. At a time when the army had come round
to agreeing that the city wall be partially demolished, a new and
more permanent obstruction was being set up by these railway
lines and yards. They followed the curve of the wall in most cases
and thus reinforced it as a barrier to planned expansion, though
not as a line of defence. This made the hypothetical line of
defence a wider arc, because the railway lines had to be protected.

When the East India Railway was built through Delhi in the
1860s, the Municipality and public opinion had had no say in the
details of its construction. But by 1900 the situation was different.
The Municipality was very vocal about the location of railway
yards, the alignment of railway lines, the construction of level
crossings, and the reservation of land for the companies. The
economic interests of a mercantile body like the Delhi Municipality were more closely involved in these issues than on other
matters calling for policy decisions. A major land transfer took
place when a plot south of Sadar Bazaar was given to the Agra-
Delhi Chord Railway and the Municipality insisted on a barrier
between the wall and the plot, so that the Circular Road would
not be broken. In 1905 when the Municipality wanted to demolish the stretch of wall between Kabul and Ajmeri Gates, which
constituted an obstacle to the extension of the city, they found
that the railway line was now a new barrier.[47] As a *quid pro quo*
for the land, the officials insisted that the railway authorities bear
the cost of three overbridges which had become essential because
of the curving route taken by the Agra Railway. These were at
Ajmeri Gate, for general traffic, and at Farashkhana, for the convenience of the Muslims whose funeral processions left the city
for the Mehndion Ka Mazhar from that point. ('I am continually
receiving representations from the Muslims on the subject of the
overbridge,' said the Municipal President in 1907.[48]) The third
was between the main railway station and the suburban station
outside Lahore Gate, a stretch which saw the heaviest traffic in
the city. 'The approaches to Delhi city from the north-west and
the west are hampered and cut up by level crossings to a degree

which has become exasperating,' wrote the Deputy Commissioner to the Railway Engineer. 'I think the public have every right to expect that the Railway management should try to reduce the nuisance.'[49] The first and third were done, but the Farashkhana bridge was shelved on grounds of expense and until such time as the Municipality itself built the road running south-west from the Gate. 'The Committee got road improvements at little cost by suggesting many things to the Railway authorities,' said the Municipal Secretary complacently.[50]

The barrier set up by the Agra Railway should have diverted the extension of the city in a southern direction. But the pattern of westward expansion continued. The practical reason for this was that the municipal properties lay in that area. The other reason was that 'expansion' meant in concrete terms the building of factories, for which the ideal location was near the railway station, and residences, which were built near the factories, not adjacent to the crowded dwellings of Delhi Gate. Therefore, beyond Delhi Gate, the south remained green, with the 'fields smiling with holly-hocks', as one Deputy Commissioner picturesquely saw it;[51] the city wall there was intact, and was unmarred by any 'rururban fringe'.

From 1908 the appearance of the city was transformed as a result of two major decisions, together with the appropriation of land by the railway companies. These were the decision to develop the western suburban area from Mithai Ka Pul to Jhandewalan,[52] and the shifting of the Cantonment to the Ridge. The project for planned expansion was mooted in 1905 by the Municipality, which suddenly woke up to the realization that there might well be further extravagant demands for land in the manner of the Agra Railway. 'The management of the new railways will cry for more room to the east of the lines, especially near the goods sheds, and the Municipality will be justified if it firmly objected to giving them any more land.' The army's concern to retain the wall was no longer tenable and the extramural railway lines now needed to be guarded. For this, the army would have to control the western Ridge. The Lieutenant-Governor personally approved the expansion scheme but said the Imperial army authorities were obstinately opposed to removing any part of the wall ('They have always rejected, and given no reasons') and that there were also 'suggestions that the citizens themselves might be in opposition'.[53] A few months later the Commissioner, Merk, urged the Municipality that the time had come 'for taking the question comprehensively and for preparing the outlines of a general scheme to provide for roads, streets and space for buildings, during the next thirty years, taking as the basis the rate of increase in the past five years ... The Municipal Committee may benefit a great deal by buying up plots which in thirty years will rise in value, the price of "betterment" going into the pockets of the Committee as has been the case with the London County Council.' As part of the scheme, the troops were to be shifted from Daryaganj to a site north of the Ridge. A wall was to be constructed alongside the dry bed of the canal outside the south-western wall; a bazaar and ornamental gardens would be built. The Marwari merchants agitating for more *katra* room would not be given hopes of Daryaganj or the Champs de Mars being made available to them and would be expected to establish their business on the new Qutb Road. It is commendable that these plans for Delhi should have been made at this time, three years before the first town-planning bill was framed in Britain.

The generalization that Indian municipalities, unlike British ones, were 'not owners of large landed properties'[54] was not true of Delhi. The awareness of the need to plan the city's extension led to the first major survey, in 1906–8, of the *nazul* properties. Following this, the Municipality proposed to appoint a Special Officer to draw up complete records and to settle outstanding disputes. Otherwise the Municipality and the Government stood to lose, as the limitation against the Government would end in 1917.[55] The Municipality also asked the Provincial Government to hand to it the five estates and the Bela forest plantation which remained with it, in the way the other *nazul* lands had been given to the Municipality in 1874. This was intended to compensate the Municipality for the lands from the Roshanara Gardens which it had given to the Rajasthan, the Delhi–Kalka and the East India Railways.

By 1908 the sprawl of the city was large enough for the Chaplain to put in a request for a conveyance allowance, because of the distance he had to cover—nearly six miles from the new Cantonment in Rajpura to the G.I.P. Railway quarters in Paharganj.[56] From 1900 more houses were built in the Civil Lines, which were inhabited by railway and factory personnel and, in some cases, by the Indian proprietors themselves. The Club gave up the Town Hall premises in 1898 and shifted to Ludlow Castle, thus increasing the isolation of the Europeans from the 'native city'. The new office for the Commissioner was built on a plot facing Ludlow Castle, and not, as earlier planned, as an appendage to the Castle, which was the old Residency, and was now sanctified as a 'historic building'.[57] (This status was ignored later and Ludlow Castle, like so much else in Delhi, fell prey to the bulldozer in the 1960s. The bus conductors still issue tickets for 'Ludlow Castle' but nothing of the building survives.) The Indian soldiers in Daryaganj were shifted to a new site north of the Ridge and south of the pre-1857 Cantonment; from 1910 the Ridge, which separated the civilian from the military area, was regularly afforested to make the area cooler. In 1908 the Deputy Commissioner said, apropos of the northern suburbs, that 'the sites now available on Government land are nearly exhausted and land has to be considered which a few years ago would have been thought unsuitable'. Therefore, when the army asked for the land near Chandrawal north of Metcalfe House for a new Cantonment bazaar, the Municipality refused to part with it. 'The land contains the only few building sites on government land remaining in the Civil Lines.'[58]

During the Durbars of 1903 and 1911, those extravaganzas when the Imperial Government cast its gigantic shadow over the local, a city momentarily came into existence adjacent to the living organism of Delhi. Electricity and tramways and railway lines transformed acres of fields into a settlement described as being the size of greater London in 1903 and as one many times larger in 1911. Hardinge wrote of the 'miraculous change' as a result of which 'where there were cornfields there is now a large railway station with ten platforms, two polo-grounds and sunken terraces. The King's Camp (covering 85 acres) was beautifully laid out with red roads, green lawns and roses brought from England.'[59] The Municipality benefited from the rent from *nazul* lands and from the sale of water and timber (when trees were wantonly cut down to clear avenues for processions of elephants). The roads constructed for the Durbar of 1877 had not been maintained. After the 1903 Durbar the Municipality agreed to maintain the roads which had been in existence earlier, but not the newly constructed ones.[60] The Cantonment was on the point of being moved from Daryaganj to the northern site (Rajpur, Timarpur and Hindu Rao's Estate) and, as in 1873, there was controversy as to whether the Municipality or the Cantonment Committee should maintain the Durbar roads that passed through the new Cantonment area. By this time the Municipality's commitments were so heavy and its resources relatively so meagre that there was justification for its irritation with the army, as with the railway authorities, for not rendering services in return for those of which they availed themselves.

In the early years of this century, the Delhi Municipality was grappling with problems created by the Imperial Government in three respects—the railway expansion, the army's needs, and the exigencies of two Durbars within a short period of time. These were also difficult years for the Municipality in another respect— measures of public health and environmental improvement were being put through at a far more rapid pace than earlier, but the revenues were inadequate for these. Yet another Imperial exigency—the 'bold stroke of statesmanship'[61] for which Hardinge modestly took full credit—was to impose further strains on municipal services.

John Lawrence and Charles Trevelyan had suggested, some fifty years previously, that Delhi be made the capital of British India.[62] In the 1860s, such a move would not have necessitated the transfer of the massive bureaucratic apparatus which had been built up by now, and would not have aroused the strong feelings it was to do in 1911. Other capital cities had been built (Versailles, Washington, Canberra), but there was a great difference between constructing a capital for a politically integrated, independent and small country and building one for a large colonial empire, at a time of political crisis. Once the bureaucratic and legislative machinery was moved to Delhi, this was bound to be followed by an influx of the political pressure groups which had hitherto been active in Bengal, the United Provinces and Punjab, although one of the motives for the transfer of the capital had been to escape their influence. The Delhi area had been the site of many earlier towns, but these had not been built alongside a densely populated urban area with a sense of community and a high level of commercial development. For Delhi, the social and political implications of the transfer, apart from the financial and engineering

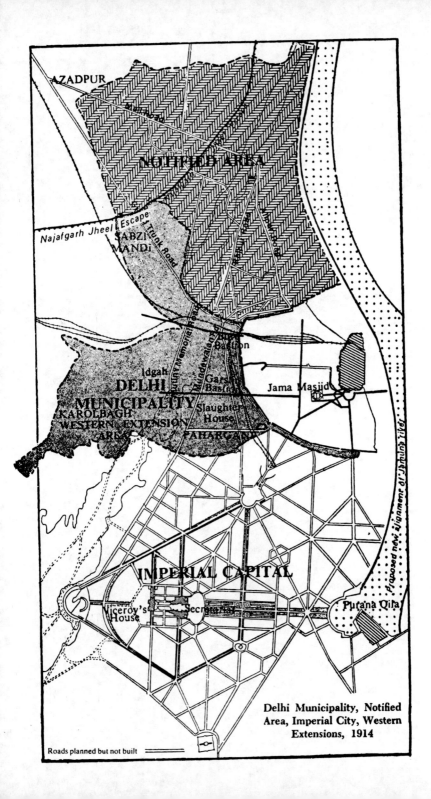

Delhi Municipality, Notified
Area, Imperial City, Western
Extensions, 1914

requirements, were likely to be very great. It would have been convenient if the Imperial Government had worked out the details of the size, location and administration of the proposed capital before announcing the decision of the transfer. There was much criticism of the proposal to shift the capital, and of the extravagances that went with it. The Bengal Chamber of Commerce suggested that Delhi be made a ceremonial capital, with Calcutta being retained as the seat of the legislature (which was exactly what the Government was anxious to avoid!).[63] If they were chafing because Calcutta's commerce would suffer, the equally vehement protest of the Governor of Punjab, Louis Dane, was a *cri de coeur* at losing Delhi District, 'a case absolutely unparalleled'. (Craddock described him maliciously as 'a lioness deprived of one of her whelps'.[64]) Like the Chamber of Commerce, he thought the Imperial Government should be satisfied with 'only such an area as would have sufficed for the dignity and administrative needs of the new capital'. But the Government made it clear that, apart from the areas specifically intended for the new city and the Cantonment, a large part of Delhi Province would be 'acquired' as a reserve. This was advisable because it was difficult to predict the demographic size of the new city. Prompt action was necessary because land values started to soar as soon as the decision about the transfer was known.

The Delhi Enclave (later called Province[65]) was 1,290 sq. miles (contrast Washington's 70 sq. miles). It included Delhi District and part of the territory of the United Provinces across the Jamuna. Craddock wanted to acquire Delhi *tehsil* and Mehrauli *thana*. 'It is clearly necessary to attach to old Delhi and to the new Capital certain environs to be administered from the headquarters at Delhi, in order that the population having the longest and closest connection with the Capital may be under the same jurisdiction as the dwellers within the actual circumference of old and new Delhi . . . It will be appreciated by the people living in the neighbourhood whose associations with Delhi are close and ancient but will also conduce to convenient and efficient administration.'[66] It would be reasonable to assume that the latter consideration weighed with him more than the former. Syed Ali Imam suggested that a strip of territory across the Jamuna be also acquired; he drew the moral from Calcutta where the smoke nuisance would have been less acute had the growth of Howrah been controlled. Looking back this appears to have been a sensible proposal. The Town Planning Committee recommended the acquisition of a large area to provide for the extension of the existing city and the Civil Lines, sanitary measures to benefit both Delhi and the capital, and 'firm control' over building activity in the environs of New Delhi.[67]

It was assumed that the new capital would be built alongside the Civil Lines. This was why the King, during the 1911 Durbar, laid the foundation stones within the precincts of the Durbar Camp, north-west of Kashmeri Gate. But the Town Planning Committee, headed by Lytton's son-in-law, Edwin Lutyens, was given complete freedom as to the choice of site. 'The stones laid by His Majesty would be treated as commemorating a great change, not to tie them to any locality. The important thing was that the new site must be Delhi—i.e. an area in close physical and general association with the present city of Delhi and the Delhis of the past.'[68] The northern site, including the Ridge and the Civil Lines, 'identified with and consecrated to the British Raj', appeared attractive. But there were many disadvantages in this site. The Durbar area was 'flat and uninteresting' and unhealthy, and liable to flooding. Sabzi Mandi was a very good site, but to acquire it meant destroying at great cost a half-square mile area covered with factories and at the risk of antagonizing the mill owners. Similarly, to acquire the Civil Lines would be expensive and would mean dislocating the whole European population, most of them businessmen (thus furnishing another grievance to the commercial interests in Calcutta). Bradford Leslie made out such a good case for the northern site that the Town Planning Committee, which preferred a southern location, had to go through the matter again, and work out a second Report. 'The battle of the sites is becoming positively bloody,' said Fleetwood Wilson. 'Angry men, hysterical women, and furious civilians are taking part in the fray.'[69]

The Town Planning Committee was adamant that the new city be south of Shahjahanabad.[70] Only there (or across the river) was it possible to secure ten square miles for the city and fifteen square miles for the new Cantonment. The site around the village of Raisina was suitable for reasons of health, for its proximity to the river, for its undulating land and the many sites of archaeological interest. It was near the area chosen for the Cantonment (at

Naraina), the cost of land was low and there were no 'business interests' who would have to be displaced. Hardinge was appalled by the extravagant plans, and urged Malcolm Hailey to investigate the possibilities of a smaller site in the north, but eventually the southern site was selected.[71]

There was something pathetic in the escapism of the officials and town-planners. Thus had Shahjahan built, for a doomed empire. The town-planners wanted 'the main features of the new city [sc. to be] as interesting, after centuries, as the older buildings in the neighbourhood area'. Even to the officials, the planning of the new city as an extravaganza in classical architecture was an attempt to compensate for the dismal political front. Hardinge could not rid himself of the conviction that 'if we allow the Town Planners to have their own way, they will make our city look ridiculous',[72] but others, like Harcourt Butler, thought it 'of the utmost imperial importance that [the financing of New Delhi] should be done on a big scale; something which will impress the Indians with our determination to stay here'.[73] Patrick Geddes, who visited Delhi in November 1914, sympathized with the town-planners, whose schemes were frustrated by 'the callous, contemptuous city bureaucrats', who were not 'open-minded'.[74]

One area of Delhi, Paharganj, was to be incorporated in the capital, since the new railway station was to be built there. But Lutyens and Baker wanted the earlier Delhis to be integrated into the layout of the city, with the architectural showpieces highlighted. A long processional avenue was planned from the Fort, through Delhi Gate, past a park and a boulevard with the houses of Indian princes lining both sides. Another was to cut through the side of the Jama Masjid from the proposed King Edward Memorial Park, and bear south-westward to the new railway station, whence another road was to lead to Kashmeri Gate. In 1913 when the Jama Masjid Committee asked to be given the Sunehri Masjid (south-west of the Fort), this was turned down because it might have 'hamper[ed] the plans under consideration to improve the City Central Avenue planned from the Fort to the new Capital'.[75] That these roads were never built (because the cost of the capital itself was far more than had been anticipated) does not reduce their interest-value. If they had materialized, there might have been a closer integration between the two cities than did occur; there might not have occurred either the tragic metamorphosis of the 'walled city' after 1947, when it became an inward-looking little world hemmed in by the galloping urbanization all round, or the thoughtless and unnecessarily hasty efforts of technocrats to 'decongest' (and dehumanize) this area in 1976.

At the same time, Lutyens and Baker felt that 'the fact that half the population of the town live outside the walls in irregularly developed suburbs made the work of co-ordinating new Delhi in balanced perspective with the present city a hard task'.[76] The disadvantages inherent in the unplanned growth of Delhi were now glaringly evident. The debate was as to whether these defects were to be remedied by drastic town-planning measures or by improvements only in those limited areas where the existing city impinged on the new. This led to discussion about the degree of centralized control needed, and its financial implications. It also brought in, implicitly and sometimes explicitly, value judgements of a racialist nature. All the participants, whether diehards (like Craddock and L. C. Porter) or possessed of some concern for the existing city (like Montmorency, a pupil and friend of C. F. Andrews), agreed that centralization would be more effective than extended self-government. Patrick Geddes is known to have written a paper about the problems of building a new city adjacent to an older one.

In England, Geddes' philosophy and the incentive provided by the passage of the Town-Planning Act of 1909 had generated a concern about planning the development of towns. Improvement Trusts were projected for Bombay in 1897 and for Calcutta in 1911, and Bombay acquired a Town-Planning Act in 1915. Porter had suggested a similar measure for Delhi in 1912. He saw this as being cheaper than the Government having to acquire land outright. A development tax would be levied on those who would benefit by the appreciation in the value of their property when the Government developed adjacent areas. Town development would be controlled by a Council with representatives of the Government, the Municipality, and landowners. 'I doubt,' said Porter, 'whether there will ever be an efficient administration in a big native city without an aristocratic officer, with a health officer and engineer as subordinates and a purely advisory council on which all interests would be represented, and not only the *banya* and landlord.'[77] Earlier, in discussions on 'self-government', the official concern had been to balance Muslims and Hindus; now in discussions on administration the concern was to balance the popular element with the 'aristocratic' British official one.

Hailey's aide, Montmorency, approved of Porter's suggestions for stricter building regulations.[78] But he thought the proposed redistribution of plots would not be acceptable to the Rajput and Jat market-gardeners and landowners living near Delhi. He also thought that acquisition and regulation would be preferable to drawing up building regulations for the suburban areas. He emphasized that the existing urban complex should not be neglected. 'We cannot afford the complaint that because of arrangements for the Capital the legitimate commercial expansion of Delhi has been checked. We must reserve land for the expansion of the present city of Delhi and fix its limits; beyond those limits we must have an open space to separate the Capital from the present city ... Delhi city must continue to flourish as a trade centre and a distributing centre for luxuries and necessities to an affluent agricultural neighbourhood and we should allow for an increase every decade of at least 25,000 people.' The possible areas for expansion were limited. Land was cheap east of the river but this would necessitate an expensive bridge. Ribbon development along the Grand Trunk Road to the north-west would mean a long and narrow settlement, too far from the heart of the city, on expensive garden-land. Both this and the possible expansion north of the Civil Lines into the 'Durbar' area would inconvenience the Civil Lines inhabitants. In the first case a road would have to be built skirting the narrow settlement, in the second 'a large Indian settlement ... would endanger the purity of the water-supply'. Extension southward from Paharganj would mean that the imperial city would be pushed further south. The remaining areas where the city could expand were those immediately to the south and west of Delhi Gate.

The combined fear of the old town encroaching on and spoiling the symmetry of the new, and of the 'Indian town' (the term now used for Delhi city, with a patently racialist overtone) polluting the imperial one led to the first serious attempt at long-term town-planning for Delhi's urban area. Good roads between the Civil Lines and Raisina were regarded as necessary. The settled areas near these roads should not be ugly and congested; therefore room had to be provided for expansion. It was these imperial considera-

tions that led the Government to take up the suggestions Cracroft
had made forty years earlier for utilizing the *nazul* lands intelli-
gently. Of the total of 1,545 acres that the Government decided
to acquire in 1913, 265 acres were *nazul* and thus belonged to the
Government already. But the officials were anxious to make it
appear that their solicitude was not merely on account of the
imperial areas. Even Hailey exerted himself to write unsigned
articles in the *Times of India* in which he argued that New Delhi
should not be dissociated from Delhi. 'The space between the
[sc. new] Railway station and the city wall will form the site of
a new suburb, which should have great commercial possibilities
and serve moreover as an admirable link between the old and the
new cities.'[79]

Though Geddes' own report was not printed, two reports made
by his colleague H. V. Lanchester are extant.[80] These aimed at
integrating New Delhi with the existing city. They detailed
schemes to accommodate those displaced by the acquisitions for
the capital and possible immigrants. The region west and south-
west of Sadar Bazaar, near Karolbagh, was selected; public buildings, places of worship, bazaars, residences and quarters for
'poorer classes' would be provided. The site (later to be called the
Western Extension Area) was approved by the Town Planning
Committee and by Indian and European traders in Delhi. Two
points were particularly 'dear to Lanchester's heart, and showed
the affinity of his thinking with that of Geddes. One was that
there should be an avenue from this area to the Jama Masjid (because if the new railway station were to be located in Ruhela
Serai, this area became important, for 'the effect of a city so
largely depended on the character of the route by which it is first
approached'); another avenue was to lead from the Jama Masjid
to the Bela near the Fort, which was to be developed as a park,
with a river-drive and playing-fields (this was done since, in the
1970s). The other point he stressed was that the architecture in
this area should be 'in the Indian vernacular style' (which he
defined as early Muslim, and not Mughal or European) for 'the
European manner would destroy the harmonious effect of the city
as a whole'. Skilled craftsmen would be encouraged to migrate to
Delhi, since 'this vernacular is less markedly developed in Delhi
than in many other Indian cities'. The Western Extension Area,
which began to be built after 1926, was to bear the mark of earlier

planning in the orderly alignment of its roads, but the proposals to regulate the style of architecture were not implemented.

NOTES

1. Smith to Underhill, 28 April 1880, Box IN/42, B.M.S.A.
2. *P.H.P.*, 11A/Dec. 1877; *R.N.P.*, 1877, p. 546.
3. *R.N.P.*, 1887, p. 551.
4. *P. Mun. P.*, 10A/Jan. 1889.
5. Ibid., 1A/May 1889 and ibid., 17–22A/Feb. 1895.
6. E. Burdon, *Monograph on Wire and Tinsel Industry in Punjab* (Lahore, 1909), p. 29. Also *A.M.R.*, 1881–82, p. 7.
7. *P. Mun. P.*, 10A/Jan. 1889.
8. Ibid., 13–14A/March 1889.
9. Ibid., 8A/April 1885.
10. *P.H.P.*, 19A/April 1878.
11. Mrs Winter to Miss Bullock, 13 March 1881 (Women's Letters from India, MSS., U.S.P.G.A.).
12. Sri Ram Mathur, op. cit., Vol. II, p. 95.
13. *P. Mun. P.*, Aug. 1890–1, 8A.
14. D.M.C. Progs., 19 Aug. 1892, n.p., and ibid., 20 Feb. 1893, n.p.
15. *A.M.R.*, 1879–80, p. 10.
16. Sri Ram Mathur, op. cit., Vol. I, p. 19.
17. *P. Mun. P.*, 3A/March 1889 and ibid., 11A/June 1889.
18. C.C.O., F. 610, Vols. I and II/Aug. 1880.
19. *P.H.P.*, Appendix/Dec. 1879; ibid., 1A/July 1884; ibid., 3A/Dec. 1884.
20. *P.H.P.*, 9–10A/Nov. 1884.
21. *P.H.P.*, 3A/June 1885.
22. C.C.O., F. 385–I/General/Q/1901.
23. P. Home (Mil.) Progs., 1A/July 1903.
24. C.C.O., F. 385–II/General/Q/1907.
25. C.C.O., Bundle 173/1907.
26. *P. Med. and San. Progs.*, 28–30A/May 1907.
27. C.C.O., F. 127, 47 (1)/1904.
28. C.C.O., F. 128, 50–B(5)/1889.
29. Sri Ram Mathur, op. cit., Vol. II, p. 96.
30. I.O.R., Hailey Papers, MSS. Eur. D. 659, F. 7.
31. N.A.I., Minto Papers, Reel 4, No. 80.
32. *P. Mun. P.*, 53A/July 1902.
33. *A.M.R.*, 1908–9, Appendix.
34. N.A.I., Minto Papers, Reel 2, W. S. Meyer to Minto.
35. *P. Mun. Review*, 1896–7, in *P. Mun. P.*, 10A/Feb. 1898.
36. Curzon, *Speeches*, Vol. I (Calcutta, 1900), p. 132.
37. 4,000 people in Delhi city (i.e. one in fifty of the total population)

paid income-tax, since their income exceeded Rs 50 p.m. (D.D.R., Bundle 51).

38. *R.N.P.*, 1899, p. 396.
39. C.C.O., F. 196/1876–8.
40. *P.H.P.*, 33A/Nov. 1889, 2A/March 1890.
41. *P.H.P.*, 15A/June 1889.
42. *P.H.P.*, 57A and Appendix/March 1893.
43. *P. Mun. P.*, 4–30A/Aug. 1891 and N.A.I., Home Progs., 10B/Nov. 1881.
44. Paul Deussen, *My Indian Reminiscences* (trans. A. King, London, 1893), p. 116.
45. D.M.C. Progs., 6 Dec. 1897.
46. N.A.I., Railways, R.C., 227–229B/March 1908.
47. C.C.O., F. 24/1906–7.
48. N.A.I., Railways, R.C., General 7809/1/1909 and ibid., General 4768/13/1909.
49. N.A.I., Railway Board, R.C., 494/1905.
50. *A.M.R.*, 1908–9, Appendix.
51. C.C.O., F. 12/L.F./1904.
52. C.C.O., F. 24/L.F./1906–7.
53. C.C.O., Home Confidential/L.F., I, 24/1906 and 1907.
54. H. T. S. Forrest, *The Indian Municipality* (Calcutta, 1909), p. 9.
55. C.C.O., Vol. I, L.F. (N)/F. 13/I/1906.
56. *P.H.P.*, 4A/Feb. 1908.
57. *P.H.P.*, 1903.
58. C.C.O., 571, General 'C'/1906.
59. Hardinge, *My Indian Years* (London, 1948), p. 42.
60. C.C.O., 18/1904.
61. Hardinge, op. cit., p. 37.
62. Ibid., p. 49.
63. *Times of India*, 2 March 1914.
64. N.A.I., Home (Delhi), 38–41A/July 1912.
65. Syed Ali Imam, 'The Indian Legislature is not familiar with the term "Enclave"'; N.A.I., Home (Delhi), Deposit No. I, Appendix 'O', Feb. 1913.
66. N.A.I., Home Progs., 38–41A, KW/July 1912.
67. *Final Report of Town Planning Committee* (P.P. 1913, Cmd. 6889), p. 7.
68. *First Report of Town Planning Committee* (P.P. 1913, Cmd. 6885), p. 1.
69. B. Leslie, 'Delhi, the Metropolis of India', *Journal of Royal Society of Arts*, Vol. 61, 1912.
70. Nethercote, the Government Irrigation Engineer, put the case succinctly: 'Why can't you have the northern site? Because dam[n] it you can't. Why must you have the southern site? Because blast it you must.' *Indian State Railways Magazine*, IV, 1930–1, Special Issue on Delhi, pp. 362–450.
71. Hardinge to Malcolm Hailey, 12 Feb. 1913 (I.O.R., G. F. Wilson Papers, fols. 96–101).
72. Hardinge to Hailey, 28 July 1913 (ibid.).
73. Butler to Mayer, 17 Feb. 1914 (I.O.R., Butler Papers, fols. 18–20).

74. P. Mairet, *Pioneer of Sociology: The Life and Letters of Patrick Geddes* (London, 1957), p. 161.

75. C.C.O., F. 658/Home/1913.

76. *First Report of Town Planning Committee*, p. 1.

77. N.A.I., Home (Delhi) Progs., Deposit No. I/Feb. 1913.

78. Ibid., 52A, KW/May 1912.

79. *Times of India*, 6 May 1914; also Hailey Papers, fols. 172–9 and fols. 213–20.

80. C.C.O., Home, F. 124B/Nov. 1915.

7

CITY, PROVINCE, AND NATION
(1911-31)

Shahjahanabad had become 'Dehli'; that had been distorted into
Delhi;* and after 1912 it was called Old Delhi.[1] And it seemed to
be in the fitness of things 'that the question of improvements
[was] taken up in earnest', in order 'that the Imperial Capital
[might] not be disfigured by a blot in the shape of old Delhi'.[2]
'Improvements' had been given high priority in the 1860s to make
Delhi a safe place for the soldiers; it was now again being given
priority, to make Delhi a safe neighbour for the capital.

'When the call of December 1911 came,' said Beadon, slipping
into the mystical language sometimes used by participants in an
unpopular despotism, 'the [sc. Municipal] committee was found
to be unready.'[3] But Malcolm Hailey was more charitable. He
congratulated Delhi Municipality for making 'much progress in
facing the problem of adapting the machinery and methods of a
provincial town to the complex needs of the capital of India'.[4]
A different note was struck by Montmorency, Hailey's aide, who
was a friend of C. F. Andrews. He later became Deputy Commissioner, when his bird's-eye view gave way to a worm's-eye view.
'You cannot expect the city to bear all the expenses of the improved administration . . . for the demand is not the demand of
the people but of the Government,' he said, while making out a
case for more aid from Government to the Municipality.[5] In 1914
the Municipality was informed that no more Imperial grants
would be given, because municipal finances were bound to increase

* I have not been able to pinpoint how and when 'Dehli' (which is the
more correct approximation to the Hindustani spelling) became 'Delhi'. It
must have been some time in the 1860s, but even as late as 1881 Lefroy
wrote home that 'Dehli' or 'Dilli' were permissible, but that 'Delhi' was
definitely wrong. Malcolm Hailey echoed this in 1913, in a letter to Har-

with the rising volume of trade after the capital was shifted. But expenditure galloped ahead of revenues. Municipal taxation, increased a few years earlier, could hardly be raised again. Whatever extra taxation was now levied fell on the lower classes, as had happened earlier. In 1914 the wheel tax was enhanced, and the protest by the *thelawalas* of Idgah was ignored.[6] In 1916 the buffalo tax was raised to a steep Rs 5 per month, to induce the *gwalas* to move out beyond the Jamuna. There were protests from impoverished *gwalas* in Sabzi Mandi and from the militant leather merchants of Sadar Bazaar. The latter, in language suggesting that they had been helped by the Vakil-e-Qaum-Punjabian, complained that the tax was illegal and onerous, and that the Commissioners had not studied 'the minds of the people or their electors'. 'The ignorant public may be led to believe that the Municipality intends to grant favours on [*sic*] the Hindus by exempting cows from the operation of this hard rule.'[7] The Municipality's methods of raising revenue did not, therefore, change as a result of the changes of 1912. In contrast, Calcutta and Bombay municipalities were able to carry through major reforms by deficit financing and by raising large loans.[8]

The electoral rules of the Municipality were revised upwards

---

dinge which is worth quoting. 'The correct spelling of the name "Delhi" has always been a matter of controversy... "Delhi" is certainly wrong. But what are we to substitute? "Dehli" or "Dihli" is a little more correct because it carries us a little further back; but the purist—and certainly such Hindus as took an interest in the matter—would not be satisfied till we had gone right back to "Dilli" or "Dhili". I myself am not in favour of making a change. As for the suggestion that the question possesses any political importance, there is so far no evidence to prove it. The use of... "Indian" and "native" stood on an entirely different basis. Indians did actually resent the use. of the word "native"... They have never to my knowledge expressed any such sentiments on the subject of the spelling of "Delhi". It is a fair working rule in politics that no injury exists till it finds expression. Secondly the change would probably involve us in a controversy. The Mohammedans would like "Dehli". The Hindus would certainly appeal for "Dilli". You will remember the long controversy which took place over the inclusion of Hindu letters in the Rupee.

'We have misliterated a great number of names in India, just as we have misliterated most of the names of continental cities. But there comes a stage when the misliteration becomes sanctified by usage. I think that Delhi has now reached that stage.' (Hailey to Viceroy's Secretary, 25 March 1913.)

in 1914.[9] The voter now needed to be the occupier or owner of premises within his ward rated at a house-tax of at least Rs 1–8 as. per annum. Candidates for election had to be owners or occupiers of premises valued at Rs 13–2 as. per annum for house-tax, or who had paid Rs 35 per annum in income-tax for the past three years.

After 1912, there was much discussion of how Delhi should be 'administered'. Craddock thought the Cantonment Code a suitable model because it gave 'many powers which are not given by the various Municipal Acts'.[10] This would mean government by a committee consisting of the Chief Commisioner and various officials; 'the best members of the present Municipal Committee could find seats on it by nomination'. 'In the hands of capable officials familiar with the people and with the administration of the town the provisions of the Code could be worked out without undue rigour.' His special reason for favouring the Code was that it incorporated 'the most recent and wide experience of the sanitary management of cantonments'. He proposed that, after the Municipality was superseded, municipal revenues would be replaced by 'the funds of old Delhi and its suburbs'. Craddock was confident that it would be easier to effect 'improvements' because 'in the case of Delhi we [sc. shall not be] hampered by the difficulties of persuading the Municipalities or persuading the Imperial Government to assist with sanitary grants'. Louis Dane, the Governor of Punjab, agreed about the need for speedy reform, but said that these could be carried through by the Provincial (i.e. Punjab) Government as effectively as by the Imperial Government, and that less disruption would be caused if Delhi were retained in Punjab.[11]

The Chief Commissioner's role in the government of Delhi city was to be considerable, because the Province was an Imperial enclave and also because his residence was in Delhi, whereas earlier the Lieutenant-Governor had been more remote, in Lahore. The Cantonment Act was not extended to Delhi, as Craddock had wanted, but the degree of effective self-government was considerably reduced. Delhi Municipality's territory and authority were truncated, and it came to be sandwiched between two 'Imperial' areas. It was shorn of the Civil Lines, which, with the addition of five hundred acres to the north, was formed into a Notified Area Committee. From 1912 to 1922 (i.e. until New Delhi was partly built) this area was maintained as a Temporary Capital. A Vice-regal Lodge was built north of the Ridge (later to become the offices of Delhi University), and a Secretariat on Alipur Road. The Commander-in-Chief's offices further south on Alipur Road are still in use today, though they were intended as a makeshift structure to be demolished by 1930. They were sold to Indraprastha College in 1932, and the only evidence of their earlier life is the horse-trough outside the wall.

The Notified Area was initially under a tripartite jurisdiction—of the Municipality, the Cantonment and the Temporary Works Directorate (the last was dissolved in March 1913). But this did not work well. 'The annual presence of the Government of India in the Civil Station will necessitate a higher standard of administration than was hitherto required, and divided authority will militate against this . . . The Sanitary Staff of the Director, Temporary Works, had no statutory powers . . . the Municipality is chary of incurring expenditure in the Civil Station which contributes little to its revenues. The Cantonment does not have the funds for the necessary improvements in the area under its management.' Therefore it gave place to a Notified Area Committee—'a greatly simplified form of Municipality'.[12] This Committee had only five members—the President (a civil servant, Indian or European), the Military Chief, the Civil Surgeon, a representative of the (largely European) Punjab Chamber of Commerce, and an Indian member. The Indian landlords of the Civil Lines (over thirty in number) pressed for an elected representative. Some demanded as many as five representatives. Hailey countered by saying that if there were elected members, there should be one to represent the tenants as well as one for the landlords. The landlords did not persist with their agitation. Though they did not count for much in the Notified Area Committee, they continued to hold positions in the Municipality.

Both the Municipality and the Notified Area received Imperial grants. Not only did the Notified Area get the lion's share, but it also exploited the Municipality. The financial setttlement as between the Municipality and the Notified Area Committee was, as Hailey admitted, 'a liberal one'. The Committee received a fixed sum of Rs 25,000 from octroi revenue as well as Rs 2,000 from hackney carriage licence fees. The house-tax, wheel tax, and water rates were collected by the Committee itself. This revenue was not adequate for the 'improvements' needed to make it 'better fitted for the occupation of the Government of India'. The Imperial Government therefore gave it generous grants till 1922. Harcourt Butler warned that 'We have silenced criticism on the big scheme. Let us not arouse general distrust by any unnecessary expenditure on temporary Delhi.'[13] The senior civil servants who clamoured for large and expensive houses in the Civil Lines, when the Viceroy was satisfied with the Circuit House, were accused of increasing the cost of the Temporary Capital. There was also tension between officials and non-official Europeans. If the Bengal Chamber of Commerce had been upset at the transfer of the capital, the Punjab Chamber of Commerce was agitated because the establishment of the Temporary Capital pushed up rents in the Civil Lines. The Imperial Government, afraid of soaring rents, wished to 'acquire' the Civil Lines houses.[14] The Indian owners protested; they were supported by the *Tribune*. 'The government should take the public into confidence as to its exact requirements and invite the leading house-owners and permanent residents to a conference before settling the matter finally.'[15] In deference to their wishes the Viceroy decided that the Government would only lease these houses, thus becoming not only the chief land-lord (by virtue of the *nazul* properties) but also the chief tenant in the Civil Lines. Many landowners found it more profitable to lease out their houses than to live in them. The Government also gave up the plan to acquire the Sabzi Mandi orchards because of the opposition of the landlords. The latter were required, how-ever, to pay taxes on these now, though hitherto these (as *sar-dara-khti* land) had been *maafi*. They pleaded that 'if the *maafis* are resumed, we will have no incentive to plant gardens and a well-known historical feature of Delhi would be lost'. This went unheeded.[16]

The World War slowed down the town-planning schemes. The southern and western extensions took time because they needed the realignment of the Agra–Delhi Chord Railway, a major opera-tion. The initiative in these schemes was taken by the Imperial Government. Hailey wanted a separate fund in the municipal accounts ('this would secure the interests of Government') and also a 'small scale Improvement Trust'—to protect the land against the people rather than to give the people the benefit of the land.[17] This was taken up by MacNabb in 1917, but he did not visualize that the Trust would have the powers that the Calcutta Trust (set up in 1911) enjoyed. He wanted it to control *nazul* lands and housing but not services. He argued forcefully for bringing the *nazul* lands once more under the Imperial Government, on the grounds that the Municipality had mismanaged them for forty years, and that any improvements after 1912 had been due to the Imperial Government. In 1924 this transfer of the *nazul* lands was carried out.

The Western Extension Area originated with a scheme to use Karolbagh for settling the families of workers employed in the construction of the capital. This would be adjacent to two settlements inhabited by those displaced by the Capital. The area between the Western Extension and the city was to be 'improved', with a wide road linking the Civil Lines and the Imperial City, through Sadar Bazaar and Jhandewalan. The Burn Bastion Road was to accommodate the spillover from crowded Khari Baoli, and the Jhandewalan Road Improvement Scheme would provide good sites for shops. The city wall from Kabul to Ajmeri Gates would be demolished and the ditch filled. Beadon wanted the western extension to be controlled by the Imperial Government. The active period in the development of the Western scheme were the years when Beadon was Deputy Commissioner. In earlier decades, the expansion of the settlement in the western suburbs had occurred largely spontaneously, but the expansion from 1912 to 1919 was due to an artificial stimulus, which went against the more natural tendency to extend south and parallel to Sadar Bazaar. New roads became necessary, and the two biggest ones planned were the new Jhandewalan Road (east–west) and the Idgah Road (north–south).

Incidental to the major schemes was the building in 1915 of a new slaughter-house at Kadam Sharif near the Idgah. This sparked off vehement protest by the Hindus who patronized the Jhandewalan Temple nearby, and made them implacably hostile to Beadon thereafter. The Shidipura cemetery was restored to the Punjabi Muslims.[18] The Anjuman Vakil-e-Qaum-Punjabian had purchased this in 1904 and the Government had bought it from them in 1915. This is, incidentally, the only known example of a separate cemetery for Punjabi Muslims in an Indian town.[19] An effort was made to develop 'more model mohullas' in pockets near Sadar Bazaar and Paharganj.

The class distinction which had been implicit in the separation of the Civil Lines from the 'Indian City' was again in evidence.

The Mutiny Memorial Road was to be used by 'superior people and high grade vehicles', and the new Mundhewalan Road by the 'city folk'[20] The Delhi Municipality nonetheless decided that the Provincial Government should pay for this latter road, since it was being done 'for the benefit of the inhabitants of Raisina and the Civil Lines'.[21]

The alternative line of communication between the Civil Lines and the new city lay through Faiz Bazaar, in Daryaganj. Since this was *nazul* property or an 'extension', the Municipality had to bear the huge cost of 'improving' Daryaganj. It was decided in 1916 that the plots in this erstwhile Cantonment property would be acquired and sold for shops and residences, and a large number reserved for schools. Plots for the first two were sold at a high premium in 1920, the year of maximum inflation, those for schools at a subsidized lower rate. There were plans to level the Jama Masjid maidan and the Parade Ground, to accommodate four football fields; a road was planned from Parade Ground to Chandni Chowk to enable the Jains to get their *Rath* to their Mandir after the annual *Jatra*. The Cantonment magistrate in 1913 ordered the Mullah of Sunehri Masjid (south of the Fort) to cease using it for prayers. Hailey toned this down by ruling that though the mosque was under army control, prayers could be held there.[22] The traditional rigidity of the Fort authorities about buildings in the 'Fort Zone' was significantly modified when the Imperial Bank asked for the land of the Pipal Park (sometimes called People's Park, and which was opposite the Jain Mandir in Chandni Chowk). 'In past years, there have been many attempts to induce us to allow buildings to encroach on the Fort zone. There would be a justifiable outcry if the most valuable site of all was given to the Bank at favourable rates,' wrote the Chief Commissioner, Barron, uneasily. 'There is no dog-in-the-manger policy in keeping this piece as an open lung between the Fort and the City. It is not only useful as a lung, but we need open ground here for all sorts of purposes. The Pipal Park is the recognized ground for the *pandals* for large Indian gatherings and is the place for travelling circuses to pitch their camp.'[23] The Park was the venue for most Congress and Home Rule meetings (the 'Indian gatherings' as Barron called them) and the military authorities obviously had little regret in donating it to an Imperial institution for a liberally low sum. (Today the site of the Park is obscured by a parking-

area and shops, and Begum Samru's Palace, occupied by the Delhi
Bauli and the then Imperial Bank, now houses the State Bank of
India.)

The Burn Bastion and Garstin Bastion schemes and the roads
projected by Beadon were financially very successful, yielding
considerable revenue in ground-rent to the Government and in
house-tax to the Municipality. The Jhandewalan Road plots were
auctioned in 1920; almost all the buyers were Marwari merchants.
The Idgah Road plots auctioned in 1921 were bought by merchants
(two Hindu cloth merchants and the rest Muslim furniture merchants and hide-sellers). As in the case of Clarkeganj (which now
appeared a modest venture compared to these major developments), these areas were settled not by immigrants but by prosperous merchants already living in the city or suburbs who needed
more elbow-room. The chief reason for the success of these ventures was that Beadon induced the Government to waive the ten-
year limit on leases which had been laid down by the Punjab
Government, and let out the plots on long leases.[24]

There was thus in this period a heightened and long overdue
recognition of the value of *nazul* properties. This led to a tug-of-
war, the Imperial Government making out that these lands were
best managed by itself, while the Indian members of the Municipality were equally determined not to part with them. The Indians
in the Municipality were irritated by the obstreperous attitude of
the bureaucrats, as Geddes had been in 1914. In the years of
'constitutional reform', officials, local and Imperial, and even the
Secretary of State, were indifferent, even hostile, to suggestions
for reform that emanated from Indians. The situation was the
reverse of that in the 1890s, when the European officials had
pressed for 'improvements' and the Indians had resisted. In 1925
Asaf Ali moved a resolution to introduce a Town Improvement
Act, on the lines of the Punjab Act of 1922, which was chiefly
concerned with street improvements and the development of
unoccupied areas. It was turned down; Abbott, the Chief Commissioner, chided the Municipality. 'Does the Municipality really
understand what it is asking for?' It would mean, he said, that
some important powers of the Municipality would be transferred
to the Trust. The Municipality reconsidered the matter and again
passed the resolution. The Deputy Commissioner then vetoed this.
He said that the Act could, at most, be extended to certain parts

13

of the city. In 1928 Johnson, the Chief Commissioner, was to dismiss Improvement Trusts as 'an expensive error'.[25] Delhi acquired an Improvement Trust only in 1937.

The Municipality suffered a serious loss in 1925 which made it impossible for it to project any schemes of planned extension on its own. This was the resumption by Government of the control of the *nazul* properties from the Municipality, at the recommendation of Abbott. He was at pains to show that he was not doing this because the Municipality had done a bad job of administering them, but because he believed that a Municipality was not equipped to act as an urban landlord. That such an objection had never been advanced earlier suggests that, after 'local self-government' became a 'transferred' department in 1921, the Imperial Government was anxious to keep as much power as possible for itself and reduce the Municipality's authority. The Municipality was compensated for the loss with a financial grant and a special allocation to defray the costs to be incurred in Paharganj, Daryaganj and the Western Extension Area (i.e. Karolbagh, Shidipura, Naiwalan and Basti Rehgaran) for the subsequent five years.[26] Henceforward Delhi Municipality often found itself in the bizarre position of being accused of encroaching on those very lands which it had hitherto protected against encroachments. The Western Extension Area was regarded as providing a safety-valve for the congested city, but the slump of the mid-1920s led to slackness in the disposal of plots; it was the strain of Partition that led Karolbagh to make its great leap forward in the late 1940s and 1950s.

The transfer of the *nazul* properties did not mean that the Imperial Government ceased to be concerned with the problems of Delhi. Lord Irwin, by contrast to earlier Viceroys, was genuinely anxious to discuss 'how best the excessive congestion in Delhi city, and its consequent evils, can be remedied'. A meeting summoned at his behest came to the conclusion that 'the best way . . . was to develop and popularize the existing city extensions and that of them the W.E.A. was the most important and that efforts should be concentrated on providing without further delay a water supply, a drainage scheme, and easy transport from the old city to this area'.[27] One follow-up measure was the introduction of a bus-service from Bara Hindu Rao to Ajmeri Gate via Karolbagh, planned 'to popularize the Karolbagh area'.[28] The Viceroy felt that 'as the congestion was largely due to the fact that the Government of India has descended upon Delhi city and thereby increased its population, it is up to the Government of India . . . to relieve the congestion'.[29] He translated his concern into grants to Delhi Municipality for improving the water supply and for slum clearance. This is significant as indicating a change in the official attitude, and it won Lord Irwin the respect and admiration of Lala Sri Ram, one of the most energetic members of Delhi Municipality. Sri Ram himself posed the issue succinctly: 'Delhi and New Delhi are controlled by separate bodies but the problem is one· the accommodation and well-being of a large population which includes the Government of India for five months a year.'[30]

The transfer of the Capital sparked off a sudden rise in the cost of living. This was further aggravated by the War. It was first felt in the prices of property and building material and the cost of labour. An estimate of Rs 6,000 in June 1912 for a building grant was raised to Rs 9,000 in 1913.[31] In August 1914 the European Association asked the Delhi Government to control prices, as the Bombay Government had done.[32] The officials refused, and showed that local products—foodstuffs and cotton—had actually become cheaper. The rise had occurred in European goods and in meat; the butchers had increased prices to compensate for the fall by 50 per cent in the demand for hides with the closure of the German market. In October 1914 Beadon appointed an informal committee, consisting of Ajmal Khan, Girdhar Lal, Wazir Singh and Amba Prasad, to enquire into the rise in prices. They blamed the European firms for hoarding grain, and exonerated Indian merchants.[33] The Punjab Chamber of Commerce complained frequently. 'The merchants are already alarmed at the increases in expenses in the shape of high rents for office and godown premises in the city and the difficulty in obtaining bungalow accommodation is becoming serious . . . There should be ample room for expansion in all directions and particularly in the areas set aside for residences of non-officials so that they might be able to obtain bungalows at all times at a reasonable rent.'[34] The edge of the Europeans' protest was taken off by 1917 when the slackness of the market and the temporary halt in some of the building schemes in the Capital led to a decrease in rents. When prices shot up again two years later, protest was to be expressed not only by the Europeans but by the Indians. This protest became linked with politics because by then a large number of people had been drawn into the politics of protest.

After the transfer of the Capital, many inhabitants who had hitherto been only lethargically interested in national politics came into contact with politicians of an all-India reputation. Slogans and ideologies that formed part of nationalist politics started to be used for local grievances.[35] Hardinge had felt that when the Legislative Assembly was located in Calcutta there was an undue degree of influence by the people of the city on the legislators. In Delhi, the reverse became true—the politicians were to exert considerable influence on various groups in the town.

There was much truth in Beadon's statement that Delhi had been a political backwater till 1911. It was only gradually that the inhabitants began to evince a sustained interest in politics. The *Tribune* protested against the plan to increase the police and army contingents in Delhi, saying that this would be an insult to the inhabitants 'who are peaceful by nature'.[36] In 1913 it was commented that C.I.D. work was at a standstill in Delhi, and the following year Allnutt said, 'The kind of meetings Amirchand attended have ceased to be held in Delhi.'[37] The spirit of 1906–9 was muted, if not dead.

For a brief time in 1912 it appeared as though the spirit of 1906–9 had been revived. This was when an attempt was made to assassinate Hardinge during the State Entry, a year after the Durbar of 1911. This was the extremists' reply to the decision to transfer the capital, which to the officials was 'something which will impress the Indians with our determination to stay here and to govern the country on imperial lines'.[38] Delhi's involvement in this conspiracy was negligible. Less than half-a-dozen local people were implicated.[39] There were formal expressions of grief made not only by the traditional loyalists but also by many organized religious and social groups, including even men like Mohammad Ali.[40] The Municipality endorsed a resolution proposing to demolish the building of the Punjab National Bank in Chandni Chowk (where the assailants were alleged to have hidden). Hailey approved the resolution, but Hardinge had the wisdom not to permit this measure. 'The action has the appearance of being vindictive.'[41] However, as a sequel to this, the beautiful trees along Chandni Chowk were cut down, and the canal bricked over. Hailey also refused to allow the imposition of a punitive police force on the city. The school-children in Delhi benefited directly from the episode. On Hardinge's own suggestion, his escape was comme-morated by distributing sweets in the local schools.

The Delhi–Lahore Conspiracy of 1914 also implicated very few men from Delhi. But great indignation was sparked off when the harsh punishments were pronounced. Amir Chand was condemned to death. Craddock's condemnation of him as 'a corrupter and perverter of young men' did not cut any ice in Delhi.[42] He was a local man who enjoyed much popularity, not an outsider like Rashbehari Bose, who had been the leader in the Hardinge bomb attempt. Extremist nationalism, associated with Bengalis, never won much support in Delhi, nor probably did the suggestion in a newspaper that one lakh Bengalis should settle in Delhi to dis-seminate Bengali influence in north India![43] From 1912, there were many politically-involved Bengalis coming to Delhi. In 1918 the police requested Rashbehari Sen, who continued Dr H. C. Sen's tradition of maintaining open house for all Bengalis visiting Delhi, to be more discriminating in his hospitality.[44]

In contrast to the poor response to extremist nationalism, the Khilafat movement was to receive a response from a large number of people in Delhi. This was chiefly because it enjoyed the patron-age of the Ali Brothers, who had established themselves at Delhi in 1912. Mohammad Ali's newspaper, the *Comrade*, had only half the circulation of the longer-established *Curzon Gazette* in 1913,[45] but both it and the Urdu *Hamdard* (which aimed to 'champion Muslim interests in the Punjab') gained ground. Shaukat Ali's Anjuman-i-Khuddam-i-Kaaba, an association formed to express sympathy with Turkey at the time of the Balkan Wars of 1913, had a fairly large membership in Delhi. In 1912 Dr Ansari, who had been in Britain for the previous ten years, returned and estab-lished a practice in Delhi; his house in Daryaganj, 'Dar-us-Salaam', became the venue for many Congress meetings. He organized a Medical Mission to be sent to Turkey, a venture supported by the Ali Brothers; the Mission had twenty local members.[46] All of them were helped financially by the local leather merchants, who since the 1870s had been zealous supporters of Turkey. An Anju-man was set up in 1918 to protect mosques, with Ansari, Abdulla Churiwala and some *maulvis* as members. Obeidullah Sindhi, for-merly of Deoband, was in charge of the Fatehpuri Mosque from

1912 to 1915, together with Saif-ur-Rahman.[47] He was eager to combine the Aligarh and Deoband traditions, neither of which had so far received much support in Delhi. He is known to have discussed this with the Alis and Ansari and with Hakim Ajmal Khan.[48]

Ansari believed that the reason why the young men in Delhi did not turn to extremist nationalism was the influence of 'constitutional agitators like Mohammad Ali'.[49] Hailey was openly uneasy because Mohammad Ali was 'mingling religion and politics'. He reported that 'there is an organized clique which follows him to the mosque where he insults the older Muslims. He has worked up the young educated Muslims.'[50] All this made it inevitable that the Khilafat question, when it was to become a political issue in 1919, had its supporters in Delhi already organized. In 1913 at the time of the Kanpur Mosque episode and also later, in 1924, Mohammad Ali was on the alert to see that Muslim graveyards and mosques were not destroyed in the process of levelling the ground to build the capital. He was able to raise an alarm when Beadon, who seems to have excelled in the art of putting his foot into things, prepared two lists of shrines, of those which were to be preserved and of the ones to be destroyed. The officials later asserted that no shrine had been or was to be demolished. A similar issue which became a major crisis for Sikhs was the proposal to take over part of the property of the Rakabganj Gurdwara for the new capital. The demolition of the mosque in Kanpur had created such tension among many Muslims in north India that the Government was unlikely to make further trouble for itself by a similar blunder in Delhi.

Despite the existence of factors to promote politicization among the Muslims after 1911, they were by no means any more homogeneous as a community now than they had been earlier. What led to a large cross-section of them becoming politically committed was the negative factor of the Government deciding in 1915 to intern the Ali Brothers. Before that, local affiliations had often clashed with larger, or nationalist ones.

In October 1913 a meeting of loyalist Muslims at the Idgah, convened by the Nawab of Rampur, was disrupted by some nationalist Muslims. Ansari saw this as a triumph for the nationalist cause. 'The attempt to cause a cleavage in the community [i.e. by the Nawab] has failed miserably,'[51] he wrote to Mohammad Ali. The degree to which local Muslims had been actively involved in this meeting is not known. There was an undercurrent of rivalry between the outsiders and the Delhi-wallahs implicit in the organization of two separate medical missions to Turkey during the Balkan Wars, one under Ansari and the other led by Ajmal Khan.[52] A similar rivalry can be discerned in Mohammad Ali's attempts to cast aspersions on the local Haj Committee which had as its President the loyalist Abdul Ahad, and as members Ajmal Khan, Abdul Ghani, Hakim Raziuddin, and Ghulam Mohammad Hasan Khan.[53] Shaukat Ali's Anjuman-i-Khuddam-i-Kaaba clashed on different occasions with the Ram Lila procession and a Sikh procession, and became split within its own ranks because of rivalry between Shaukat Ali's Central Committee and the Delhi branch. Sheikh Ataullah, a lawyer and the leader of the Anjuman Islamia, declared that no Muslims should join the Anjuman-i-Khuddam-i-Kaaba.[54] An association called the Vakil-i-Islam was formed in 1916, under Abdul Rahim, a shoe merchant, to recover the money the Delhi Anjuman was alleged to have embezzled.[55] The same year, another rupture occurred between the Muslim *chamars* and the shoe merchants, as had happened in 1901; this was exploited by the Arya Samaj and the Christian missionaries, who offered to lend money to the *chamars*. A foretaste of the Khilafat agitation was seen in 1916 when the local nationalist Muslims Abdul Aziz and Rauf Ali (both lawyers) and Maulvi Kifayatullah held a meeting attended by five hundred people to condemn the revolt of the ruler of Mecca. It is significant that Umrao Mirza and Abdul Ghani, both Municipal Commissioners, and Ajmal Khan expressed their sympathy but stayed away from the meeting. Prayers for the Sultan were said at the Fatehpuri Mosque but not at the Jama Masjid.[56]

The Hindus of Delhi did not have any major issue which served as a rallying-point in the way the Turkish problem and the Jama Masjid did for many Muslims. When the capital was shifted to Delhi, the *Parkash* of Lahore wanted to make Delhi the headquarters of the Arya Samaj and the Pratinidhi Sabha thought of starting a branch of the Gurukul Kangri there.[57] Arya Samaj influence increased in the city and, more markedly, among the Jats of the rural hinterland. A close connection between the Gurukul and some members of St Stephen's College developed because of the friendship between Munshi Ram (later known as Swami

Shraddhanand) and C. F. Andrews.[58] The students of this College had been sympathetic to the Arya Samaj from the 1890s. Andrews wrote that a Hindu and a Muslim Society were established in the College after 1912 to balance the Christian element.[59] A visitor wrote that 'At St Stephen's case after case where something might easily have become sedition under the control of less enlightened Englishmen, became an earnest enthusiasm for a fuller national life.'[60] Shraddhanand's popularity in the College must have been a factor in his popularity in Delhi during the Satyagraha of 1919. For the Hindus generally, however, grievances against the local government were the main basis on which larger political affiliations were to be built.

There were some instances of opposition to the local Government, which are significant because they overlap with larger political issues. The municipal bye-laws regulating the sale of meat provoked opposition from many more people in 1913 than in 1908. The Muslim merchants supported the butchers. The 'Muslim public' represented on the Municipality by Chaudhries Bashiruddin, Nasiruddin and Abdul Ghani, protested at the coercion implied in the attempt to force the butchers into the municipal markets. 'If the advent of Government has increased the expenses of Delhi Municipality, the Government should pay, not the poor public.'[61] Even after the Municipality had made a partial concession (by allowing meat to be sold by hawkers, 'in *mohullas* in the occupation of Muslims') the butchers went to the law. They lost their case because Hailey refused to interfere. He held that the Municipality had imposed only the 'minimum of control'. The *Tribune* scolded the butchers for being unreasonable: 'The inhabitants of Delhi ought to remember that they are no longer a provincial, isolated or insular people but enjoy the dignity of being citizens of an important metropolis.'[62] Another type of protest was that of 1915, when many Hindus and Jains (led by Sultan Singh) protested against the establishment of the new slaughter-house near the Idgah, because of its proximity to the Jhandewalan temple.[63]

Between 1915, when the Ali Brothers were interned, and 1917, political activity in Delhi was at a very low pitch. In 1917, there were a large number of political meetings in the city, in anticipation of the visit of Montagu, Secretary of State for India. In the process, some citizens became interested in the Home Rule League movement and the National Education Movement of Mrs Besant. Those actively involved were Miss G'Meiner, an Australian and the Principal of the Indraprastha School, doctors (Ansari and A. C. Sen) and lawyers (R. S. Pearey Lal, Abdul Rahman, Asaf Ali, Abdul Aziz, Shiv Narain and S. N. Bose), and some bankers and merchants.[64] Nearly all of them had in common the background of an anglicized education at St Stephen's College. Sultan Singh, a prominent banker and industrialist and a Home Rule sympathizer, was a friend of C. F. Andrews, who induced him to contribute to Gokhale's South African Fund.[65] In 1917 Asaf Ali condemned as 'an act of drastic repression' Hailey's ban on a proposed meeting of the Delhi Bar Association to protest against the internment of Mrs Besant.[66]

Ajmal Khan was respected by the Home Rule Leaguers, and himself evinced sympathy for the movement. He himself was, from 1917, interested in making out a case for a national Muslim university to be located at Delhi. In this he was supported by Muslims who otherwise were divided amongst themselves—Ansari and Abdul Rahman (both Home Rule Leaguers) and Sheikh Ataullah, who publicly condemned the League's tactics (at a meeting convened by Abdulla Churiwala). In 1921 this took shape in the establishment of the Jamia Millia Islamia, with Mohammad Ali as its first Vice-Chancellor.

The first political organization of a nationalist character to originate in Delhi was the Indian Association formed in 1917 by two lawyers, and used by Ajmal Khan to present the views of the Moderates to Montagu. The subtle distinction between Home Rule Leaguers and Moderates at the all-India level was not obvious in Delhi, because many members of the Home Rule League also joined the Association.[67] Apart from supporting the Congress–League scheme for India, they put forward specific demands relating to Delhi Province. These were aimed at asserting the city's individuality and making it the administrative centre of its cultural and linguistic hinterland, by enlarging the province to include Rohilkhand, Agra, Meerut and Ambala—those areas which shared with Delhi 'a common language and social life'. (This demand was to be repeated in 1928 by the local Congress organization and by the Municipality.) Delhi should be made a Gov-

ernor's Province, with a Council, since as things stood it had no
representation either in a Provincial Council or in the Imperial
Council. The administrative and judicial dependence on the Punjab should be ended, and Delhi should have its own court, as
well as a separate university. The Municipality should have fifty
elected members, and should elect its own President.[68] In December 1917 the Association decided to put up candidates for municipal elections. Its members, mostly lawyers, challenged the loyalist
Punjabi merchants of the Municipality; both the lawyers and the
merchants were Muslims. The local leaders, who met the Secretary of State, were Pearey Lal, Home Rule Leaguers, and Pirzada
Mohammad Husain, a member of the Muslim League. When the
Government proposed to ban political meetings in Delhi that
year, individuals as diverse in their political and class affiliations
as Dr Ansari, Dr A. C. Sen, Sheikh Ataullah, and Lala Ram Kishen
Das protested strongly.[69]

A possible explanation for the ban on meetings was that in mid-
1917 there had occurred a fracas between the people of Delhi
and the local government authorities. The latter were probably
already on edge because many political meetings were being held
in the city. They became tense at the prospect of Ram Lila and
Mohurram occurring at the same time that year. The 1916 *Administration Report* had highlighted the achievement of 'more
efficient control of traffic in the streets, and of processions and
fairs generally'. This 'efficient control' meant police escorts being
provided for all festive processions. The Deputy Commissioner,
Beadon, complained that the crowds grew larger every year, but
that the streets were still narrow; also, there were more processions, with the increasing numbers of Sikhs and Bengalis. Fearing
a riot, he decreed that on those days when Mohurram and Ram
Lila coincided, the Ram Lila celebrations should be held at the
Tis Hazari Maidan outside Mori Gate. But that year, in July,
Ajmal Khan and Sultan Singh had led the Hindus and Muslims
in reviving the practice of an earlier generation, of the days of
Ajmal Khan's brother Abdul Majid and Sri Kishen Das, when
Hindus had greeted the Muslims with refreshments after the Id
prayers. Beadon's decision led to a ten-day hartal by the Hindus,
led by Ram Lal, a cloth merchant, Pearey Lal, a merchant, and
Sri Ram, a lawyer, the last two being Home Rule Leaguers. This
protest was backed by Home Rule League members, including

Asaf Ali and Abdul Aziz, and by the students of St Stephen's and Hindu College.[70]

There was nothing to justify the reply made to Surendranath Banerjea in the Legislative Assembly, that there was 'no solution which would have been fully acceptable to both Hindus and Muslims and at the same time have offered adequate safeguards against a breach of the public peace'.[71] A Lahore newspaper gave a more realistic appraisal: 'Such a muddle could never have happened if the leaders of the people had been associated with the administration in a responsible manner ... [sc. It] could happen more easily at Delhi than elsewhere because here there was no consciousness on the part of the officials that they might be called upon to publicly account for their actions.'[72] The episode indicated that many individuals who were on good terms with the officials had become supporters of the Home Rule League. It marked the beginning of Beadon's general unpopularity. His only supporter in Delhi was Islamullah Khan, whom he had nominated as a Municipal Commissioner, and who believed that those Muslims who supported the hartal were falling into a Hindu trap.[73] Another crisis in 1918 was caused by the Government proposing an alternative route for the Congress procession. To this the local Congress Committee protested in a manner reminiscent of the Tennis-Court Oath of the Third Estate in France in June 1789. Asaf Ali was prohibited from addressing meetings.[74] The grant-in-aid and Government recognition to Indraprastha School was suspended because of the political activities of its Principal, Miss G'Meiner. She wrote to Hailey, whom she had known for many years, 'Knowing your real sympathy for the Indian people, I look to you for protection and help'.[75] That Hailey's chivalry did not rise to the occasion is evident from C. F. Andrews' reference to 'Miss G'Meiner's ... hard struggle with Mr Hailey who is threatening her school'.[76]

The officials became tense because nationalist political organizations were trying to rouse enthusiasm in the city, to provide a fitting local reception to the Congress and Muslim League sessions which were to be held in Delhi in December 1918. In addition, the Khilafat agitation won much support. In 1918 imperial fiat and local grievance confronted each other on a more impressive platform than had been possible earlier, when the Muslim League at its Delhi session demanded that the restrictions on the use of the

Jama Masjid be removed. Hailey countered by saying that the Masjid was controlled by the Masjid Committee, which consisted entirely of Muslims.

More people in Delhi city were involved in politics from the end of 1918 than ever before. This can be explained in the context of the unprecedented rise in prices between 1918 and 1921 and of rentals, the slump in the cloth market, the imposition of income-tax and super-tax, and of the tragic influenza epidemic of October 1918.

The incidents in the Rowlatt Satyagraha in Delhi in March–April 1919 are worthy of examination as much as for what they signified as what they did not. The episodes were not part of an Indian, nor even of a Punjab–Delhi conspiracy; there was less emphasis on any aspect of nationalist ideology than on local grievances. These, as listed by Raj Narain, a Delhi lawyer, during .he Hunter Committee enquiry, were a combination of minor and major ones, but all of a local nature.[77] Those that he specified were the strict enforcement of municipal building bye-laws, the closing of the city wells, the cutting down of the trees in Chandni Chowk after the Hardinge Bomb attempt, the inadequate compensation in some cases for the land taken for the Capital, the imposition of income-tax and super-tax and the manner in which the objections to the income-tax assessment were dealt with, the imprisonment of the Ali Brothers, the action taken at the time of the Ram Lila in 1917, the methods employed to recruit soldiers during the War and the activities of the C.I.D.

Above all, the Satyagraha was to mark the nadir in relations between officials and inhabitants. Ajmal Khan indicated that Hailey had not been very popular. The episode of the Ram Lila was cited by many witnesses as a major grievance. The most unpopular figure was Beadon. He was criticized because 'his general treatment was harsh and he mostly devoted his attention to municipal affairs'. Beadon's problem was that he could not come to terms with the changes brought about in Delhi as a result of its enlargement from a provincial town to a focal point for political activity. He was particularly irritated at the fact that 'we have had billeted on Delhi several *outside* agitators'. The local people probably felt that an excessive number of officials had been billeted on them! He claimed that not more than thirty inhabitants in the city were actively involved in politics. But the volume of political activity and conspiracy made the District Magistrate's position 'an impossible one'. Ajmal Khan put it in his own way when he said that after 1911 political awareness has been growing in Delhi and that it had been on 'strictly Constitutional lines'; the people were law-abiding and the leaders had kept them so. Beadon's excessive reliance on the police was perhaps the greatest grievance of the Delhi people. Almost every witness examined by the Hunter Commission was to refer to the great dislike of the police. One of the rumours circulated about the Rowlatt Bills had been that they would give much power to the police. A European bank manager said that merchants and bankers were extremely worried on this score; this same group had suffered most during the War and the following depression, and were therefore sympathetic to the Satyagraha.[78]

The Satyagraha movement gathered momentum after a meeting addressed by Gandhiji on 7 March. One hundred and twenty people in Delhi signed the Satyagraha pledge (the list was subsequently destroyed by the Satyagraha Sabha, as a precautionary measure). The signatories as well as those who did not sign but who sympathized with Gandhiji (Sultan Singh, Ajmal Khan) were to be described by the local authorities as the 'leaders' of the city. This label could be questioned, for few of the individuals referred to had earlier exercised any 'leadership', few had attempted to use public oratory to mould opinion, and their association with such a recently-formed political organization could not confer on them the status of leaders of the community. The only person with a charismatic appeal somewhat like Gandhiji's was Swami Shraddhanand. On 27 March he took control of the Satyagraha Sabha, replacing Dr Ansari. It has never been adequately explained why the Delhi hartal occurred on 30 March, when all the others in the country had been postponed till 6 April. A possible explanation could be that Swami Shraddhanand wanted to enjoy the kudos of his area being the first to carry out the hartal, or that he was apprehensive that the hartal might be a failure if it was postponed. The C.I.D. reports made the Government complacent, for they were confident that the hartal would fail in Delhi, since all the Muslims and some of the Hindus seemed to be opposed to it. Other than Shraddhanand (whom the Chief Commissioner did not name at all) Barron's so-called 'major' leaders (obviously in terms of respectability *vis-à-vis* the British) were

Ajmal Khan, Ansari, Sultan Singh and Pearey Lal; the 'minor' leaders were Shankar Lal (Secretary of the Satyagraha Sabha and brother of Lala Sri Ram), Abdul Majid, an outspoken *maulvi*, and Abdulla Churiwala, a shoe merchant. Asaf Ali was under a vow of silence because of the ban on his making speeches (the ban also applied to Neki Ram Sharma); this must have been why he was not mentioned. The names of Shuaib Qureshi, Mohammad Ali's son-in-law, K. B. Desai, Pandit Ram Chand and Dr Abdul Rahman were not mentioned, possibly through ignorance.

From the first confrontation between the Satyagrahis and the police on 30 March, through all the subsequent episodes till mid-April, the Indians' line was that it was the presence of the police which provoked a riot on each occasion, while the authorities comforted themselves with the thought that the chief leaders of the Home Rule League were not involved, and that all the mischief was being wrought by the 'minor leaders'. The Police Superintendent once used the term 'a riot against me', which to the Indians seemed to prove the point that the police themselves were the cause of turning into riots what were otherwise peaceful hartals. The implementation of the hartals was partly done by the many volunteer organizations which had been formed in 1918, in all of which Home Rule members were active. This recruiting of the young was a new feature in Delhi politics. There were three episodes on 30 March—a fracas at the railway-station (when the police fired on a crowd which was seeking to make a vendor shut his shop), an encounter between the police and a crowd in Chandni Chowk (which led Asaf Ali to propose that the Clock Tower square be renamed Khooni Chauraha), a meeting in Pipal Park, on returning from which Shraddhanand had an encounter with some Manipuri soldiers (which his son Indra publicized in his newspaper, the *Vijaya*). In each of these the police and the vocal participants were convinced that the other was guilty of provocation. There was strong indignation in Delhi and elsewhere at the use of the police and the troops on such a large scale.

The following week was an uneasy one, with a sense of wariness on both sides. Both Shraddhanand and Beadon became increasingly intractable. Shraddhanand's local reputation became quickly enhanced because of the powerful speeches he delivered at the funeral of those killed in the police firings. Rudra, the Principal of St Stephen's College, described these as the most remarkable speeches he had ever heard, and the funerals themselves as very moving, particularly the sight of Muslims carrying the Hindu dead. The Satyagraha Sabha decided that there would be no hartal on 6 April. But Shraddhanand (who appears to have been at variance with the Home Rule League members, who regarded 30 March as the Satyagraha accomplished) kept up the fever-pitch of popular excitement and sense of participation by meetings and speeches, and most of all by his dramatic appearance at the pulpit of the Jama Masjid on 4 April at a gathering where the Imam was insulted for being a loyalist.* Ajmal Khan was not happy about this episode (he and Shraddhanand had met for the first time on 31 March and had not found each other's company congenial). Shraddhanand repeated this performance on 6 April, at the Fatehpuri Masjid. The Government banned all meetings at Jama Masjid other than those for worship. On 5 April the volunteers succeeded in carrying through a boycott of trams. The officials saw in this an anti-British attitude, but the Indians explained that this was done as a symbol of respect for those killed on 30 March.

Beadon's classic *faux pas* was his statement (in Urdu) on 2 April describing the hartal of the 30 March as 'foolish and unnecessary'. 'A crowd of *badmashes* created a disturbance at the railway station. The so-called Passive Resistance turned at once into active rioting, which the *Sirkar* cannot allow.' The effect of the use of the word *badmashes* is difficult to exaggerate. Most of the witnesses examined by the Hunter Commission said that this had made many 'respectable people, cloth merchants and others' indignant. The very appearance of Beadon at the head of a posse of police or soldiers was enough to make shopkeepers lower their shutters and declare an impromptu hartal. The police built up these episodes into a piece of horrifying fiction where the British families in the Civil Lines were 'in a state of siege' on 6 April. Barron vehemently denied this later.

The local officials, then the higher Government officials, rationalized the state of suspended animation in the first two weeks of April as caused by the fact that 'the leaders had lost control of their followers, and the lower-class Muslims had taken charge'.

* More recently, in February 1977, there was another instance of the Jama Masjid being used as a political platform and Hindus being asked to address the audience.

This appears to be partly borne out by a later remark of Principal
Sushil Rudra that the episodes of early April had made the *rais*
and the students ashamed of the excesses of the mob. What had
actually happened was that Shraddhanand (who was not included
among Beadon's 'secondary leaders') had established his local
reputation, helped greatly by the abysmal blimpishness of Beadon.
As a result, many merchants, artisans and shopkeepers became not
anti-Government but strongly anti-Deputy Commissioner. Therefore Shraddhanand could press his demands for another hartal on
6 April, and for the withdrawal of the extra police and military
force. He did so with the confidence that he had the sympathy
of most of the citizens, who had traditionally hated the police,
and now also Beadon. A man who described the Satyagraha
leaders as *badmashes* had forfeited popular respect.

The hartal of 10 April was a protest against the arrest of
Gandhiji. From 13 to 16 April the Government observed a hartal
by declaring these days to be public holidays, because they feared
trouble for English banks and other establishments (particularly
after the news of Jallianwala became known). The officials, whose
panic outstripped their sense of realism, feared an attack on the
civil station (shades of 1898!) and withdrew the police from the
city as a precautionary measure. Beadon comforted himself with
the hope that 'the very protraction of the period of discomfort
has brought home to the local populace of Delhi that the political
leaders have feet of clay and government alone can keep order'.

Ultimately the Chief Commissioner, Barron, decided to have
serious talks with the Home Rule League members, who were
now regarded as the only people with authority in the city. These
individuals replied by holding a large meeting (on 13 April) where
it was stated that 'this mass meeting of the citizens of Delhi protests against the investigations instituted by the Delhi executive
of the incidents of 30 March'—a popular vote of no-confidence
in the local government. On 14 and 15 April the officials met the
League leaders and Shraddhanand at the Town Hall. Rumour-
mongering was at its height on these two days and was on a par
for absurdity with the fears of the officials. There was a widespread canard that the leaders were to be arrested and spirited
away in an aeroplane, which happened to fly over the city. These
rumours whipped up popular hysteria, seen in the attack on a
C.I.D. man at a meeting in Edward Park on 14 April, and in the

large crowds outside the Town Hall, which conspicuously included Jats from Sadar Bazaar carrying *lathis*, who had gathered to give moral support and defence if necessary to the leaders within the Hall. On 15 April, one hundred and fifty traders were also called in to meet the officials. Beadon was as pugnacious as before. 'I told Ansari, Ajmal Khan and Sultan Singh that we could not tolerate this mob law, and that if the hartal continued, I would ask the military to take charge.' He went on to say, 'If they made an effort to open the shops, I guaranteed to isolate the city from the suburbs.' The only explanation for this would be that by 'the suburbs' he meant Sadar Bazaar with its predominantly Jat population. C. F. Andrews spoke of the harm being done to relations between the people and the officials by the *agents provocateurs*.[79]

The tension eased chiefly because of a deft act by the Chief Commissioner which saved the situation. Shraddhanand himself had high praise for this. Barron wanted to explain that the Government had declared a hartal because 'the people are suspicious that the Government intended to arrest the leaders'. (The word 'arrest' was changed to 'do harm to' when Ajmal Khan protested.) Barron assured the people that this had never been their intention. In return, the leaders wanted it conveyed to the Supreme Government that they had declared a hartal on 10 April only as a protest against Gandhiji's arrest. The people were assured by the officials that Gandhi was in good health. The desultory hartal continued for some days, always occurring when Beadon made his appearance. Barron felt that the return to normalcy was taking time because of the propaganda of Shraddhanand and his son Indra, and their contacts with the Jats.

On 16 April Beadon and Hare-Scott (the Police Chief) again invited trouble by deciding that fourteen prominent leaders (including Sultan Singh, Pearey Lal and other League members) should act as 'special constables'. The Police Superintendent after a few days said that these individuals were not functioning satisfactorily, and should wear uniforms and stay in the *thana*. The indignant 'constables' and the people at large felt this had been done to humiliate the leaders. The officials' intention was possibly that, since the ordinary police was so obviously disliked, these men with local knowledge could act as a link between the Government and the people and exercise a calming influence. As in the case of the notice of 4 April, the manner in which this policy

14

was put through was blundering and clumsy, and alienated men like Sultan Singh and Pearey Lal, who had earlier been sympathetic to the Government's attempts at restoring normalcy. An even more clumsy act, reminiscent of 1886, was the decision to impose a fine on Delhi. Barron was in a dilemma as to how this should be collected. He exempted 'poor houseowners' and then found that he would also have to exempt the 'substantial houseowners' because they had not participated in the 'riot'. The way out of the embarrassing dilemma was to drop the charges altogether. But this was done after a delay of two years, at the cost of much goodwill.

Ajmal Khan and Ansari, as well as Pearey Lal and Sultan Singh, were irritated at the manner in which the officials handled the April Satyagraha, but (unlike the Ali Brothers, who were freelancers) they were essentially *en rapport* with the officials and had occasion to work with them in many different contexts. This was seen in the meetings organized by Hindus and Muslims, chiefly of the Home Rule League, in May 1919, to express support for the Government in the Afghan War. C. F. Andrews reported that 'Ajmal Khan [sc. had] implored me to ask at Simla that there might be peace, in the face of the Afghan invasion'.[80] The Indian Association of Ajmal Khan thanked Barron formally at a meeting in July for the manner in which he had handled the Satyagraha. The mediatory style of politics (as between the *rais* and the officials) could not develop further because feelings were embittered again by two acts of the Government. The first was the proclamation of the Seditious Meetings Act in Delhi in June 1919, at a time when there was no reason for it; secondly, the punitive levy was imposed on the people so belatedly that no one was prepared to tolerate it. The sittings of the Disorders Committee were held at Delhi in the winter of 1919. The combination of all these led to a general revulsion against the Government. Maulvi Kifayatullah, a Khilafat leader, followed Abdul Bari's lead in urging Muslims not to participate in the Peace celebrations. Many members of the Municipality, including the eminent Dr Shroff, who was very close to the Home Rulers at Delhi, induced the Municipality to cancel the contributions allocated earlier for the Peace celebrations. Thereupon Barron indignantly 'withdrew [sc. his] grant to the Municipality and left the city alone'.[81] Shroff was to be the person chiefly responsible for the Municipality's decision to boycott the visit of the Duke of Connaught in 1921. (In 1922 Shroff was granted a site in Daryaganj for his hospital, after the officials had satisfied themselves that he had 'seen the error of his ways'.[82]) The celebration in which all the people of Delhi did participate with enthusiasm was the welcome accorded to the Ali Brothers when they were released and entered Delhi in a triumphal procession in December 1919.

Even before the Ali Brothers' return, the Khilafat movement had got off the ground, with a meeting on 17 October 1919, at which only the local Khadim-ul-Islam association protested its loyalty to the British. Muslim pleaders (Abdul Aziz and Abdur Rahman), the novelist Rashid-ul-Khairi and some merchants were active.[83] Shraddhanand and Shankar Lal, Secretary of the Delhi Home Rule League, participated in the observance of Khilafat Day in March 1920.

The Non-Co-operation activities began in August 1920. There was some difference of opinion between the Congress sympathizers (Ansari, Ajmal Khan and Asaf Ali), who wanted to support the Non-Co-operation Movement and the commercial boycott, and the extremists, led by Abdulla Churiwala and Maulvi Kifayatullah. Pearey Lal and Ajmal Khan gave up their titles, and the Principal of Hindu College, Gidwani, resigned. Ajmal Khan got the Non-Co-operation Committee's permission to retain his connection with the Government in the interests of the Tibbia College. As in 1918, so again in 1920 and on a bigger scale, 'volunteering' was organized by various political or quasi-political bodies. The implementation of the Nagpur programme of the Congress was effective in Delhi from 1921 to 1922 but by 1923 it was in a state of collapse, and much loss had been incurred on the Khaddar programme.[84] The Delhi Piece-Goods Association (which had European and Indian members) passed a cautious resolution in July 1921 that a boycott of foreign goods 'should not be directed against the existing stocks in the country'.[85] The Non-Co-operation Movement was characterized by the Muslims abandoning cow-slaughter (only 29 cows were slaughtered in 1920, as against 250 in 1919, and 130 in 1918), and both Hindus and Muslims boycotting the *Gulfaroshan* at Mehrauli (because it was patronized by officialdom).[86] In October the Anglo-Arabic School (also associated with the Government), whose secretary Abdul Ahad had refused to go along with the supporters of the Khilafat, was stormed by Asaf Ali and Abdulla Churiwala and their supporters, to induce it to close.[87] Simultaneously, Ajmal Khan started a 'national school' in the Jama Masjid, which attracted many of the students of the Anglo-Arabic School. This school did not last long.[88] The vendetta against Abdul Ahad was continued after his death in December 1920, when the Non-Co-operation enthusiasts (not Ansari or Asaf Ali but Muslims who were not Home Rule League members) denied him a funeral until his family stated that on his death-bed he had 'recanted' and accepted the N.C.O. creed.[89] There was an official case about this, and the Government's interference was deeply resented by nationalist Muslims. These episodes were more ugly than earlier incidents of conflict (1863, 1886) and feelings were more exacerbated than in earlier verbal feuds between sections of Muslims.

Local grievances were not completely forgotten in these years. Delhi's *Morning Post* complained in August 1920 (i.e. at the time the N.C.O. movement was launched) that the 'leaders' of the Satyagraha and the N.C.O. had neglected the distress of tenants in Delhi. 'For the past few years, the Provincial Civil Service officers transferred from Punjab to Delhi have represented that owing to the sustained rise in the already heavy rents in Delhi, it was becoming increasingly difficult for them to obtain accommodation.'[90] The Satyagraha 'leaders' were themselves chiefly landlords, the officials were not interested, and the tenants were servile, said the newspaper. The vernacular press also made similar complaints, and there had been a meeting in February 1920 to express protest. Perhaps in response to the *Morning Post's* criticism, some of the leaders of the N.C.O. (Ansari, Daya Shankar) teamed up with Indian bankers and merchants and European residents (i.e. all well-to-do people) to form a Citizens' Deputation (led by Rauf Ali, a barrister).[91] They petitioned Barron for a Rent Act on the Bombay model. They had done some research into rental increases and were also able to show the vicious circle which pushed up prices, which raised rents and in turn led to prices being further increased. Rents had increased two-fold and, in some cases, four- or five-fold between 1905 and 1921. The question was raised in the Legislative Assembly. The Government spokesman's answer was that building activity in the Imperial City and in the extensions near Delhi city, which would be intensified in the following four years, would help to make rents fall. The retort to this was that the pressure of outsiders who wanted houses in the capital city or in the older city and the Civil Lines was pushing up rentals. But Barron refused to introduce rent control.

Economic distress might also have been as much of a factor as politicization in explaining the five or six strikes in Delhi in 1920–2 in the mills and in the Tramway Company. Asaf Ali and K. A. Desai (both Congress members) were active in these. The Home Secretary's proposal to Barron ('if the City is helping the strikers, cut off the city lights') was not carried out.[92]

Municipal elections remained fairly quiet, with stray instances of political issues obtruding on them, as in 1915 when the Punjabi pleader Sheikh Azizuddin was challenged (unsuccessfully) by young Islamullah Khan, a Muslim League member; at a later date he was brought into the Municipality as a nominated member by Beadon who said he wanted to 'unearth some of the younger Muslims'.[93] Dr Ansari and Dr Shroff, whose politics were later to be often anti-establishment, were also nominated members. The Punjab Chamber of Commerce repeated its request of 1907 for a special seat on the Municipality. Beadon refused, saying that a body which claimed that it was not a local society but a regional one (and thereby secured a seat on the Punjab Legislative Council) could not also make out a case for municipal representation on the strength of its local character. A European lobby thus did not necessarily secure preferential treatment, particularly if it had been agitating with regard to houses in the Civil Lines shortly before.[94] In 1923, when the officials needed more 'safe' supporters, the Chamber was given special representation on the Municipality. The loyalists who were nominated as honorary magistrates were drawn from among bankers, merchants and landlords, and adopted a stance of servility just as their predecessors of the 1860s and 1870s had done. When any of them secured nomination, servile thanks were tendered by their supporters organized at 'command' meetings of ward members or occupational groups. This excessive display of loyalism could well have irked people like Ajmal Khan, Ansari, or Pearey Lal, who were *en rapport* with the officials but would not be servile.

From 1918 the question of reforming Indian municipalities as part of the Reforms Scheme, and following the recommendations of the Decentralization Commission, was under discussion. Hailey was prepared to allow an elective majority for the Municipality. But his successor Barron, who had earlier been Deputy Commissioner, warned in 1919 that 'the new constitution of the Municipality cannot be introduced with confidence and safety unless provision is made for appointing an official, in the person of a Municipal Commissioner or an Executive Officer, with statutory powers to carry on the daily work of administration under the general control of the Municipal Committee and its non-official chairman'.[95]

It was not so much about the Presidentship of the Municipality as over the question of separate electorates that controversy occurred. The statements by the Deputy Commissioners (Beadon, followed by Bolster) evoke a *déjà vu* sensation. Smyth's statement of 1882 was echoed by Beadon in 1918 when he said that it was 'folly to disguise the fact that Hindu–Muslim feeling is strong. Since I have known Delhi [i.e. since 1907] there has never been a contest between a Hindu and a Muslim, and there can be no stronger condemnation of mixed electorates than this fact'. It is difficult to see how this proved the existence of communal feelings. The real consideration should have been whether Muslims got elected from Hindu-majority wards; they did, and this indicated that there was cross-communal voting. Beadon's statement led Hailey to qualify his own, which had accepted the need for elected majorities by adding that 'the circumstances of Delhi involve the necessity of securing something like an equal representation of Muslim and Hindu interests... It is a matter for consideration whether the equal representation of Muslim and Hindu interests can be left to the chance of the polls or must be arranged for by nomination or otherwise.'[96] This implied that the officials were afraid of inter-communal amity, and were trying to prevent it. The municipal sub-committee (appointed at the end of 1919, the traumatic year of the Rowlatt Satyagraha) suspected this ulterior motive and took a firm stand. It declared itself to be 'strongly opposed to the... establishment of separate electorates, because these would result in the return of persons who will not be the fittest available... and who will always bear in mind that their future election will depend entirely on advancing the interests of the particular com-

munity which has elected them'. Beadon had wanted a Municipality with twenty-six members, and Smith suggested thirty
(twelve 'double constituencies' and six nominated members). The
'double constituencies' were devised because 'in the present conditions it is imperative to avoid contests between Hindus and Muslims'. The Municipality's own suggestion was for twenty wards,
ten to elect Hindus and ten Muslims, with three other members
to be returned by trading interests (one Hindu, one Muslim and
one European), and one member to be elected by professionals.
Even Pirzada Mohammad Husain, a government pensioner and a
member of the Muslim League, wanted mixed electorates. He
added that the anomaly by which three wards with Hindu majorities were to choose Muslim candidates should be corrected. The
only members of the sub-committee who wanted separate electorates were Govan and Walker, European members of the Punjab
Chamber of Commerce; they also disagreed with the majority in
that they wanted an official chairman, and no special representation for professionals. Beadon was prepared to widen the franchise
by reducing the qualifications to an income of Rs 4 per month,
the Municipality wanted Rs 3, and Pirzada Mohammad Husain
wished for Rs 2 as the floor (to benefit poorer Muslims).

The 'minorities' and the groups needing special representation
were now, unlike in 1882, subgroups—Shias, Sikhs, merchants, professionals, bankers. To these Beadon added another—the Imperial
Government. He felt that Delhi, as the capital and enclosed as it
was by the property of the Imperial city, and *nazul* and railway
land, should have representation for these interests on its Municipality. The Chief Commissioner snubbed the Municipality when
it asked, tongue-in-cheek, how many seats should be allocated to
these interests. The Deputy Commissioner finally converted the
loyalist Pirzada Mohammad Husain to the principle of separate
electorates. But (like Smyth earlier) he distorted the sense of the
Municipal sub-committee's discussions by making out that the
committee as a whole had asked for separate electorates. Thus the
'procedure laid down by the Chief Commissioner in a hurry' (as
the *Comrade* described it) was carried through in 1922. The last
election under the old system, that of 1921, yielded significant
results. Both the members elected in each of three wards were of
a religion different from that of the majority of electors in those
wards. The Municipality was puzzled about the manner in which

to work the new law, which laid down that one Hindu and one Muslim each should be returned from each double-member constituency. They asked the Chief Commissioner to interpret it, and were told that the rules meant that Hindus could vote only for a Hindu candidate, and Muslims for a Muslim. 'The point of introducing two members in each ward was to avoid friction caused by Hindu–Muslim contests. It follows that in each ward Hindus must vote for a Hindu candidate, and Muslims for a Muslim. Otherwise in some of the wards where Hindus predominate, they would control the election not only of the Hindu candidate but of the Muslim also.' Of the existing system he said that members were 'free to give unreserved expression to communal demands resulting in considerable communal tension in the committee's deliberations . . . I am not prepared to take a step which might extend the tension from the Municipality to the electorate.'[97] These arguments were soon seen to be spurious, and the policy of having separate electorates remained an official, not a popular, one.

Once the principle of separate electorates was forced on the Municipality, the latter was flooded with requests for sectional representation—by factory owners, the Hindustani Mercantile Association (who wanted representation separate from the Piece-Goods Association which had only a hundred members, as against their four hundred and fifty), the depressed classes (organized by Ramanand Sanyasi under Swami Shraddhanand's patronage), the Anjuman Islamia (for Shias), Indian Christians, the Anjuman Muhafiz Auqaf (saying that the Municipality did not understand 'Muslim matters') led by Pirzada Mohammad Husain, the Anjuman Vakil-e-Qaum-Punjabian, the bankers' consortium and the Sundries Goods merchants.[98]

For various reasons, from 1922 municipal politics became more and more affected by national political issues. Beadon's farewell address to the Municipality had a little homily addressed to 'you who call yourselves Home Rulers'. In 1921, on the infrastructure of the Home Rule League, the Congress–Khilafat entente gained more and more of a hold over the city. Ansari, Ajmal Khan and Asaf Ali were the local leaders of the Congress. In 1923 a split occurred when Ajmal Khan set up a branch of the Swaraj party, which was opposed by Ansari. In 1923 Pearey Lal, Vice-President of the Municipality and Secretary of the local Bar Association, was elected to the Legislative Assembly on the Swaraj ticket.[99] The Ali Brothers visited Delhi occasionally, and the *Comrade* resumed publication from 1924. Asaf Ali became a municipal member from 1924, but from 1921 the Congress leaders prepared panels of names of candidates for elections. The pattern of the communal electorates of 1922 was such that rivalries now were between the Hindus themselves or between different sections of the Muslims. In October 1924 the Municipality by a majority (14 to 9) passed a resolution in favour of joint electorates.[100] By this proposal, each voter was to have two votes (as the Municipality had wanted in 1922) on condition that he cast one vote for a Hindu and one for a Muslim. Those who opposed it said that the proposal was engineered by the Congress, and went against the interests of the Muslims. A meeting of the Muslims at Jama Masjid declared that the interests of Muslims would be safeguarded only by separate electorates. This was endorsed by Mohammad Ali and other Muslim Congressmen. Mohammad Ali at the same time created some ambiguity saying that since the number of Muslim votes in Delhi was roughly equal to that of the Hindus, the safeguard of separate electorates was unnecessary. The Municipality needed 'good city Fathers and not game-cocks who make municipal meetings the cockpit of Hindu–Muslim wranglings'.[101]

The dissident view gave the Chief Commissioner the excuse to reject the municipal resolution. The resolution was given publicity by the press, and held out as an example to the rest of the country. The *Hindustan Times* adjured the citizens of India's capital to protect their self-respect by seeing to it that their municipal commissioners did their duty. 'If they fail and but help in the perpetuation of the mummery of their Municipality, they will have only themselves to blame . . .' The *Tribune* and the *Bombay Chronicle* (which had Asaf Ali as its Delhi correspondent) agreed with this view, but Muslim newspapers were inclined to support the separate electorates programme.

Another rebuff that the Chief Commissioner administered to the Municipality in 1924 was to reject its proposal that the Punjab Municipal (Amendment) Act of 1923 be extended to Delhi, to make the Municipality an 'empowered local body'. Any legislation must be postponed, he said, 'till conditions throughout urban Delhi become more stable'.[102]

The explanation for the Chief Commissioner's arbitrary action as well as for the change in Mohammad Ali's attitude on the question of separate electorates lies in the occurrence of a riot in 1924.[103] In early 1924 there was no political activity in the city, though nationalist leaders were frequently in Delhi and many conferences took place. These did not disturb 'the calm surface of the local life of the city'. But in July 1924 a riot occurred during Bakr-Id. Local officials saw this Hindu–Muslim tension as a reflection of a development common to all of north India since 1922. In Delhi the disintegration of the Congress–Khilafat entente led to a weakening in the hold of men like Ajmal Khan on the local people. But in Delhi there was now, as in 1919, a local factor which complicated issues. This was the setting up of the new slaughter-house near the Idgah in 1916; Hindus and Jains had protested because of its being near the Jhandewalan temple. The development and settlement of the Idgah-Jhandewalan area made it highly probable that friction would occur when sacrificial cows were led to the slaughter-house. In 1924 the Pahari Dhiraj road was added to the routes which were to be closed to the passage of cows being taken for sacrifice. This was the shortest route to the slaughter-house for Muslims living in Sadar Bazaar, and they therefore decided to challenge the municipal order. That this might lead to a clash was apprehended for some time, and the Congress–Khilafat Unity Board made efforts to avert it.[104] But they were powerless to stop the scrimmage in Bagh Diwar snow-balling into a free-for-all in Chandni Chowk, with lathis and brickbats in evidence. Mohammad Ali, Ajmal Khan, Ansari and Shankar Lal were in the tragic situation of respected men present at the affray and unable to restore calm. 'For the first time after many years,' wrote the embittered Mohammad Ali to Gandhiji, 'I have come in touch with a section of the Muslims who have held back from N.C.O. and the Khilafat—and Mohammad Ali and Shaukat Ali and Maulvi Kifayatullah are losing their hold over them.'[105] With a supreme sense of humiliation he confessed: 'We the Congress have decided to admit defeat and leave the maintenance of peace to the guns of the police.' As things began to return to 'normal', he said, 'Business relations cannot be resisted, but hearts have been torn asunder.'[106] The Muslims refused to accept refreshments from Hindus after Id. Gandhiji suggested that a committee of enquiry be set up under the Congress, but some members, including the Secretary of the local Congress Committee, Indra (Shraddhanand's son), were half-hearted about the utility of such an enquiry.

The *Shuddhi* and *Tabligh* movements must have sharpened tension between orthodox Hindus and Muslims in Delhi as elsewhere in north India. But local factors were equally important in explaining this riot. The main protagonists in 1924 were the butchers of Pahari Dhiraj and the Jats of Sadar Bazaar. These Jats for centuries had had little contact with the dwellers of the walled city except encounters during acts of brigandage by them in periods of political instability; in the decade before 1924 they had come under the influence of the Arya Samaj. They had also come closer to the city when the wall started to be demolished and the city started moving westward into what had hitherto been agricultural land or wasteland. The butchers had been a disgruntled group since the Municipality enacted its regulations about the sale of meat. These factors, combined with the unhappy choice made by Beadon for the new slaughter-house, were as important in explaining the riot of 1924 as was the collapse of the Khilafat movement. But the disillusionment of Mohammad Ali and of Ajmal Khan (who was to retire from politics soon after and died three years later, in 1927) contributed to keeping the tension simmering so that for the next few years non-involved inhabitants feared that riots could occur again. The officials were also on the alert, and were so alarmist that in 1925 a clash between two Hindu candidates for municipal elections was hastily misreported as a communal riot. Rauf Ali (who had in 1921 organized the protest against high rents) resigned from the Municipality in order to defend the Muslims accused in the 1924 riots. Asaf Ali, who had been elected to represent Delhi Province in the Imperial Council, was unseated in 1926 by Lala Rang Behari Lal, also a lawyer, who got many Hindu votes because he had defended the Hindus in the 1924 riots. When the Pahari Dhiraj route again became a matter of contention in 1925, the Muslim municipal members did their best to defuse tension, first by appealing to fellow-Muslims to forego the route, then by asking for a new slaughter-house at Bara Hindu Rao. The first appeal met with resistance from more militant Muslims, the second was not accepted by the officials. 'The result is that the shops are closed and ... the machine-guns are allowed to patrol . . . through the city.'[107] In 1932 Sri Ram was to condemn the 'exhibition of strong communal feelings' in the administration of the city.[108]

New Delhi Municipality was set up in 1916, but it became an effective body (of ten members) only in 1925. Delhi's Deputy Commissioner was given charge of developing the city and managing the *nazul* properties (which were resumed that year by the Imperial Government), but in 1928 this responsibility of the Deputy Commissioner ceased. The reason given was that he was already President of an enormous Municipality 'with more serious problems of its own';[109] this was said by Johnson (who had at one time been Deputy Commissioner himself). The time was past, he added, when this official could even devote himself chiefly to that Municipality and its problems. He also thought that the New Delhi Municipality would be 'in a favourable position—in the close neighbourhood of the long-established Delhi Municipality and will be able to profit by the lessons there learned and by the ripe experience of a very capable officer [i.e. Sohan Lal, then Secretary of the Municipality and earlier President of the Notified Area Committee]'. In the first joint service worked out for the two Municipalities—the Joint Water Board set up in 1925, under the Chief Commissioner and administered by the P.W.D.—friction soon developed. The charges were made arbitrarily, and the Delhi Municipality refused to pay.[110] They were also dissatisfied with the reduced quantity of water available to them (a large portion was going to the Notified Area, New Delhi, and the new Cantonment). The Delhi municipal representatives on the Water Board Committee were militant Congress sympathizers—Asaf Ali, Lala Pearey Lal, Lala Sri Ram—and they were able, by taking a firm stand, to get better terms for the Municipality. By 1930, the political polarization in Delhi was complete. As Ansari commented despairingly, the Congress could not hope for much support in a city where 'all the well-to-do people . . . are connected with the cloth trade . . . the lawyers, doctors and *hakims* are all ultra-loyalists . . . the Muslim shopkeepers are under the influence of Maulana Mohammad Ali'.[111]

By 1931 certain implications of the transfer of the capital had become clear. Urban government in the Delhi area was now more concerned with the maintenance of the capital than with the upkeep of the 'old city', except where the latter was in close proximity to the former. The most well-developed municipal service, the water supply system, was turned to the benefit of the new town at the cost of the 'old'.

After Delhi became the seat of the Central Government, political activity was constant and on occasion, when connected with local problems, affected the local inhabitants. This political activity was carried on in the 'old city', which remained the political heart of the urban area, though sandwiched between the arid stretches of New Delhi and the apolitical bureaucratic island of the Civil Lines. The officials were more anxious now than before to maintain a balance between various political groups and between the two major communities. The blinkers they wore led them very often to make erroneous analyses, and these were used to justify strong Imperial control. The net result was that the hold of the Chief Commissioner over the local government robbed it of much of its 'self-government' even though after 1919 this element had in theory been 'increased'. The loyalists remained numerous and the general tone of the city was a quiescent one. But sporadic acts of violence and the credibility-gap between the truly secular leaders and the people who participated in these acts of violence augured ill for the future. Delhi's splendid isolation was coming to an end—politically, and also ethnically (with the increasing number of Punjabis and Bengalis coming to the city). From this time onwards, Delhi became increasingly part of India, though many of its people did not quite shed their sense of being a different breed, and their general indifference to national politics.

NOTES

1. C.C.O., Home, 185–6B/April 1913.
2. C.C.O., Home, F. 2A/Feb. 1917.
3. C.C.O., Education, F. 4A/Feb. 1914.
4. Ibid., F. 241B/1914.
5. Ibid., F. 4A/Feb. 1914.
6. Ibid., F. 86–90B/1914.
7. Ibid., 1–2A/March 1916.
8. Lala Sri Ram, *Municipal Problems in Delhi* (Delhi, 1932), p. 17.
9. C.C.O., Education, 94–97B/May 1914.

10. N.A.I., Home (Delhi), Deposit No. 1/Feb. 1913.
11. Ibid., 38–41A/July 1912.
12. C.C.O., Education, 1A/March 1913; N.A.I., Home Public, 34–46A/May 1913.
13. N.A.I., Home (Delhi), 38–41A/July 1912.
14. Ibid., 15A/March 1913.
15. *R.N.P.*, 1912, p. 111.
16. C.C.O., Rev. and Agr., F. 18B/1914.
17. N.A.I., Education, 3–6A/Oct. 1916.
18. C.C.O., Education, F. 8A/Sep. 1921 and ibid., 115–116B/July 1922.
19. I am grateful to Professor Nurul Hasan for this point of information.
20. C.C.O., Education, F. 8A/Sep. 1921.
21. Ibid., F. 13A/April 1926.
22. Ibid., 44–47B/Nov. 1916.
23. C.C.O., Military, F. 24B/1922.
24. C.C.O., Education, F. 92B/1920; ibid., F. 8A/Sep. 1921.
25. C.C.O., Education, F. 4(17)/1926.
26. N.A.I., Education, Health and Lands (L.S.G.), 28–29A/Nov. 1924.
27. Ibid., 1–6B/Nov. 1927.
28. C.C.O., Home, F. 37B/1925.
29. N.A.I., Education, Health and Lands (L.S.G.), 1–6B/Nov. 1927.
30. Lala Sri Ram, op. cit., pp. 70 and 78.
31. C.C.O., Home, F. 55B/1913.
32. C.C.O., Home, 132–137B/Sep. 1914.
33. C.C.O., Home Confidential, F. 34/1914.
34. N.A.I., Home (Delhi), 15A/March 1913.
35. There is a detailed account of the political developments in Delhi between 1911 and 1922 in D. W. Ferrell's unpublished Ph.D. thesis 'Delhi 1911–22: Society and Politics in the new Imperial Capital of India' (Australian National University, 1969). There is room for different analyses, however, because he tends to accept the two-community theory and the value-judgements made by British officials. He admits his debt to Rudé, and uses that author's categories even though the type of evidence which were used by Rudé are not available for Delhi. Another work on the political history of Delhi is Sangat Singh's *Freedom Movement in Delhi* (Delhi, 1972). This is based chiefly on the Confidential Reports, and is painted with a zealously nationalist brush. For a detailed critique, see my review of this book in *Indian Historical Review.* Vol. I, No. 2 (September 1974), pp. 431–4.
36. *R.N.P.*, 1912, p. 856.
37. *Times of India*, 13 July 1914.
38. I.O.R., Butler Papers, fols. 18–20.
39. N.A.I., Home Poll., 11A/Dec. 1914.
40. N.M.L., Mohammad Ali Papers, Deputy Commissioner, Delhi to Mohammad Ali, 27 Dec. 1912.
41. I.O.R., Hailey Papers, fols. 8–104.
42. N.A.I., Home Poll., 345–419B/May 1916.
43. *R.N.P.*, 1912, p. 425.

44. *Adu Babu (Dr Rashbehari Sen)* (Delhi, 1964), p. 15.
45. *The Curzon Gazette's* circulation in 1913 was 4,340, that of the *Comrade* 2,247 *(P.A.R.,* 1913–14, p. 68).
46. Ansari to Mohammad Ali, 28 Nov. 1912, Mushirul Hasan (ed.), *Muslims and the Congress* (Delhi, 1979), p. 2.
47. N.A.I., Home Poll. Progs., 494–487B/June 1919.
48. A. Ahmad, *Islamic Modernization in India and Pakistan* (London, 1967), p. 196; Ch. Khaliquzzaman, *Pathway to Pakistan* (Lahore, 1961), p. 31.
49. N.A.I., Home Poll., 549–552B/June 1915.
50. C.C.O., Home Confidential, F.34/1914.
51. Ansari to Mohammad Ali, 9 Oct. 1913 (Mohammad Ali Papers, MOH/L/1086).
52. C.C.O., Home Confidential, F.10/1913.
53. N.A.I., Home Poll., 259–262B/Aug. 1914; Mohammad Ali Papers, 1556 and 1560.
54. N.A.I., Home Poll. 412–415B/April 1915; ibid., 547–552B/June 1915.
55. C.C.O., Home Confidential, F.4/1916.
56. Ibid., and also F.4/1917.
57. *R.N.P.,* 1912, p. 494; N.A.I., Home Poll., 1–4B/July 1912.
58. N.A.I., MSS., Munshi Ram – C. F. Andrews Letters.
59. *Guardian,* 13 May 1921 (cutting in U.S.P.G.A.).
60. M. Sykes and B. D. Chaturvedi, *C. F. Andrews—A Narrative* (London, 1949), p. 52.
61. C.C.O., Education, F.160B/1914.
62. *R.N.P.,* 1913, p. 631.
63. C.C.O., Education, F.8A/Sep. 1921.
64. N.A.I., Home Poll., 399–402B/March 1918.
65. C. F. Andrews to Munshi Ram, 15 Nov. 1913, (Munshi Ram – C. F. Andrews Letters).
66. *New India,* 12 July 1917 (cutting in C.C.O., Home Confidential, F.4/1917).
67. Ibid.
68. I.O.R., Montague Papers, Enclosure.
69. C.C.O., Home Confidential, F.4/1917; ibid., F.48/1918, *R.N.P.,* 1917, p. 849.
70. *D.A.R.,* 1916–17, p. 8; C.C.O., Home, 111–113B/Dec. 1917; ibid., F.320B/1917; *R.N.P.,* 1917, p. 838.
71. N.A.I., Home (Police), 154–155B/April 1918.
72. *R.N.P.,* 1917, p. 876.
73. Letter to *Morning Post,* 23 Nov. 1917 (cutting in C.C.O., Home Confidential, F.4/1917).
74. N.A.I., Home Poll., 160–163B/Jan. 1918; ibid., 491–494B/June 1918.
75. C.C.O., Education, 118–119B/Nov. 1917.
76. C. F. Andrews to R. Tagore, 14 May 1917 (Viswa-Bharati MSS., Andrews – Tagore Letters).
77. *Disorders Inquiry Committee* (Delhi, 1920), Vol. I, Minutes of Evidence, p. 183.

78. Before giving an account of the Satyagraha, it would be useful to indicate what I consider to be the lacunae in Ferrell's analysis ('The Rowlatt Satyagraha in Delhi', in R. Kumar (ed.), *1919: Essays in Gandhian Politics* (London, 1971)). These can be summed up as follows:

   1. He uses the concepts of 'mob', 'crowd' and 'audience' but his police reports, unlike those of Rudé's for the French Revolution, are often impressionistic and therefore cannot be called accurate.
      (a) He speaks on one occasion of 50,000 by-standers [*sic*] at a funeral ceremony (p. 233).
      (b) He describes crowds as 'largely Muslim' or 'chiefly Hindu', without explaining how this was estimated. For instance, he speaks of an audience of 'Hindu artisans' though he has himself stated that artisans in Delhi were chiefly Muslim (p. 214).
   2. He does not notice the significance of the part played by rumours in this period. Here Rudé's *guru* Lefebvre (*La Grande Peur de 1789*, Haute-Marne, 1932, p. 87) has an instructive parallel to offer from Revolutionary France.
   3. There are intriguing juxtapositions, as on p. 233, when he says that communal harmony was absent, and that no violent speeches were made. Were 'violent speeches' an indication of 'communal harmony'?
   4. To prove that the 'secondary leaders' seized power from the 'primary leaders' (Beadon's categories) he says Ansari opposed the hartal, while also stating that Ansari's house was used by the hartal leaders!

79. Sykes and Chaturvedi, op. cit., p. 130.
80. N.A.I., Home Poll., Deposit 48/July 1919; also C. F. Andrews to R. Tagore, 14 May 1919 (Andrews–Tagore Letters).
81. C.C.O., Home Confidential, 4B/1919.
82. C.C.O., Education, F. 16B/1924.
83. D.C.O., Home Poll., p. viii (17)/46-General (old).
84. Ibid. Also Asaf Ali to Mohammad Ali, 14 Dec. 1923 (Mohammad Ali Papers).
85. N.A.I., Commerce (Int. Trade), 4/Aug. 1921.
86. C.C.O., Home Confidential, F. 3/1920.
87. D.C.O., Home Poll., p. viii (17)/46-General (old).
88. C.C.O., Home Confidential, F. 3/1921.
89. *Khan Bahadur Ka Janaza*, Vol. I (Delhi, 1920), and N.A.I., Home Poll., 35B/Feb. 1921.
90. N.A.I., Home (Ests.), 265–269B/1920.
91. C.C.O., Home, F. 238/1921.
92. C.C.O., Commerce and Industry, 26(a)B and 33B/1921.
93. C.C.O., Education, 94–95B/Jan. 1917.
94. C.C.O., Education, F. 141/May–Aug. 1915.
95. N.A.I., Home (Ests.), 204–205B/May 1921.
96. C.C.O., Education, 3–49A/Oct. 1921.
97. C.C.O., Education, 1–2A/March 1922.

98. C.C.O., Education, 59–79A/May 1929.
99. C.C.O., Home Confidential, F. 1/1923; ibid., F. 1/1924.
100. C.C.O., Education, 59–71A/May 1925.
101. *Comrade*, 6 Feb. 1925, in C.C.O., Education, 59–71A/May 1925.
102. N.A.I., Education, Health and Lands (L.S.G.), 11–12B/Nov. 1924.
103. C.C.O., Home, F. 25B/1925; N.A.I., Home Poll., F. 249/11B/1924 and ibid., F. 336B/1924.
104. Mohammad Ali to M. K. Gandhi, 12 July 1924 (M. Ali Papers, MOH/ L/24).
105. Same to same, 21 July 1924 (ibid., MOH/L/4709).
106. Same to same (MOH/L/4702 and 4709).
107. Abdur Rahman Siddiqi to M. A. Ansari, 1 July 1925, M. Hasan (ed.), *Muslims and the Congress* (Delhi, 1979), p. 14.
108. N.A.I., Home Poll., F. 106/iii/1925; N.A.I., Home Judicial, F. 250/1925; N.A.I., Home Public, F. 697/1925; C.C.O., Legis., F. 38/1926; Sri Ram, op. cit., p. 18.
109. N.A.I., Home Public, F. 414/1930.
110. C.C.O., Education, F. 4(35)B/1925.
111. M. A. Ansari to Jawaharlal Nehru, 19 Oct. 1929, M. Hasan (ed.), op. cit., p. 88.

8

CONCLUSION

'A city is as much a personality as a human being...There are cities whose histories are always an expression of violence. There are others which are renowned for their breadth of mind, others for their industry, yet others for their skill and craftsmanship and so on, until you begin to see in the mind's eye a picture of the...inner life of the city long before you visit it...'

—*Philip Paneth*

The cross within the circle, the Egyptian symbol for the city, is fundamental for any study of Delhi. The circle of the city wall insulated the inhabitants from much that went on outside and separated them from the rural hinterland and from other towns. It also created a sense of community which cut through communal and class groups. 'The texture of the circumvallation was as much· of the spirit as it was of stone and mortar.'[1] Time and again, from Bernier to Abdul Hai, observers have commented on the fact that the people of Delhi were quite unconcerned about anything beyond their walls. Together with this went a great love for the city. *Kaun jaye Zauq par Dilli ki galian chhorkar* (How can anyone forsake Delhi and its lanes?).[2] This concept of belonging to Shahjahanabad, an urban island in a rural sea, the aesthetically pleasing creation of an emperor's whim, was bound to undergo a change when the British began to rule Delhi.

The character of Delhi city emerges clearly in the tranquil years before 1857—a civilized, cultured community with non-competing and mutually respecting élites. There was a close rapport between different sections of society, because Muslim *umara*, Hindu *kayasths*, Muslim and Hindu merchants, European and Indian intellectuals, even some British officials, partook of the common diet of Delhi's Urdu culture. The narrow two-dimensional Victorian vision of some Englishmen led them to paint a dismal picture of a 'decadent' Mughal Court in the years 1803–57. This was far from true. Bahadur Shah's long reign, particularly, saw a vigorous flowering of Delhi's Urdu literature. His pensioner's existence and the political security led the Court to develop as a cultural centre, a surrogate for political power. From the 1830s this was supplemented by the work of the Delhi College, where the Vernacular Translation Society fostered a rich and many-sided education, and developed Urdu as a medium for transmitting Western science and classical learning. In these decades the original sense of the word 'urbanize'—'to civilize'—was appropriate for Delhi. Western civilization was regarded not as a superior culture to be copied but as one from which much that was useful might be learnt.

As in culture, so with British concepts of municipal government now and later, the impact in Delhi was less than in the Presidency towns, which were colonial settlements. When the British publicized the concept of using local taxes for municipal services, this was only a variation of the administration by the *Kotwal* in the two centuries preceding. But in the years between 1803 and 1857, the very fact of the administration of the city being in the hands of two governments made it inevitable that the interaction would give rise to some features which would affect government and race-relations in the future. Here, as elsewhere in India, the British became victims of the tendency to think in stereotypes, which the Mughals had not done. The British regarded the Muslims and Hindus as two separate and antagonistic communities which they had to balance. This, coupled with their phobia of crowds, made them unduly alarmist when any fracas occurred during religious celebrations and at times of Waha'bi excitement, though in Delhi, Waliullah's theological doctrines had a stronger appeal than his revolutionary teaching. The army was often used as a deterrent, but since the more fearsome enemy was the Punjabi, the Cantonment was on the Ridge facing the north-west. The events of 1857 took the British completely by surprise.

The trauma of the Revolt and Counter-Revolt snapped the links between political and cultural institutions, widened the gulf between the British and the Indians, and implanted a lasting fear of revolt in the minds of the Europeans. The cosmopolitanism that had existed before 1857 was adversely affected by the decision of the officials to live away from the city in a Civil Lines. Even the missionaries rather shamefacedly opted to live there rather than in the city, where their work would have been more effective. From the 1890s the Club and the offices which had been inside the city were also moved out, probably because of the fear of plague. This deliberate exclusiveness heightened the alarmism shown by officials during festivals—an alarmism magnified by their continuing to think in stereotypes about Hindus and Muslims. This made them depend on the army and the police to suppress any excitement covered by the portmanteau word 'disturbances', and on the loyalists as a means of communicating with the people of the city. They failed to appreciate the resentment caused by the presence of the army and the police, and the fact that the loyalists were not 'leaders', as the officials optimistically termed them, but merely men of substance whose presence did not necessarily carry weight with the people.

The officials expected the loyalists to act as mediators between themselves and the people. But on the occasions when there was tension in the city the loyalists did not back the administration in its attempts to maintain 'order', nor did the officials treat them as colleagues. This was so during the *Rathjatra* episode in 1863, the riot of 1886, the plague-scare of 1898, the 1919 Satyagraha and the riot of 1924. It was impossible for Indians and Britons to work together as long as the officials feared a repetition of 1857 and also acted ham-handedly *vis-à-vis* the Indians, most obviously when they enrolled some of the most respected citizens as 'special constables' in 1919.

The Municipality instituted in 1863 in place of the *kotwali* was different in that its primary function was to maintain law and order, not through the *chowkidars* but through the police, imposed by the Provincial Government but paid for with local taxes. It also differed from the Mughal system in that it included some of the inhabitants as participants, first by nomination and later by election. The choice of people nominated was determined by an individual's loyalty to the British in 1857. Those of proved loyalty were boosted by being given municipal office and *durbari* status. But such kudos, while gratifying, was not essential for these men, who were nearly all rich landowners, bankers and merchants. Some of them, the mercantile community, found British patronage useful but the others did not really need it.

The loyalists singled out by the *Herrenvolk* could have become an incipient new élite. But wealth and official favour could not upset the traditional hierarchy of status, which had been shaken but not destroyed by the events of 1857–8. This shone through the dust of poverty and grief, and till the 1890s it helped to maintain the social harmony which was such a marked feature of Delhi. To the members of the traditional *rais*, recognition by the British *per se* was meaningless, sometimes even distasteful. The officials offered a caricature substitute for the Court by forming the Delhi Society. Starting as a rallying-point for the loyalists, in the 1870s and 1880s this Society showed promise of developing as a forum of public opinion, but its most articulate members migrated to Lahore, where there were more opportunities for professionals. The Delhi College continued the ethos of the 1850s in the second phase of its existence (1864–77). The vacuum it left after 1877 was partially filled by religious reformist associations, Christian, Muslim and Hindu, thus beginning the process of decreasing the sense of community.

Delhi was at once a military post and a commercial entrepôt. But because it was not a provincial capital, environmental services came a low second in the order of priority in municipal spending, and medical and educational expenditure still further down. By the 1890s the pressure of population in the limited area of the walled city and the uncontrolled expansion of the suburbs made it imperative to introduce public health services. After 1911 to this was added a new urgency, the need to make Delhi a respectable neighbour to the new capital city. The inhabitants did not agitate for municipal reform, chiefly because they regarded the British innovations as unnecessary or unwelcome superimpositions on their beloved city. Many British concepts were contrasted unfavourably with earlier institutions—the police system with the *chowkidari* system, Western medical facilities with that afforded by Delhi's eminent hakims, the new sewerage system with the Shahjahani drains, the piped water supply with the canal, the barren Civil Lines with the glittering Palace, Western education, particularly missionary schools and colleges, with that of the *madarsas;* direct taxation was unpopular.

After 1858, the cross cut gashes into the circle, when trunk roads and railways were built, but because the wall was retained, the urban area did not have its edges blurred in a 'rural–urban continuum' except in the west. There were individual officials in the 1870s and 1880s who were ahead of their generation in perceiving the need for ecological planning and phased extensions. Lack of concern on the part of the Government and the obduracy of the military authorities prevented these being implemented. From the 1890s the blue-prints prepared earlier began to be translated into reality, a process hastened by the two Durbars. The city extension schemes were taken seriously after 1912 because it was vital to avoid the embarrassment of unhygienic and jerry-built areas between the northern and southern wings of the capital. After 1911, when the number of professionals interested in serving on the Municipality increased, Indian commissioners showed more interest in ecological development. When 'local self-government' became a transferred subject in 1921, the Indians were anxious for an Improvement Trust, and were zealous in guarding the Municipality's rights in those public services which were shared with the New Delhi Municipality. In Delhi, even though municipal government had been made a 'transferred' subject, official control was so great that schemes to integrate the old and new cities were shelved, even when they had been made by an Englishman like Geddes, who found the ruler of princely Indore more responsive. One marvels at the lack of realism on the part of men who blithely planned a city that would last five hundred years, and treated as a minor inconvenience the human element—the people of Delhi, who were living cramped in a town with the highest population density in India. Goaded by the rising cost of living brought on as much by the transfer of the capital as by the War, they protested on 30 March 1919 in a massive and disciplined fashion which surprised the officials.

The degree of official control in Delhi was so great as to make meaningless the argument that 'the work of local government bodies acted as some kind of counterpoise to the apparently all-pervading influence of the official administration'.[3] This statement, made in old age, was Hailey's, one of the most imperialistic bureaucrats Delhi had known! Financial limitations were also a reason why municipal services did not expand in proportion to the growth in prosperity in the town. The generalization made for British India that between 1882 (the year of Ripon's Resolution on Local Self-Government) and 1908 (the year the Decentralization Commission met) municipal income doubled but did not lead to any expansion in the scope of public services[4] is true for Delhi. In the case of Delhi various reasons can be given to account for this slow growth. In this period the Municipality was saddled with the medical and educational charges and also continued to bear the cost of the police force, because the Provincial Government did not carry out its side of the bargain. The crown lands were not utilized to increase revenue until after 1911; when their value became obvious, the Imperial Government asserted possession of them. Provincial and Imperial loans were seldom given to Delhi Municipality, though the European-dominated Notified Area Committee after 1911 subsisted largely on these, a degree of preferential treatment possible only in a colonial situation.

Since the Municipality was dominated before and after 1884 by the mercantile and banking groups, the burden of taxation fell chiefly on the professional and lower-paid sections. The rich were, however, generous in their philanthropy, because of which the Municipality was able to execute many public works and carry out effective famine-relief. Donations, not taxes, had been the traditional method of contributing to public services, and this continued to be evident in the late nineteenth and early twentieth centuries.

The loyalists were in a majority in the Municipality in these decades. They did not need to make much special effort to win votes. Because the situation was so placid, we cannot agree with the view that in Delhi the Municipality 'fulfilled [its] educative purpose even when [it] fell short in administrative achievement'.[5] The sons and grandsons of the loyalists of 1863 opted for an English education in missionary schools and colleges, and later for professional careers, but remained securely cushioned by the family wealth. Anglicization did not bring them closer to the officials, in whose minds fear of Delhi's position as the old Mughal capital was added to the fear of modern political developments in India.

The British stereotype of two distinct Hindu and Muslim communities was not applicable to Delhi because this usually holds good in a situation where one community is in a distinct minority or if the communities are identifiable with particular classes. The Muslims did become a minority as a result of death and exile in 1858, and they had reason to be bitter because many of them had been impoverished, all of them were under suspicion and their mosques were confiscated and desecrated. But as a community they were invigorated by the immigrant Punjabi Muslim merchants, who stridently took up pan-Islamic issues and whose wealth fed the mosques and *madarsas*. There was not always consensus between them and the older-established Muslim families. Similar tension occurred between the established Hindu families and the immigrant Jains, and later, as the Arya Samaj–Sanatan Dharam ideological rivalry showed, between Punjabi and Delhi Hindus. Muslim *chamars* defied Muslim merchants, and a 'riot' occurred when the supporters of rival Hindu candidates clashed during municipal elections. There were, therefore, many occasions of tension in the city, but these did not run along distinct religious, class, or provincial lines.

The absence of communal separatism is indicated by the lack of any demand for separate electorates. In the 1880s, the 1890s, and again in 1907, the limitation of the *rais* and the loyalists was the same—they all wanted special weightage for wealth and property. The officials on these occasions speciously claimed that communalism was so strong in Delhi that Government control was necessary in the Municipality to ensure a balance; in 1920 they forced the Municipality to accept separate electorates on the basis of religion, a measure the Municipality itself revoked later. Therefore in Delhi at least it does not hold true that 'the extended elective system naturally served to aggravate communal differences... Modern communalism in its organized form may be said to have begun from the introduction of the elective principle.'[6] Mohammad Ali wrote in 1912 that 'Moslem Delhi is beyond the skill of the restorer... The Hindus of Delhi can hardly be distinguished from their Moslem brethren.'[7]

The issues on which public opinion expressed itself collectively in Delhi were more often local than national. The most sustained and broad-based agitations were those for the restoration of Delhi College in 1876–82 and for the revocation of the house-tax in 1902–9. The large audiences that collected to hear speeches on nationalist, non-local subjects after 1912 were symptomatic of the dilution of the sense of community which the walled city had fostered. Two factors were responsible for this. One was the suburban sprawl, which diffused the population over an area too large to permit a sense of community in an age of slow communications. The other was the influence of revivalist and nationalist ideologies. The use of the Idgah as the venue for a meeting in 1910 had a dual significance—it symbolized the growth of the western suburbs, with the Idgah a more accessible rallying point than the Jama Masjid. It also indicated the growth of politicization, the opposition of nationalist Muslims to the loyalist *rais* who controlled the Jama Masjid.

Most cities have a heart, and Delhi's was Chandni Chowk, even after the growth of the western suburbs and the artificial development of the northern suburbs. In 1858 Ghalib had bemoaned the ending of an age, symbolized for him by the Canal in Chandni Chowk abruptly ceasing to be a hub of social activity. The walled city, which had an ecological rationale of its own, appeared doomed to extinction in 1858; the gallows set up in Chandni Chowk seemed to portend this. But the East India Railway line gave the city new life, and commercial activity picked up, particularly in Chandni Chowk. Municipal administration was introduced to Delhi and formally installed in the Town Hall. The opposition to urban government was symbolized by the meetings in Queens Gardens and Pipal Park in 1898, 1906, 1908, and in 1919. These protests indicated the strains being put on a medieval city by increasing congestion and inadequate services. But the protests were expressed with little elbow-room, because though they were made to the authority located in the Town Hall, they were under the shadow of guns in the Fort trained on Chandni Chowk, a threat that even sympathetic officials were not prepared to see removed. The increasing congestion also caused clashes when the Mohurram and Ram Lila processions collided in Chandni Chowk, clashes which occasionally flared up into riots. The Durbar and the State entry cavalcades, the British equivalents of the Mughal processions, evoked interest among the inhabitants, but no sense of identification. The Satyagraha leaders clashed with the police in the Chowk in 1919, the Jats and the butchers indulged in violence in 1924. The failure of Ajmal Khan's attempts to restore calm after the riot of 1924 marked the end of an epoch. After that episode, the spirit of Shahjahanabad was to glimmer more and more faintly. At the same time, because of government policy, Delhi was to become more and more a neglected appendage to a pampered capital city.

NOTES

1. A. Gerschenkron in O. H. Handlin and J. Burchard (eds.), *The Historian and the City* (Massachusetts, 1966).
2. Zauq (1790–1854).
3. Hailey, in Foreword to H. Tinker, op. cit., p. xiii.
4. Ibid., p. 51.
5. T. G. P. Spear (ed.), *The Oxford History of India* (Oxford, 1958), p. 722.
6. B. B. Misra, *Administrative History of India 1834–1947* (Delhi, 1970), p. 609.
7. *Comrade*, 13 Jan. 1912.

MEMBERS OF DELHI MUNICIPALITY,
1863-1931
(classified by occupation)

The dates indicate the years each member served on the Municipality. Names of English officials and of Indians who were members of the Municipality by virtue of their official positions have been omitted.

The first elections under 'local self-government' took place in 1885. After 1922 the rules of 1921 (setting up separate communal electorates) were in force.

Titles like Lala, Mir, Hafiz, Haji and Sheikh have been omitted.

Bankers
1. Sahib Singh, 1863-9, 1871-86
2. Chunna Mal, 1863-70 (related to 4, 11 and 22 below)
3. Ummed Singh, 1863-9
4. Umrao Singh, 1864-76
5. Mahesh Das, 1863-74
6. Ajodhya Pershad, 1864-74 (brother of 7 below)
7. Dharm Das, 1874-84
8. Rammi Mal, 1870-80
9. Narain Das Gurwala, 1870-4 (related to 14 and 29 below)
10. Shiv Sahai Mal, 1875-97
11. Hardhyan Singh, 1880-1911
12. Jagannath Naharwala, 1884-6
13. Girdhar Lal, 1885-98
14. Sri Kishen Das Gurwala, 1886-1914
15. Pyare Lal, 1887-97
16. Jawahar Lal, 1893-1912
17. Nihal Singh, 1893-5
18. Sultan Singh, 1901-26 (son of 17 above)
19. Lachmi Narain, 1902-14
20. Ishri Prasad, 1906-9
21. Amba Prasad, 1911-29
22. Jageshwar Nath Goela, 1915-18
23. Radha Mohan, 1915-18
24. Madho Pershad, 1918-22 (son of 11 above)

25. Sri Ram, 1920–31
26. Ram Lal Khemka, 1922–5
27. Lachman Das, 1922–31
28. Nanak Chand, 1925 (son of 3 above)
29. Sat Narain Gurwala, 1925–31
30. Ram Krishan Das Chandiwala, 1928–9
31. Laxmi Narain Gadodia, 1929–30

Merchants

1. Baldeo Singh, 1874–80
2. Hazari Mal, 1881–2, 1898–1902
3. Bala Prasad, 1885–93
4. Shimbhu Nath, 1890–1903
5. Jai Narain, 1893–1901
6. Nathu Ram, 1904–16
7. Niadar Mal, 1910–13
8. Mina Mal Sohani, 1913–22
9. Gur Prasad Kapur, 1918–26
10. Pearey Lal Motorwala, 1922–7
11. Madan Mohan Lal, 1922–31
12. Ram Pershad, 1922–31
13. Baldev Singh, 1922–7
14. Risal Singh, 1922–5
15. Manohar Lal Bhargava, 1922–31
16. Bulaqi Das, 1922–6
17. Deshbandhu Gupta, 1929
18. Mahbub Bux, 1863–88
19. Vilayat Husain Khan, 1863–9
20. Nur Husain, 1880–93
21. Nur Mohammad, 1885–1900
22. Hafizullah, 1885–1901
23. Nur Ilahi, 1893–1905
24. Qamaruddin, 1906–10
25. Abdul Ghani, 1909–13
26. Abdul Ahad, 1911–15
27. Nasiruddin, 1912–19
28. Ghiyasuddin, 1919–22
29. Mahbub Ilahi, 1915–22
30. Zamir-ul-Haq, 1922–5
31. Mir Mohammad Husain, 1922–7

32. Abdul Khaliq, 1922–5
33. Abdur Razzaq, 1922–7
34. Mumtaz Husain Khan, 1922–5
35. Mohammad Tamizuddin Khan, 1922–31
36. Azizuddin, 1927

Lawyers

1. Gopal Singh, 1875–84
2. Jugal Kishore, 1896–1907
3. Basheshar Nath Goela, 1903–12 (related to 22 in list of bankers)
4. Wazir Singh, 1908–17
5. Shiv Narain, 1906–16, 1918–22
6. Rup Narain, 1915–18
7. Pearey Lal, 1918–25 (son of 13 in list of bankers)
8. Sri Ram, 1922–9 (son of Kanhaiya Lal, cloth merchant)
9. Rang Behari Lal, 1925–7
10. Bishen Dayal, 1925–31
11. Harish Chandra, 1928–31
12. Mohammad Ismael Khan, 1896–1902
13. Azizuddin, 1911–31
14. Abdul Aziz, 1915–31
15. Abdul Rahman, 1911–30
16. Rauf Ali, 1922–4
17. Mohammad Aminuddin, 1925–7
18. Asaf Ali, 1925–9
19. S. M. Abdulla, 1923–31
20. Mohammad Rashiduddin, 1928–31
21. Mirza Ijaz Husain, 1927

Aristocrats

1. Diwan Inamullah Khan, 1863–9
2. Nawab Shahabuddin Khan Loharu, 1864–9
3. Nawab Mohammad Husain Khan, 1870–3
4. Mirza Suleiman Shah, 1874–88 (son of Mirza Ilahi Bux)
5. Nawab Mohammad Najaf Khan, 1884–5
6. Mirza Iqbal Shah, 1888–95
7. Syed Sultan Mirza, 1888–98 (of the family of Nawab Itmad-uddaula)
8. Syed Fakruddin, 1891–6

9. Mirza Surayya Jah, 1892-1912 (brother of 4 above)
10. Mohammad Ilahi Bux Khan, 1892–1906
11. Ghulam Mohammad Hasan Khan, 1896–1914 (father of 34 in list of merchants)
12. Syed Umrao Mirza, 1914–18, 1921–2
13. Pirzada Mohammad Husain, 1919–27
14. Nawab Abul Hasan Khan, 1925-31

Hakims and Doctors

1. Hakim Ghulam Raza Khan, 1870–6
2. Hakim Zahiruddin Ahmad Khan, 1874
3. Hakim Ahmad Syed Khan, 1898–1913
4. Dr M. A. Ansari, 1915–17
5. Dr S. P. Shroff, 1918–21
6. Dr Hari Ram, 1925–31
7. Hakim Nasiruddin Ahmad Khan, 1925–7
8. Hakim Mohammad Zafar Khan, 1925 (son of Abdul Majid Khan)
9. Dr C. R. Jeyna, 1928–30

Educationists

1. Mohammad Ikramullah Khan, 1875–1907
2. Rev. J. C. Chatterji, 1927–31

It has not been possible to ascertain the occupations of 12 members; their names have been omitted.

GLOSSARY

Ahl-e-Hadis   an Islamic sect
akhara   place for wrestling
anjuman   association
badmash   rascal
bajra   fireworks display during Mohurrum
Bakr-Id   Muslim festival commemorating Abraham's proposed sacrifice of Ismael
bakshi   paymaster
bakshish   gratuity
bania   trader
banjar   uncultivated
bara   house
baradari   spacious house set in garden
barbhunja   corn-chandler
basti   a cluster of houses
bela   riverine land
biradari   fraternity
chabutra   platform
chamar   tanner
chaprassi   office attendant
chowdhuri   head of caste guild
chowkidar   watchman
dalal   broker
Darbari   courtier (title given by the British entitling holder to a place at official levées)
daroga   police superintendent
dar-ul-Harb   literally, 'land of war', region not under Islamic law (term used by Wali'allah)
dar-ul-Islam   land of Islam
Dassehra   Hindu festival celebrating Rama's defeat of Ravana
dastan-go   story-teller
doli   closed litter
ekka   small one-horse carriage
farman   royal mandate

fatwa   judicial decree under Islamic law
ganj   market-place
gharry   cart, carriage
ghazal   ode, short poem
ghee   clarified butter
ghosi   cowherd
gora   white (an Englishman)
gota   gold or silver thread
gwala   milkman
hakim   physician practising one of the Muslim systems of medicine
halwai   sweetmeat-seller
Hanafi   a Muslim sect
hartal   ceasing work or closing shop as a sign of protest
haveli   a large traditional house
Holi   Hindu spring festival
hundi   bill of exchange
Idgah   a place of assembly and prayer for Muslim festivals, always situated outside a town
Id-ul-Fitr   Muslim festival marking the end of the month-long fast in the month of Ramzan
ilaka   area
imam   preceptor
imambara   a place of worship where Mohurrum is celebrated
jagir   estate
jamadar   guard
jangal-baahar   on the edge of the forest
jharoka   small window
kabutarbazi   pigeon-flying
kachahri   court
kandlakash   making of gold-wire
karkhandar   artisan
katra   market
khandani   family
Khilafat   spiritual leadership of Islam; also, the pan-Islamic movement after the First World War to maintain the authority of the Sultan of Turkey
khillat   a robe or some other mark of honour
kotwal   chief of police in a town
kucha   lane

kuchabandi   gate, shutting off one lane from another
kumhar   potter
Kursi-nashin   title given by the British entitling holder to a seat at official levées
lakh   one hundred thousand
lala   prefix used for *khatri* and *vaishya* members of the trading community
lathi   baton, stout stick
maafi   freehold land
madarsa   school, usually attached to a mosque
mahajani   a form of Hindi script used by businessmen and shop-keepers
maidan   open grassy field
mali   gardener
maulvi   master of Muslim law
mauza   village
mela   festival, fair
mirza   member of a royal family
mohulla   identifiable separate area of town; neighbourhood
Mohurrum   ten days of mourning observed by Shias to com-memorate the death of Hasan and Hosain
mullah   Muslim priest
naib   deputy
namak-haraam   traitor
nawab   aristocratic title
nazar   gift given as homage
nazul   royal estate
nekzaat   honest
pakora   vegetables fried in batter
panchayat   committee of arbitration, with five members
parwana   command
patangbazi   kite-flying
pathsala   primary school
pinjrapole   charitable hospital for animals
punsaria   small shopkeeper
purdah-nashin   woman who observes purdah
qasida   eulogium
rais   term used to indicate respectability/wealth
Ram Lila   pageant depicting life of Rama, enacted during Dassehra

16

Rathjatra religious festival of the Jains

raunaq gaiety

sabha association

sahib-log Englishmen

sahukar moneylender

saiban canopy

sardarakhti garden with trees

sarkar/sirkar government

satta a gambling game

satyagraha political movement of non-violent resistance associated with Gandhi

serai inn

Shuddhi movement for reconversion to Hinduism

sufed posh gentleman (literally, one who wears white dress)

Swadeshi literally, made in one's own country; a political movement to promote Indian manufactures and to boycott foreign products

Tabligh Muslim conversion movement of the nineteen-twenties

tai-khana cellar

tarkashi wire-drawing

tazia symbolic shrines of Hasan and Hosain used in Mohurrum celebrations

teh-bazari tax levied on pavement vendors

tehsil administrative sub-division of a district

thana police station

thanadar officer in a police station

theka/ticca on hire

thela cart pushed by hand

tonga horse-drawn carriage

ujar desolate

ulema learned men

umara nobility

unani the ionian system of medicine

vaidya Hindu physician

vakil pleader/advocate

zaildar superintendent of a group of villages

zamindar landowner

zenana that part of a house which is inhabited by women (opposite of *mardana*)

zillah an administrative unit, like district

BIBLIOGRAPHY

A. UNPUBLISHED SOURCES

(*a*) Official records, classified according to repository (arranged alphabetically)

Delhi Archives:
  Miscellaneous files of records for the period 1857–1912;
  Proceedings of the Chief Commissioner, 1912–30, particularly in the Departments of Home, Education, Revenue and Agriculture, Industry and Commerce, Military;
  Some files from the Deputy Commissioner's Office.
Delhi Municipal Corporation, Records Department:
  Delhi Municipal Proceedings, 1879 onwards, with some volumes missing.
India Office Records:
  Punjab Proceedings, A Series, in the Departments of Home, Education, Judicial, Military, Police and Municipalities for the period 1860–1912;
  Bengal Political Consultations, 1856–8;
  India and Bengal Despatches, 1857–8.
National Archives of India:
  Proceedings of the Government of India in the Department of Home, especially the following branches: Education, Judicial, Military, Police, Political, Public ('Delhi'); also other Departments: Foreign, Education, Health and Lands, especially the branches of Municipalities,. Commerce and Industry.
Punjab Records Office, Patiala:
  Records of the old Delhi Division, in the Political, Revenue, General, Education, Military and P.W.D. Departments for the period 1857–80.

(*b*) Private papers of individuals and institutions, arranged alphabetically and followed by name of repository

C. F. Andrews – Rabindranath Tagore Letters, Rabindra Bhavan, Visva-Bharati University.
Papers of Dr M. A. Ansari, Nehru Memorial Library, Delhi (in microfilm).
Browne MSS, National Library of Scotland, Edinburgh.
Papers of Lord Canning, India Office Library.
Papers of W. M. Hailey, India Office Library.
Papers of Lord Hardinge, Nehru Memorial Library (in microfilm).
Memoir of Rev. M. J. Jennings, typescript, U.S.P.G. Archives, London.
Papers of Lord John Lawrence, India Office Library.
T. T. Metcalfe Papers, India Office Library (in microfilm).
Papers of Lord Minto, National Archives of India (in microfilm).
Papers of Mohammad Ali, Nehru Memorial Library (in microfilm).

Papers of Edwin Montagu, India Office Library.
Munshi Ram – C. F. Andrews Letters, National Archives of India.
Papers of Charles Saunders, India Office Library.
'Waqa-e-Sri Ram' (manuscript memoirs), in the custody of Mr Naresh Dayal.
Warner MSS, India Office Library.
Papers of G. Fleetwood Wilson, India Office Library.
Women's Letters from India, U.S.P.G. Archives.

(*c*) Theses, some since published after revision

Bayly, C. A., 'Development of Political Organization in Allahabad Locality, 1880–1925' (D.Phil., University of Oxford, 1970).
Bhadra, Gautam, 'Some Socio-Economic Aspects of the Town of Murshidabad, 1765–93' (M.Phil., Jawaharlal Nehru University, 1973).
Bose, Ashish, 'Process of Urbanization in India, 1901–51' (Ph.D., Delhi University, 1959).
Ferrell, D. W., 'Delhi, 1911–22: Society and Politics in the New Imperial Capital of India' (Ph.D., Australian National University, 1969).
Holmes, Jessie, 'Administration of Delhi Territory, 1803–32' (Ph.D., London University, 1955).
Oldenburg, Veena Talwar, 'Peril, Pestilence and Perfidy: The Making of Colonial Lucknow, 1856–77' (Ph.D., University of Illinois, 1979).

B. PUBLISHED SOURCES

(*a*) Official reports and publications

Annual Reports, Delhi Municipality.
Census of Delhi, 1913.
Census of Punjab, 1881, 1891, 1901, 1911 and 1921.
Census of North-Western Provinces, 1853.
Delhi Administration Reports, 1913 onwards.
Delhi Residency and Agency Records, 1807–57 (Lahore, 1915).
Gazette of India.
Gazetteer of the Delhi District, 1883–4.
Gazetteer of Punjab, 1913, volume on Delhi District.
Imperial Gazetteer, Vol. XI, 1908.
Master Plan for Delhi, 2 vols. (Delhi, 1960).
Military Report on Country around Delhi (Simla, 1909).
Nazul Lands Administered by Delhi Municipality (Lahore, 1908).
Punjab Administration Reports, 1850–1912.
Report of Disorders Enquiry Committee (Calcutta, 1920).
Report of Punjab Provincial Committee, with minutes and memorials submitted to the Education Commission, 1882 (Calcutta, 1884).
Three *Reports of the Town Planning Committee to Select a Site for the the New Capital* (Parliamentary Papers Cmd. 6881, 6885 and 6889 of 1913).

Report on the Famine in the Punjab, 1869–70.

Report of the Indian Factory Labour Commission (Parliamentary Paper 74 of 1908).

Report of the Indian Industrial Commission (Parliamentary Paper 17 of 1919).

Report on the Crown Lands at Delhi (Lahore, 1910).

Report on the Selections from the Records of the North-Western Provinces (Calcutta, 1849).

Report on the Working of the Income Tax in the Punjab, 1868, 1869, and 1896.

Report on the Settlement Operations at Delhi, 1872–80.

Report on the Third Regular Settlement of Delhi District, 1906–10.

Reports on Native Newspapers published in the Punjab, 1864–1925.

Report on the Disease of Cholera in Delhi Division (Lahore, 1861).

(b) Other reports

Annual Reports, Cambridge Mission to Delhi, 1881 onwards.

Annual Reports, Union Society for the Propagation of the Gospel.

(c) Newspapers, with location indicated

Civil and Military Gazette	India Office Library
Comrade	Nehru Memorial Library (in microfilm)
Delhi Gazette	India Office Library
Friend of India	India Office Library
Hindustan Times	Nehru Memorial Library, Delhi
Illustrated London News	British Library, Colindale
Lahore Chronicle	India Office Library
Mofussilite	India Office Library
Times of India	National Library, Calcutta

(d) Books in English

Ahmad, Aziz, *Islamic Modernization in India and Pakistan* (London, 1967).

Ahmed, Qayamuddin, *The Wahabi Movement in India* (Calcutta, 1966).

Ali, Ahmad, *Twilight in Delhi* (New Delhi, 1973).

Amar Nath, *The Development of Local Self-Government in the Punjab, 1849–1900* (Lahore, 1930).

Andrews, C. F., *Zaka Ullah of Delhi* (London, 1929).

Ashworth, W., *Genesis of Modern British Town Planning* (London, 1954).

Aziz, K. K., *British and Muslim India, 1887–1947* (London, 1963).

Bailey, T. G., *A History of Urdu Literature* (London, 1932).

Banerjee, P., *Provincial Finance in India* (Calcutta, 1929).

Bayly, C. A., *Local Roots of Indian Politics : Allahabad, 1880–1930* (Oxford, 1973).

Bernier, A., *Travels in the Mogul Empire, 1656–68* (Delhi, 1968 edn.).

Bopegamage, A., *Delhi : A Study in Urban Sociology* (Bombay, 1957).

Bradshaw, *Through Routes Overland to India* (London, 1890).

Breese, G. (ed.), *The City in Newly-Developing Countries: Readings on Urbanism and Urbanization* (Englewood Cliffs, N.J., 1969).

Brief History of the Family of Rai Chunna Mal (Delhi, 1930).

Briggs, Asa, *Age of Improvement* (London, 1959).

——, *History of Birmingham*, Vol. II (*1865–1938*) (London, 1952).

——, *Victorian Cities* (London, 1963).

Burdon, E., *Monograph on the Wire and Tinsel Industry in Punjab* (Lahore, 1909).

Burke, Peter (ed.), *A New Kind of History, from the Writings of Lucien Febvre* (London, 1973).

Chandra, Jag Parvesh, *Delhi: A Political Study* (Delhi, 1969).

Chhabra, G. S., *Social and Economic History of the Punjab, 1849–1901* (Jullundur, 1962).

Choudhuri, Keshab, *Calcutta: The Story of its Government* (Calcutta, 1973).

Chunder, Bholanath, *Travels of a Hindoo* (London, 1869).

Cities: A 'Scientific American' Book (Harmondsworth, 1967).

Colchester (Lord) (ed.), *History of the Indian Administration of Lord Ellenborough in his Correspondence with the Duke of Wellington* (London, 1874).

Cooke, C. N., *Rise and Progress and Present Conditions of Banking in India* (London, 1863).

Cooper, F., *Handbook for Delhi* (London, 1863).

Cornish, Vaughan, *The Great Capitals* (London, 1923).

Curzon, George Nathaniel (Lord), *Speeches*, Vol. I (Calcutta, 1900).

David, M. D., *History of Bombay, 1661–1708* (Bombay, 1974).

Dayal, Maheshwar, *Rediscovering Delhi* (Delhi, 1975).

Deussen, Paul, *My Indian Reminiscences* (London, 1893).

Dobbin, Christine, *Urban Leadership in Western India* (Oxford, 1972).

Doshi, H., *A Traditional Neighbourhood in a Modern City* (New Delhi, 1974).

Dyos, H. J. (ed.), *The Study of Urban History* (London, 1968).

Dyos, H. J., and Wolff, M. (eds.), *The Victorian City: Images and Realities*, 2 vols. (London, 1973).

East India Gazetteer (London, 1815).

Eden, Emily, *Up the Country* (Oxford, 1937 edn., with an introduction by Edward Thompson).

Jones, Emrys, *Towns and Cities* (Oxford, 1966).

Fanshawe, H. C., *Delhi, Past and Present, ...with maps and illustrations* (London, 1902).

Febvre, Lucien, *A Geographical Introduction to History* (London, 1925).

Fergusson, J., *India, Ancient and Modern* (London, 1868).

Fraser, Lovat, *At Delhi* (Bombay, 1903).

Forbes, J., *Oriental Memoirs*, Vol. IV (London, 1813).

Forrest, G. W., *Cities of India* (London, 1903).

Forrest, H. T. S., *The Indian Municipality and Some Practical Hints on its Everyday Work* (Calcutta, 1909).

Gallagher, J., Johnson, G., and Seal, A., *Locality, Province, and Nation: Essays on Indian Politics, 1870–1940* (Cambridge, 1973).

Gazetteer of the East India Company (London, 1854).

Geddes, Patrick, *Cities in Evolution* (London, 1854).

Ghalib, Mirza Asadulla Khan, *Dastanbuy*, trans. K. A. Faruqi (New Delhi, 1970).

Gillion, Kenneth L., *Ahmedabad: A Study in Indian Urban History* (Berkeley, 1968).

Ginsburg, Norton S. (ed.), *Patterns of Asia* (Englewood Cliffs, N.J., 1958).

Graham, G. F. I., *Life and Work of Syed Ahmad Khan* (Edinburgh, 1885).

Greathed, H. H., *Letters Written during the Siege of Delhi* (London, 1858).

Greathed, W. H., *Report on the Drainage of the City of Delhi and on the Means of Improving it* (Agra, 1852).

Griffiths, C. J., *Narrative of the Siege of Delhi*, ed. H. J. Yonge (London, 1910).

Hall, Peter G., *The World Cities* (New York, 1966).

Handlin, Oscar, and Burchard, J. (eds.), *The Historian and the City* (Cambridge, Mass., 1966).

Harcourt, A., *New Guide to Delhi* (Allahabad, 1866).

Hardinge (Lord), *My Indian Years, 1910–16* (London, 1948).

Hasan, Mushirul, *Nationalism and Communal Politics in India, 1916–28* (New Delhi, 1979).

——(ed.), *Muslims and the Congress: Select Correspondence of Dr M. A. Ansari, 1912–35* (New Delhi, 1979).

Hauser, Philip M., and Schnore, Leo F. (eds.), *Study of Urbanization* (New York, 1965).

Hayward, V. E. W., *The Church as a Christian Community* (London, 1966).

Hearn, Gordon R., *Seven Cities of Delhi* (London, 1906).

Heber, R. R., *Narrative of a Journey through the Upper Provinces of India*, Vol. I (London, 1828).

Hennock, E. P., *Fit and Proper Persons: Ideal and Reality in Nineteenth-Century Urban Government* (London, 1973).

Hussey, C., *Life of Sir Edwin Lutyens* (London, 1953).

Hutchins, Francis G., *Illusion of Permanence: British Imperialism in India* (Princeton, N.J., 1967).

Imperial Coronation Durbar, Delhi 1911, 2 vols. (Lahore, 1911).

Irvine, W., *The Later Mughals* (London, 1922).

Joshi, Arun, *Lala Sri Ram: A Study in Entrepreneurship and Industrial Management* (Delhi, 1975).

Joshi, V. C. (ed.), *Ram Mohun Roy* (Delhi, 1975).

Kaye, John W., *History of the Indian Mutiny, 1857–8*, ed. Colonel Malleson (London, 1888).

Kaye, J. W., *Life of Charles Metcalfe*, Vol. I (London, 1858).

Keene, H. G., *Handbook for Visitors to Delhi* (London, 1874).

Kellett, J. R., *Impact of Railways on Victorian Cities* (London, 1969).

Ker, J. C., *Political Trouble in India, 1907–17* (Calcutta, 1973, reprinted from the original 1917 edition).

Khaliquzzaman, C., *Pathway to Pakistan* (Lahore, 1961).

King, A. D., *Colonial Urban Development* (London, 1976).

Kumar, Ravinder (ed.), *Essays on Gandhian Politics* (Oxford, 1971).

Lal, Raja, *Life of Jiwan Lal* (Delhi, 1888).

Lapidus, Ira M., *Muslim Cities in the Later Middle Ages* (Cambridge, Mass., 1967).

Leasor, James, *Red Fort—An Account of the Siege of Delhi in 1857* (London, 1956).

Mairet, Philip, *Pioneer of Sociology: The Life and Letters of Patrick Geddes* (London, 1957).

Makdisi, G. (ed.), *Arabic and Islamic Studies in Honour of H. A. B. Gibb* (Leiden, 1965).

Masselos, J., *Towards Nationalism* (Bombay, 1974).

Matheson, J., *England to Delhi* (London, 1870).

Metcalfe, C. T., *Two Native Narratives of the Mutiny in Delhi* (London, 1898).

Minturn, R. B., *New York to Delhi* (London, 1858).

Misra, B. B., *Administrative History of India, 1834–1947* (Delhi, 1970).

Mitra, A., *Delhi: Capital City* (New Delhi, 1970).

Monk, F. F., *History of St Stephen's College, Delhi* (Calcutta, 1935).

Montgomery, H. H., *Life and Letters of G. A. Lefroy* (London, 1920).

Mujeeb, M., *Indian Muslims* (London, 1966).

——, *Islamic Influence on Indian Society* (Delhi, 1972).

Mukherjee, C., *Urban Growth in a Rural Area: Case Study of a Town in West Bengal* (Santiniketan, 1972).

Mumford, Lewis, *The City in History: Its Origins, Its Transformation, and Its Prospects* (London, 1961).

Napier, C. J., *Defects, Civil and Military, of Indian Government* (London, 1863).

Naqvi, H. K., *Urban Centres and Industries in Upper India, 1556–1803* (Delhi, 1968).

——, *Urbanization and Urban Centres under the Great Mughals* (Simla, 1971).

Narang, G. C., *Karkhandari Dialect of Delhi Urdu* (Delhi, 1961).

Nath, R., *Monuments of Delhi: Historical Study* (based on *Aasar-us-Sanaadid*) (New Delhi, 1979).

Nehru, Jawaharlal, *An Autobiography* (London, 1938).

Nigam, N. K., *Delhi in 1857* (Delhi, 1957).

Nilsson, Sten, *European Architecture in India, 1750–1850* (London, 1968).

——, *The New Capitals of India, Pakistan and Bangladesh* (Scandinavian Institute of Asian Studies, 1973).

Ookhtomsky, E., *Travels in the East of Nicholas II, Emperor of Russia, when Cesarevich, 1890–1* (London, 1891).

Page, J. A. (ed.), *List of Mohammedan and Hindu Monuments, Delhi Province*, 4 vols. (London, 1913).

Panikkar, K. N., *British Diplomacy in North India* (Delhi, 1968).

Parks, F., *Diary of the Wanderings of a Pilgrim in Search of the Picturesque* (London, 1950).

Pascoe, C. F., *Two Hundred Years of the S.P.G.: An Historical Account of the Society, 1701-1900* (London, 1901).

Pershad, Madho, *History of the Delhi Municipality, 1863-1921* (Delhi, 1921).

Qamber, Akhtar, *The Last Musha'irah of Dehli* (Delhi, 1979).

Rao, V. K. R. V., and Desai, P. B., *Greater Delhi: A Study in Urbanization, 1940-57* (Delhi, 1963).

Records of the Intelligence Department, Government of the N.W.P., during the Mutiny of 1857, 2 vols. (Edinburgh, 1902).

Richards, D. S. (ed.), *Islam and the Trade of Asia* (Oxford, 1970).

Roberts, F. S., *Forty-One Years in India, from Subaltern to Commander-in-Chief*, 2 vols. (London, 1897).

——, *Letters Written during the Indian Mutiny* (London, 1924 edn.).

Robinson, Francis, *Separatism among Indian Muslims: The Politics of the Muslims in U.P., 1860-1923* (Cambridge, 1974).

Robson, W. A., *Great Cities of the World—Their Politics and Planning* (London, 1954).

Russell, Ralph (ed.), *Ghalib: The Poet and His Age* (London, 1972).

Sadiq, M., *History of Urdu Literature* (Oxford, 1964).

Shan Mohammad, *Sir Syed Ahmad Khan: A Political Biography* (Meerut, 1969).

Singh, Sangat, *Freedom Movement in Delhi* (New Delhi, 1972).

Singh, Khushwant, and Joshi, Arun, *Shri Ram: A Biography* (Bombay, 1968).

Sinha, Pradeep, *Nineteenth-Century Bengal* (Calcutta, 1965).

Sjoberg, Gidson, *The Pre-Industrial City: Past and Present* (Illinois, 1960).

Society for the Propagation of the Gospel, *Story of the Delhi Mission* (London, 1908).

Sovani, N. V., *Urbanization and Urban India* (Bombay, 1966).

Spear, Percival, *Delhi: Its Monuments and History* (Bombay, 1945).

——, *Twilight of the Mughals* (Cambridge, 1951).

Sri Ram, *Municipal Problems in Delhi* (Delhi, 1932).

Stedman-Jones, Gareth, *Outcast London* (Oxford, 1971).

Stephen, Carr, *Handbook for Delhi* (Calcutta, 1876).

Sterndale, R. C., *Municipal Work in India* (Calcutta, 1881).

Stocqueler, J. H., *Handbook of India* (London, 1845).

Sykes, M., and Chaturvedi, B. D., *Charles Freer Andrews: A Narrative* (London, 1949).

Temple, R., *Men and Events of My Time in India* (London, 1882).

——, *Story of My Life* (London, 1896).

Thacker's Directory (Calcutta, annual).

Tinker, Hugh, *Reorientations: Asia in Transition* (Bombay, 1965).

——, *Foundations of Local Self-Government in India, Pakistan and Burma* (Bombay, 1967 edn.).

Trevaskis, H. K., *The Land of the Five Rivers : The Economic History of the Punjab till 1890* (Oxford, 1928).

Trevelyan, H., *The India We Left* (London, 1974).

Troll, C. W., *Sayyid Ahmad Khan : A Reinterpretation of Muslim Theology* (New Delhi, 1978).

Turner, Roy, *India's Urban Future* (Berkeley, 1962).

Tyrwhitt, Jacqueline (ed.), *Patrick Geddes in India* (London, 1947).

Urwick, W., *Indian Pictures Drawn with Pen and Pencil* (Delhi, 1972 edn.).

Wheeler, S., *History of the Delhi Coronation Durbar of 1903* (London, 1904).

Wilberforce, R. G., *An Unrecorded Chapter of the Indian Mutiny* (London, 1894).

Wilmott, P., and Young, M., *Family and Class in a London Suburb* (London, 1960).

Young, K., *Delhi—1857* (London, 1902).

Zakaria, Rafiq, *Rise of Muslims in Indian Politics* (Bombay, 1970).

(e) Works in Indian languages

Aarzu, Mukhtaruddin Ahmad (ed.), *Ahwal-e-Ghalib* (Aligarh, 1953).

Adu-Babu : Sri Rashbehari Sen (Delhi, 1964).

Bashir-ud-din Ahmad, *Waqa'yat-e-dar-ul-Hukumat-e-Delhi*, 3 vols. (Delhi, 1919).

Delhi College Urdu Magazine (Old Delhi College Number) (Delhi, 1953).

Dilli Jain Directory (New Delhi, 1961).

Ghalib, Asadullah Khan, *Khutoot-e-Ghalib*, ed. Meher (Lahore, n.d.).

Hai, Abdul, *Safarnama* (Delhi, 1894).

Hali, Altaf Husain, *Yadgaar-e-Ghalib* (Delhi, 1892).

Haq, Abdul, *Marhum Dehli College* (Delhi, 1945 edn.).

Haq, Syed Moinul (ed.), *Akbar-e-Rangeen* (Lahore, 1962).

Hasan, Mohammad, *Dehli Shairi Ka Fikri Aur Tahzibi Pesh* (Delhi, 1964).

Khan, Syed Ahmad, *Aasar-us-Sanaadid* (1854 edn.).

Khan Bahadur Ka Janaza (Delhi, n.d.).

Risala-e-Anjuman-e-Rashidin-e-ahl-e-Islam (Delhi, 1877).

Risala-e-Anjuman-i-Rifah-e-Ra'ayan (Delhi, 1875)

Sabri, Imdad, *Asaar-e-Rehmat* (Delhi, 1967).

——, *Dilli Ke Yaadgar Hastian* (Delhi, 1972).

Subuhi, Ashraf, *Dilli Ke Chand Ajib Hastian* (Delhi, 1943).

Tagore, Debendranath, *Atma-Jeebani*, ed. S. C. Chakravarty (Calcutta, 1964).

Urdu-e-Mo'alla, ed. K. A. Faruqi, Vol. 3 (1969).

(f) Articles

Ahmad, Enayat, 'Origins and Evolution of the Towns of Uttar Pradesh', *Geographical Outlook*, 1 (January 1956).

Andrews, C. F., 'The King's Visit to Delhi', *The East and the West* (October 1907).

Aziz, A., 'A Study of Indian Towns', *Geographer*, 7 (Summer 1955).

Banerjea, S. N., 'Lord Macaulay and Higher Education', reprinted in *Nineteenth-Century Studies*, 5 (1974).

Banerjee, Tarasankar, 'Trevelyan and the Abolition of Octroi Duties in 1833', *Visva-Bharati Quarterly*, 32, no. 2 (1966–7).

Bhatia, Shyam Sunder, 'Historical Geography of Delhi', *Indian Geographer*, August 1956.

Chawla, Indernath, 'Urbanization of the Punjab Plains', *Indian Geographer*, 3 (December 1958).

Cohn, B., 'The British in Benares', *Comparative Studies in Society and History*, 4 (1961–2).

Ghurye, G. S., 'Cities in India', *Sociological Bulletin*, 2 (1953).

Gist, Noel P., 'Ecology of Bangalore, India: An East–West Comparison', *Social Forces*, 34 (May 1957).

Gupta, Narayani, 'Military Security v. Urban Development: A Case Study of Delhi, 1857–1912', *Modern Asian Studies*, 5 (1971).

Indian State Railways Magazine, special Delhi issue (February 1931).

Jones, P. I., 'Coming of the King to Delhi', *Church Missionary Review*, 63 (1912).

King, A. D., 'The Colonial Bungalow-Compound Complex: A Study in the Cultural Use of Space', *Journal of Architetctural Research*, 3, no. 2 (May 1974).

——, 'The Language of Colonial Urbanization', *Sociology*, 8, no. 1 (January 1974).

Leslie, B., 'Delhi—the Metropolis of India', *Journal of the Royal Society of Arts*, 61 (1912).

Leonard, John G., 'Urban Government under the Raj: A Case Study of Municipal Administration in Nineteenth-Century South India', *Modern Asian Studies*, 7 (1973).

Lewandowski, S. J., 'Urban Growth and Municipal Development in the Colonial City of Madras, 1869–1900', *Journal of Asian Studies*, 34 (February 1975).

Metcalfe, T. R., 'Notes on the Sources for Local History in North India', *Journal of Asian Studies*, 26 (August 1967).

Mukerjee, S. N., 'Caste, Class and Politics in Calcutta, 1815–38', in Leach, E., and Mukerjee, S. N. (eds.), *Elites in South Asia* (London, 1970).

——, '*Daladali* in Calcutta in the Nineteenth Century', *Modern Asian Studies*, 9 (Februry 1975).

Neild, Susan M., 'Colonial Urbanism: The Development of Madras City in the Eighteenth and Nineteenth Centuries', *Modern Asian Studies*, 13, no. 2 (April 1979).

Nigam, M. N., 'Evolution of Lucknow', *National Geographical Journal of India* (March 1960).

Redfield, R., and Singer, M. B., 'Cultural Role of Cities', reprinted in *Man in India*, 36 (1956).

Russell-Wood, A. J. R., 'Local Government in Portuguese America: A Study in Cultural Divergence', *Comparative Studies in Society and History*, 16 (March 1974).

Sanial, S. C., 'The It'maduddaulah Institution at Delhi', *Islamic Culture*, 4 (April 1930).

Sen Gupta, Kalyan K., 'Bengali Intelligentsia and the Politics of Rent, 1873–85', *Social Scientist*, 3 (September 1974).

Sheehan, J. J., 'Liberalism and the City in Nineteenth-Century Germany', *Past and Present*, 51 (May 1971).

Singer, Milton, 'Beyond Tradition and Modernity in Madras', *Comparative Studies in Society and History*, 13 (1971).

Singh, K. N., 'Territorial Basis of Medieval Town and Village Settlement in Eastern U.P.', *Association of American Geographers*, Annual, 58 (June 1968).

Singh, Ujagar, 'Origin and Growth of Kanpur', *National Geographical Journal of India*, 5 (March 1959).

Spate, O. H. K., 'Factors in the Development of Capital Cities', *Geographical Review*, 32 (1942).

Spear, T. G. P., 'British Administration of Delhi Territory, 1803–57', *Journal of Indian History*, 19 (August 1940).

Thrupp, Sylvia L., 'Creativity of Cities', *Comparative Studies in Society and History*, 4 (November 1961).

Upadhyaya, R. D., 'Delhi As It Was 100 Years Ago', *Modern Review*, 117 (March 1965).

INDEX